Dr. Johnson's
Dictionary

Engraved by Heath, from an Original Painting by Opie, in the Possession of Mr. Harrison
The Sarcophagus, and other Ornamental Parts designed by Mr. R. Smirke.

London. Published as the Act directs, March 14, 1786 by Harrison & C. N. 18, Paternoster Row.

Dr. Johnson's Dictionary

Essays in the Biography of a Book

By JAMES H. SLEDD *and* GWIN J. KOLB

THE UNIVERSITY OF CHICAGO PRESS

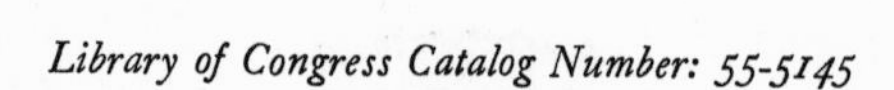

Library of Congress Catalog Number: 55-5145

THE UNIVERSITY OF CHICAGO PRESS, CHICAGO 37
Cambridge University Press, London, N.W. 1, England
The University of Toronto Press, Toronto 5, Canada

Published 1955. Composed and printed by THE UNIVERSITY OF CHICAGO PRESS, *Chicago, Illinois, U.S.A.*

Preface

THIS collection of essays is intended to commemorate the bicentennial of Johnson's *Dictionary*, and we hope it is not unworthy of the occasion. That it contains many faults we neither would nor could deny. To a severe scrutator, it may appear that we have fiddled a pious tune at the festival of the intellectual lowbrow. Our long-suffering wives have passed a gently ambiguous judgment, remarking only that this is not a book for the common reader. To us, our fiddling has been pastime with good company; and where the company has been so good, we trust that the fiddling has not been altogether bad.

However that may be, we heartily thank our good companions, whose kindness and generosity have had no limits. To the Rockefeller Foundation and Mr. Chadbourne Gilpatric, to the Guggenheim Memorial Foundation and Mr. Henry Allen Moe, to the University of Chicago and Dean Napier Wilt we are grateful for financial support. We have worked happily in the Library of the University of Chicago, the Bodleian Library, the British Museum, and the John Rylands Library; and we have had special help from Miss Katharine M. Hall, of the University of Chicago; Mr. David F. Foxon, of the British Museum; Professor Edward Robertson and Dr. Frank Taylor, of the Rylands Library; and Mr. Frederick R. Goff, of the Library of Congress. We are grateful to them and to their colleagues. The list of our own colleagues and teachers who have patiently borne and wisely answered our inquiries is too long for repetition here; giving due thanks to all, we must particularly mention Professor R. C. Bald, Professor Fredson Bowers, Professor Richard

T. Bruère, Professor James L. Clifford, Professor Gösta Franzen, Professor Arthur Friedman, Professor Allen T. Hazen, Professor W. R. Keast, Mr. Herman W. Liebert, Mr. Robert F. Metzdorf, Professor Gertrude E. Noyes, Professor D. T. Starnes, and Professor Charles L. Wrenn of Pembroke College, Oxford, at whose invitation earlier drafts of some of our essays were read as lectures at Oxford early in 1954. Some of the material in those essays was drawn from the ledgers of the printers William and Andrew Strahan, to which we had access through the kindness of their present owners, Spottiswoode, Ballantyne, and Company; and it was also at Oxford that we enjoyed the hospitality and helpful criticism of Dr. L. F. Powell. No one, finally, has helped us more than Mr. and Mrs. Donald F. Hyde, who made available to us the resources of their unique collection of Johnsoniana and who gave us the benefit of their personal advice and assistance in a quite extraordinary way.

With so much help from so many helpers, we can offer no excuses for our blunders, for which we alone are responsible. We wish only to say that we are aware of a certain amount of repetition and overlapping from chapter to chapter. It was caused by the fact that the chapters were written separately over a period of some three years. The first, which we reprint from *Modern Philology* by permission of the editor, Professor George Williamson, was written in the autumn of 1951, the last in the autumn of 1954. The circumstances of the writing made it necessary that each essay should be able to stand alone, and in revision we have judged it wise to preserve that independence. Adequate cross-references, we hope, have been supplied.

University of Chicago
February 6, 1955

Table of Contents

Chronological Table

April 30, 1746—Johnson probably completes "A Short Scheme for compiling a new Dictionary of the English Language."

June 18, 1746—Johnson signs his contract for the *Dictionary* with the booksellers.

October 29, 1746—Chesterfield becomes a secretary of state.

March 20, 1747—The *Dictionary* is advertised as in "great forwardness."

Early August, 1747—*The Plan of a Dictionary* is published.

August, 1748—Birch writes that Johnson's amanuenses have almost finished transcribing the authorities.

September, 1749—Birch reports some part of the *Dictionary* as "almost ready for the Press."

October, 1750—Birch reports the printing of the first 120 sheets.

May, 1752—Millar and Dodsley have paid their shares of Strahan's charges for printing sheets 1–120.

April, 1753—Johnson has completed the first volume of the *Dictionary* (except for the Preface, the grammar, and the history of the language).

October 4, 1753—Strahan charges Hitch for printing sheets 121–420.

Summer, 1754—Johnson's work on the *Dictionary* draws to an end.

November 28–December 5, 1754—Chesterfield puffs the *Dictionary* in two papers in *The World*.

Early February, 1755—Johnson writes the "celebrated letter."

February 20, 1755—Oxford confers the M.A. degree on Johnson.

Late February or early March, 1755—The octavo edition of *The Plan of a Dictionary* is published.

April 15, 1755—The *Dictionary* is published.

June 14, 1755—Publication of the second folio edition of the *Dictionary* begins.

December 13, 1784—Johnson dies.

October 22, 1785—Publication of Harrison's edition of the *Dictionary* begins.

Late October, 1785—Fielding publishes the first number of his edition.

November 19, 1785—The proprietors' sixth edition begins to appear.

December 10, 1785—The first number of the proprietors' seventh edition is published.

I

Johnson's *Dictionary* & Lexicographical Tradition: I

It is now two hundred years since Johnson published his *Dictionary*. Though its immediate success was not phenomenal,[1] its publication was undoubtedly a great event for Johnson, for the booksellers, and for what their century proudly called "the republic of letters." Johnson became "Dictionary Johnson," and his *Dictionary* became *the* dictionary. As Noah Webster somewhat invidiously said, a half-century later: "Johnson's writings had, in Philology, the effect which Newton's discoveries had in Mathematics, to interrupt for a time the progress of this branch of learning; for when a man has pushed his researches so far beyond his cotemporaries, that all men despair of proceeding beyond him, they will naturally consider his principles and decisions as the limit of perfection on that particular subject, and repose their opinions on his authority, without examining into their validity."[2] Johnson, in short, realized one of the great scholarly and literary ideals of his age, to the considerable discomfort of competing lexicographers but to the eventual admiration of his own and succeeding generations.

Perhaps, then, it is really not surprising that even after so long a time the traditional accounts of the *Dictionary* leave something to be desired. The *Dictionary* was the culmination of a long development, and the culmination was so impressive that the development was naturally forgotten. When at last the new knowledge and new ideals of the nineteenth century might have made it possible to see the *Dictionary* in its historical perspective, the Johnsonian tradition—the cult of Johnson the man—was there to block inquiry. The philologist busied himself with making new dictionaries or revising Johnson's; the Johnsonian, with reading Boswell; and the traditional accounts show the effects of these preoccupations.

The term "traditional" is not improperly applied to the modern historian's rather condescending tributes, for which a fairly definite pattern has been established. The historian mentions the contents of the *Dictionary*—Preface, history of the language, grammar, the dictionary proper—briefly dismisses the history and the grammar, and devotes himself to the body of the text and to the Preface. Johnson's word-list is criticized as bookish, a little remote from the crudities of daily life, sometimes almost un-English; but it may equally be praised for its inclusiveness. It is noted that though Johnson marked the accents of words, he said little about pronunciation, and his etymologies and his fussy remarks on usage are treated as rather ludicrous but typical of his age. To Johnson's definitions, his careful distinction and classification of the different senses of words, the historian gives high praise, but praise a little tempered by references to tart Johnsonian humor or stilted Johnsonese. Unlimited praise is given to his industriously collected illustrative quotations, which are represented, with his definitions, as his grand contribution to the technique of English lexicography; but not much is made of possible models, especially foreign models, for this English development. The influence of the French Academy or the Accademia della Crusca is more likely to be discussed in connection with Johnson's Preface, when it is said that Johnson, like the academies, hoped to fix his language; that Johnson realized, sooner than the academies, that a language cannot be fixed; but that whatever the academies did for French and Italian, Johnson did for English. A few comments are made on Johnson's predecessors and imitators, and the historian closes his account with some further remarks, generally rather vague except with regard to spelling, concerning the linguistic influence of the *Dictionary*.

To this pattern, of which the preceding is hardly too gross a caricature, there are honorable exceptions. One would not like to say that after two centuries historians of the English language and of English literature continue to neglect the plain clues which Johnson gives us to the sources of his ideas and techniques; that in attributing to Johnson some notable influence on the language, they have perpetuated a characteristic but untenable eighteenth-century theory; or that in neglecting his sources and judging him by the standards of the century which followed, they have distorted the history which they set out to write and have made a balanced judgment of Johnson's work unnecessarily difficult. As a matter of fact, in the last fifty years or so a great deal has been learned about the rise of English philology, about English grammatical traditions, English ideas of language, and the development of lexicography in England. What is needed is an attempt to bring this new knowledge to bear on Johnson, and that is the purpose of the present essay. The statement which it offers is admittedly incomplete, and no pretense is made of changing beyond recognition the broad outlines of the traditional account of Johnson's *Dictionary*. Rather that account, it is hoped, is here clarified, modified in some of its details, and enriched with some new lore. Specifically, it will be argued that the *Dictionary*, a booksellers' project, gave its age what the age demanded; that, with few exceptions, Johnson, as lexicographer, asked no questions, gave no answers, and invented no techniques which were new to Europe, though they may very well have been new to English lexicography; and that the acceptance of these two propositions will force a revaluation of his work.

To begin in the most general way, the whole history of English lexicography makes one slow to accept a claim of striking originality for any dictionary-maker. As early as 1600, almost any two dictionaries prepared in England, whether Latin, French, Italian, Welsh, or what not, were likely to be related in some way; and the first dictionaries purely English, when they appeared, pillaged the earlier Latin-English works.[3] The same story can be told for the English dictionaries of the seventeenth and early eighteenth centuries, for the bilinguals, the polyglots, and the etymological dictionaries. Certainly there were innovations from time to time; but English lexicographers often lagged behind their Continental fellows, and the proportion of innovation to copying and conformity was never high. The student who is squeamish about plagiarism had simply better not study the old wordbooks, to which the concepts of plagiarism and literary property are hardly applicable. Dictionaries were gathered one from another: Johnson himself worked from an interleaved copy of Nathan Bailey's *Dictionarium Britannicum.*[4]

The congenital inertia of lexicographers helps to explain what might seem a curious fact in the history of Johnson's *Dictionary:* the fact that so many pleas and false starts were necessary before the demand was finally met for a dictionary like those of the academies. At least as early as

Mulcaster in the sixteenth century, Englishmen had been calling for a good dictionary of their language and toying with the notion of its official regulation;[5] and when, in the seventeenth century, the influence of the French and Italian academies began to make itself felt, the demand for an authoritative English dictionary became more insistent. The lexicographers themselves were naturally quick to recognize the significance of the Continental undertakings. Already in his 1650 edition of Cotgrave's French dictionary, James Howell mentions the intention of the French Academy to "put such another Dictionary to light as Crusca in Italian";[6] and in 1671 the editor of Stephen Skinner's *Etymologicon* expresses the hope that Englishmen will some day emulate politer nations, establish an academy, and make English the rival of Latin by freeing it of solecisms and improprieties. In such an undertaking, he says, the *Etymologicon* would be of the greatest value;[7] and that his ideals and ambitions for English were not unshared by other antiquarians appears from Wanley's note that "a *Dictionary* fixing the English language as the French and Italian" would be a desirable book.[8]

If the desire for an authoritative dictionary had been confined, however, to etymologists and antiquarians, hard-headed booksellers would have been unimpressed, and a contract like that into which Johnson entered would never have become possible. The real pressure was built up in other quarters, in the Royal Society and among leading men of letters. In 1664 the Royal Society named its committee for improving the English language; and in 1665 Evelyn, who had visited the Accademia della Crusca, wrote Wyche his famous letter on the work of that committee, calling, among other things, for "a more certaine Orthography" and an authoritative grammar and lexicon.[9]

Somewhat later, Dryden, in the dedication of *Troilus and Cressida*, emphasized the importance of such works by declaring that "propriety must first be stated, ere any measures of elegance can be taken"; and in 1693 he again remarked that "we have yet no English *prosodia*, not so much as a tolerable dictionary, or a grammar; so that our language is in a manner barbarous. . . ."[10] Such ideas suggest those of Swift, who was to become the great advocate of an English academy and who strengthened the demand for authority in language. That demand was again heard typically in 1724, from the anonymous authors of *The Many Advantages of a Good Language*, who repeated the complaint that there was no good dictionary of English to fix what was right in the language and "to bring it into method, with an account of the Derivations, and Senses and Uses of Words";[11] similarly, Warburton, in 1747, noted the lack of a standard for English, "for we have neither GRAMMAR nor DICTIONARY, neither Chart nor Compass, to guide us through this wide sea of Words";[12] and while Johnson was actually at work on his *Dictionary*, Chesterfield remarked, in a letter perhaps of 1752, "that though we have ten thousand Greek and Latin grammars and dictionaries, we have not yet a single one on English."[13]

Taken literally, Chesterfield's statement was, of course, false. By 1752 there were many English grammars and many dictionaries. Their number, indeed, measures the strength of the demand that the national honor be redeemed by a dictionary matching the performances of France and Italy, just as the persistence of the demand measures the failure of English lexicographers to meet it, and that despite the fact that men like Ambrose Philips, Addison, and Pope had not thought themselves above some lexicographic labors. Johnson himself records the activities of Addison and Pope. Addison, Johnson says in his *Lives of the Poets*, "had once a design to make an English dictionary," chose his authorities, and collected some quotations; and Pope, according to Johnson's *Plan* for the *Dictionary*, had also been concerned with some such project and had likewise drawn up a list of authorities.[14]

Philips had actually gone so far as to issue "*Proposals for Printing an English Dictionary* in Two Volumes in Folio," in which he had promised to explain the whole language by giving right spellings, etymologies, and definitions of the different meanings and uses of words, phrases, and idioms; by distinguishing levels of usage; and by including proverbs, technical terms, and obsolete words and phrases.[15] Like Addison and Pope, Philips never completed the dictionary which he had planned, but it should be noted that his *Proposals* have much in common with Johnson's statement of his own achievement in the Preface to his octavo edition of 1756. What Philips and so many others had wanted done or had proposed to do, Johnson did. "Having been long employed," he wrote, "in the study and cultivation of the English language, I lately published a dictionary, like those compiled by the academies of Italy and France, for the use of such as aspire to exactness of criticism or elegance of style"; and the justice of his comparison was acknowledged by the academicians themselves, who recognized his achievement, after the fashion of academicians, by sending him copies of their dictionaries.[16]

It should be clear, then, that, before Johnson, the seventeenth and eighteenth centuries had evolved a fairly clear lexicographic ideal, an ideal which Johnson largely shared and, to anticipate, largely realized. In the 1740's, the booksellers could hardly have failed to see the opportunity which was afforded by the state of the market, the state of the public taste, and the presence in London of Samuel Johnson. There is ample evidence that a number of them were willing to take advantage of that opportunity. According to Boswell, the bookseller Dodsley had suggested to Johnson the possibility of his preparing an English dictionary some time before Johnson published his *Plan* in 1747: "I have been informed by Mr. James Dodsley, that several years before this period, when Johnson was one day sitting in his brother Robert's shop, he heard his brother suggest to him, that a Dictionary of the English Language would be a work that would be well received by the publick; that Johnson seemed at first to catch at the proposition, but, after a pause, said, in his abrupt decisive manner, 'I believe I shall not undertake it.' "[17]

Though Johnson was in two minds about the project, it must certainly have appealed to him as a means to improve the English language by bringing English lexicography abreast of that of France and Italy; and his early writings, especially the *Miscellaneous Observations on the Tragedy of "Macbeth,"* which he published in 1745, must have recommended him to the booksellers as a good man for the editorship. In the words of Sir John Hawkins, "By this and other of Johnson's writings, his reputation as a scholar and a philologist was so well established, that the booksellers of greatest opulence in the city, who had long meditated the publication of a dictionary, after the model of those of France and the Academia [*sic*] della Crusca, looked upon him as a fit person to be employed in such an undertaking."[18] In 1792, Arthur Murphy, in his essay on Johnson, repeated the gist of Hawkins' statement and Boswell's,[19] which is further confirmed by Horne Tooke's vicious criticism of the *Dictionary:* "It appears to be a work of labour, and yet is in truth one of the most idle performances ever offered to the public: compiled by an author who possessed not one single requisite for the undertaking, and, being a publication of a set of booksellers, owing its success to that very circumstance which alone must make it impossible that it should deserve success."[20]

Of Horne Tooke's criticism, something must be said later, but he was perfectly right that "a set of booksellers" did what they could to make the *Dictionary* financially successful. Some time in the 1740's, Johnson began the making of his book; in April, 1746, he wrote the first sketch of the *Plan* or prospectus which he addressed to Lord Chesterfield; in June of the same year he signed a formal contract with the booksellers, who published the *Plan* in August of 1747; by April, 1753, he had finished his first volume, except for the Preface, the grammar, and the history of the language which it was to contain; and two years later he published the complete work, in two volumes folio, priced at ninety shillings.[21] Some three thousand pounds had been spent on the *Dictionary*, and, though the two thousand copies which had been printed were not immediately sold out, proposals were soon issued for a reprint in cheap weekly numbers.[22] That a stir had been made in the publishing world is indicated by the competition which developed between Johnson's *Dictionary* and its rival, likewise a booksellers' project, the Scott-Bailey *New Universal*.[23]

All the available external evidence combines, then, to show that Johnson, with his *Dictionary*, satisfied himself, the booksellers, and ultimately the public by realizing an established but difficult ideal. "Scarcely any man," he was to write in his Preface to Rolt's *Dictionary of Trade and Commerce*, "publishes a book, whatever it be, without believing that he has caught the moment when the publick attention is vacant to his call, and the world is disposed, in a particular manner, to learn the art which he undertakes to teach"; but he himself had done what others merely hoped to do. As he said to Boswell long afterward: "I knew very well what I was undertaking,—and very well how to do it,—and have done it very well."[24] He was saying no more of himself than the reviewers had said. Though individual Englishmen rather commonly compared their single-handed works with the joint productions of the academies,[25] the commonplace was quickly and permanently applied to Johnson by others than himself. In the *Edinburgh Review* of 1755 Adam Smith could already say of the *Dictionary:* "When we compare this book with other dictionaries, the merit of its author appears very extraordinary. Those which in modern languages have gained the most esteem, are that of the French academy, and that of the academy Della Crusca. Both these were composed by a numerous society of learned men, and took up a longer time in the composition, than the life of a single person could well have afforded. The Dictionary of the English language is the work of a single person, and composed in a period of time very inconsiderable, when compared with the extent of the work."[26] The forty French, at least in the judgment of Englishmen—and Scotsmen—had been well beaten.

All this is sufficiently obvious and by no means new; but before turning to the *Dictionary* itself it was necessary to review the external evidence, so that fruitless questions might not be asked in the remainder of this study. Though it is natural and proper to ask what Johnson's original contribution to English lexicography may have been, the attempt to prove that Johnson was in this or that respect an innovator is likely to end in disappointment and distortion. The same question may be answered, more accurately and with greater satisfaction, by asking rather how Johnson united the best lexicographic theory and practice current in his time in order to realize his time's ideal. With that question in mind, one may begin by looking first at the general structure of his book.

One expects, and one finds, nothing surprising. A lexicographer's stock in trade included a preface explaining his aims and methods, discussing his predecessors, and pondering the likely reception of his work: Johnson could produce one for a dictionary of commerce which he had never read.[27] Histories of the English language had been included in Edward Phillips' *New World of English Words* (1658), *Cocker's English Dictionary* (1704), Nathan Bailey's *Universal Etymological English Dictionary* (1721), and his *Dictionarium Britannicum* (whose 1736 edition traces the history from Babel to contemporary English).[28] The list is by no means exhaustive and deliberately excludes one of Johnson's most notable predecessors, Benjamin Martin, since his *Lingua Britannica reformata*, which appeared in 1749, may have been influenced by Johnson's known intentions. Martin, however, included in his dictionary the *Physico-grammatical Essay on the Propriety and Rationale of the English Tongue*, which he had published separately in the preceding year; and in that essay one finds, among other things, both a history of English and an English grammar. The four divisions, then, of Johnson's *Dictionary* had each its counterpart in Martin's; and if it were necessary to labor Johnson's traditionalism at this point, the fact could be cited that Edward Phillips, who apparently first introduced a history of the language into an English dictionary, had drawn, for his account, on Davies' Welsh-Latin and Latin-Welsh *Dictionarium* of 1632.[29]

Though Benjamin Martin deserves some credit for combining a careful preface, history, grammar, and dictionary within a single volume, he, too, had had ample precedents —to pass to the third item in Johnson's *Dictionary*, the English grammar—for at least part of that combination. Histories of English and grammars of English had long been linked, notably in the *Grammatica linguae Anglicanae* (1653) of the great John Wallis, whose work had become a quarry, to the unnecessary consternation of modern students, for several following grammarians.[30] In addition, to say nothing of such works as Sewel's large Dutch-English and English-Dutch *Dictionary*, which Johnson probably knew and which included grammars both of Dutch and of English,[31] or of the *Etymologicum Anglicanum* of Francis Junius, which again was familiar to Johnson and which was published together with a grammar of Anglo-Saxon, English grammars had already made their way into the common dictionaries of modern English. This innovation was apparently made by Thomas Dyche and William Pardon, in their *New General English Dictionary*, a mere schoolbook published in 1735; and their example had been taken, before Johnson published, by other compilers.[32]

Clearly, tradition demanded that Johnson include a grammar and a history of the language. The contents of his grammar and history are equally traditional. Neither has been much discussed, and in itself neither is worth much discussion. Horne Tooke was wrong, but not hopelessly wrong, when he called them "contemptible performances; and a reproach to the learning and industry" of the nation.[33] Even at its worst, however, Johnson's work was not altogether unimportant. Both history and grammar, it is said, supplied materials for his rival, the Scott-Bailey *New Universal*,[34] and his history was used by the makers of the *Encyclopédie* as well.[35] Negatively, his scanty treatment of

English syntax, which he dismissed with some eleven lines in his grammar, prompted Bishop Lowth to prepare the extensive syntax in his own more famous analysis of the language.[36] For the present argument the very weakness—and the peculiar kind of weakness—of Johnson's grammar and history is significant; for the two pieces show him at work in fields where, for once, he could realize neither his own ideals nor those of others but where, as usual, he tried to make the most of the traditional materials at his command.

The hastiest reading of the grammar and history shows that Johnson's heart was not in them. The history consists almost wholly of voluminous specimen texts, representing the language in its development from the age of Alfred to that of Elizabeth and interspersed with brief comments which are quite lost in the mass of quotations; and the grammar ends on anything but a triumphant note: "Thus have I collected rules and examples, by which the English language may be learned, if the reader be already acquainted with grammatical terms, or taught by a master to those that are more ignorant. To have written a grammar for such as are not yet initiated in the schools, would have been tedious, and perhaps at last ineffectual."

Perhaps Johnson remembered the argument for the utility of Germanic studies which had been made by George Hickes in his *Thesaurus*, where it is demonstrated that such studies are necessary for lexicographers, etymologists, grammarians, and historians of the ancient and modern Germanic dialects and where corrections are made of the egregious errors into which otherwise learned men have fallen for want of the proper training.[37] In any case, Johnson knew his own limitations and the dangers of his undertaking a linguistic history. He would not be like Dryden, who, in discussing the language and meter of Chaucer, "mistakes genius for learning, and, in confidence of his abilities, ventured to write of what he had not examined."[38] Johnson's few remarks in the history are, on the other hand, quite chaste and free from wild speculation. Where he had some independent knowledge, he wrote with his usual good sense, as in his discussion of Skinner's charge that Chaucer had vitiated the language by introducing numerous loan-words from the French. Johnson is equally dubious of Skinner's blame and Dryden's praise for Chaucer's alleged introduction of such loans: "Some innovations he might probably make, like others, in the infancy of our poetry, which the paucity of books does [not] allow us to discover with particular exactness; but the works of *Gower* and *Lydgate* sufficiently evince, that his diction was in general like that of his contemporaries."[39]

More often, however, Johnson seems to rely not on independent knowledge but on established commonplaces; his statements have parallels and sources in authorities like Wallis, Hickes, and Junius, who were regularly quoted by the grammarians of the day. Thus his family tree for the Germanic languages is taken, with due acknowledgment, from Hickes, who had given it, in 1689, in his *Institutiones grammaticæ Anglo-Saxonicæ* and who, it may be added, includes in his *Thesaurus* several of the specimen texts which Johnson also quotes.[40] The use itself of specimen texts was, of course, much older than the *Thesaurus*. On the flyleaf of a manuscript Anglo-Saxon vocabulary by Laurence Nowell, one of the sixteenth-century pioneers of Anglo-Saxon studies, is a scheme for studying English by reading texts of successive ages, "by the w^{ch}, and suche like it may appeare, how, and by what steps, our language is fallen fro*m* the old Inglishe, and drawen nearer to the frenche";[41] and specimen texts had been used in historical accounts of the language by many writers, including Camden in his *Remaines*, Alexander Gill in his *Logonomia Anglica*, Hickes in the *Thesaurus*, Bailey in his *Universal Etymological English Dictionary*, James Greenwood in his well-known *Essay towards a Practical English Grammar*, and Benjamin Martin in his *Physico-grammatical Essay*. All in all, Johnson's thoroughly conventional history seems the work of a man who realized that he could contribute little to the stock of knowledge and was determined to add nothing to the burden of error.

In his grammar, though it, too, is conventional, he is more at home and more at ease. He makes some notable and familiar blunders, as when he says that *H* "seldom, perhaps never, begins any but the first syllable"; his notions on etymology as a guide to the spelling of Latin, Greek, and French loans seem not altogether consistent; and he is definitely eighteenth century in his confused phonetics, his preference for spelling pronunciation, and his prescriptive emphasis. Some modern writers have even accused him of retarding the simplification of the English verbal system by his advocacy of distinct participial and preterit forms in the strong verbs.[42] Yet the grammar has its merits. It is brightened by occasional pungent sentences, as when Johnson speaks of the grammarian and spelling reformer Charles Butler, "a man who did not want an understanding which might have qualified him for better employment";[43] and it is steadied by Johnson's knowledge of grammatical tradition, not only in English, but in Latin, Greek, French, and Italian: among the books advertised for sale from his library at his death was the laconic item, "Thirty grammars, &c."

This is indeed the main point to be made about the

grammar, that at every step Johnson considers what his predecessors had done. Under the influence of two main traditions—the ancient tradition of Latin grammar and the more modern tradition begun by John Wallis, who had attempted to make English grammar less Latinate—Johnson is as likely to be copying when he is right as when he is wrong.[44] Thus his explanation of the genitive in *'s*, which he refuses to derive from the pronoun *his* in usages like "Ulysses his bow," may be traced at least as far as to Wallis and to Hickes, who in his Anglo-Saxon grammar had remarked that the modern genitive represents the Old English genitive of nouns like *smið:* Johnson, like Greenwood before him, uses the same word for his illustrative paradigm.[45] Furthermore, Johnson includes traditional material, because it *is* traditional, even when he doubts the value of its inclusion. An example is his discussion of the alphabet. It had long been a habit among grammarians and lexicographers to offer learned "dissertations" on the letters—their names, shapes, "powers"; the articulation, "properties and gradations" of the corresponding sounds. Johnson cannot force himself to such a display of possibly wasted learning. He refuses to discuss the form of the letters, "as an antiquarian," the articulation of the corresponding sounds, "as a mechanick, anatomist, or physiologist," or the properties and beauties of sounds, "as a writer of universal and transcendental grammar"; yet he is equally unwilling to turn his back altogether on the past. The result is a rather unsatisfactory compromise: "I consider the English alphabet only as it is English; and even in this narrow view I follow the example of former grammarians, perhaps with more reverence than judgment, because by writing in English I suppose my reader already acquainted with the English language; and because of sounds in general it may be observed, that words are unable to describe them. An account therefore of the primitive and simple letters is useless almost alike to those who know their sound, and those who know it not."[46] Whereupon the "useless" account is duly inserted.

There is no need to say much more about the grammar. Its traditionalism, overshadowing any possibly original contributions which Johnson may have made, cannot be missed; for Johnson proclaims it in his opening paragraph. The established grammatical terms and distinctions had been questioned already in the eighteenth century; so in the grammar called Brightland's, such innocent terms as *noun* and *verb* are branded affected, foolish, and awkward.[47] Johnson will have none of these ridiculous innovations. Having divided grammar into orthography, etymology, syntax, and prosody, he bluntly continues: "In this division and order of the parts of grammar I follow the common grammarians, without enquiring whether a fitter distribution might not be found. Experience has long shown this method to be so distinct as to obviate confusion, and so comprehensive as to prevent any inconvenient omissions. I likewise use the terms already received, and already understood, though perhaps others more proper might sometimes be invented." Again, the neglect of syntax which set Lowth to work is justified, perhaps not altogether fairly, by the example of Wallis, whose contribution also to Johnson's section on "etymology" is so large that modern readers would be happier if acknowledgments more adequate by modern standards had been made. Johnson refused to emulate the "painful churning" with which his namesake Ben had once tried to bring order into the English verb; instead, under the heading "Of Irregular Verbs," he gives a good deal of direct translation, but not directly acknowledged translation, from Wallis' "De verbis anomalis."[48]

Johnson's rather puzzling relation to Wallis cannot be treated here,[49] though in justice it must be said that the relation was not always one of slavish copying. The high point of the grammar is probably reached when Johnson, after transcribing a number of Wallis' etymologies, adds some terse comments: "In these observations it is easy to discover great sagacity and great extravagance, an ability to do much defeated by the desire of doing more than enough. It may be remarked,

"1. That Wallis's derivations are often so made, that by the same licence any language may be deduced from any other. . . .

"4. That some of his derivations are apparently erroneous."

One more illustration of the debt to Wallis may be given, if only because it affords a transition from Johnson's grammar to his Preface. Writing of abstract nouns like *depth*, *truth*, *height*, *flight*, and *fright*, Wallis had said that the last three should be spelled with final *-th* instead of *-t* except that custom forbids the *h* to be twice written. Johnson, in his grammar, dutifully transcribed Wallis, and remembered him when he came to write his Preface, where his own conservatism had freer play. Complaining, on the first page of the Preface, of bad spellings too long established to be reformed, Johnson cites several examples, including a number of Wallis' abstract nouns in *-th*. "Of this kind are the derivatives *length* from *long*, *strength* from *strong*, *darling* from *dear*, *breadth* from *broad*, from *dry*, *drought*, and from *high*, *height*, which *Milton*, in zeal for analogy, writes *highth; Quid te exempta juvat spinis de pluribus una;* to change all would be too much, and to change one is nothing."[50]

For the details, then, of Johnson's work in his history and grammar, as well as for their broad outline, one can discover expected and unexpected sources and parallels. No one would be able, and no one has really tried, to make much of an argument for Johnson's originality as historian of the language or as grammarian. The Preface and the body of the *Dictionary* are a different matter. Of the Preface, Horne Tooke himself spoke highly,[51] for it is one of the finest things that Johnson ever wrote, a moving personal document and an excellent statement of the aims, methods, and difficulties of one kind of eighteenth-century lexicography. Its excellence cannot be rightly understood, however, if it is read as too many Johnsonians have apparently read it, in isolation from its historical context; for the basis of its merit is not originality. The eighteenth century was an age of dictionaries—dictionaries of all kinds, from horsemanship to mathematics; and critical and self-critical lexicographers and encyclopedists produced, in the course of the century, many discussions of the problems and purposes of lexicography. One such discussion which Johnson certainly knew and almost certainly admired was the Preface to the famous *Cyclopædia* of Ephraim Chambers. Johnson once considered making a revision of the *Cyclopædia*, which was in his library at his death and for which, in a typically Johnsonian way, he expressed a liking; and the tradition has persisted that he "formed his style" on that of Chambers, either on Chambers' original proposal for the *Cyclopædia* (now lost), on the Preface to the *Cyclopædia*, which Johnson was said to have imitated when he wrote his own *Plan*, or on Chambers' *Considerations Preparatory to a Second Edition.*[52] Whatever the truth of that may be, a number of topics and a number of statements on those topics are common to Chambers' *Considerations* and Preface and to Johnson's Preface and *Plan.*

In the first place, the attitudes of the two men toward the academies are strikingly similar. As Flasdieck has shown, Johnson's rejection of the idea of an English academy was a turning point in a line of thought which had its beginning in the sixteenth century;[53] but Chambers, surprisingly enough, is not listed in Flasdieck's Index, although he had rejected the academy notion quite as vigorously as Johnson. In his *Considerations*, Chambers declared that the scheme for an English academy was unsuited to the present state of the nation and that in France and Italy the academies had but slowly produced works which at last were disappointing. Some of his statements are more than a little Johnsonian, as when he speaks of "Royal, Imperial, Cæsarian, and Ducal Academies, Palatine Societies, and the like: Splendid Names, pompous Titles, but rarely productive of Fruits answerable thereto! Many of our private Clubs," he adds, "might vie with their Academies; and much of the Conversation at certain Coffee-house Tables, with their Conferences in Form."[54] Again like Johnson, Chambers can reject the idea of an English academy while hoping that his individual work would accomplish some of the purposes for which academies had elsewhere been instituted. In the *Considerations* he maintained that the plan of an encyclopedia like his, if well executed, would fix "the Use and Acceptation of an infinite Number of Words" and would thus supply, "in some Measure, the Want of an *English Academy*";[55] and the Preface to the fifth edition of his work, the edition which Johnson owned, opens with the same comparison:

"The Vocabulary of the academy *della Crusca* was above forty years in compiling, and the Dictionary of the French academy much longer; and yet the present work will be found more extensive than either of them in its subject and design, as much as it falls short of them in respect of years, or of hands employed in it."[56] Clearly, Johnson's self-estimate of *his* accomplishment, in the Preface to his octavo edition, was by no means unique.

How had Chambers been able to accomplish such things? His explanation is precisely that which the present essay would offer for Johnson's achievement. Chambers, like Johnson, had some pride in his work; both gave to England books of a kind which England had not had before. Yet Chambers had no illusions about the powers of the individual lexicographer. Though the toils of lexicography, he said in the *Considerations*, are such that Scaliger could hardly find terms fit for them, no credit is allowed to lexicographers but "that of being laborious Compilers." The lexicographer cannot hope for perfection: "If nothing of this Kind were published till a Man had made it as perfect as he was able, he must never publish it; and . . . if this were the Condition of writing a Dictionary, No-body would be found to undertake it."[57] The single-handed dictionary-maker must therefore strengthen himself by enlisting the co-operation of the living and the dead. In the *Considerations*, Chambers appealed to his readers to aid him by informal, voluntary contributions, just as Johnson wrote later to Chesterfield in his *Plan:* "I here lay before your Lordship the plan of my undertaking, that more may not be demanded than I intend; and that, before it is too far advanced to be thrown into a new method, I may be advertised of its defects or superfluities."

Appeals like these were likely to bring small response,

but the lexicographer had a more valuable resource. To borrow from his predecessors, Chambers wrote in his Preface, "is a kind of privilege attached to the office of lexicographer; if not by any formal grant, yet by connivance at least"; and so he becomes "an heir, to a large patrimony, gradually raised by the industry and endeavours of a long race of ancestors. What the French and Italian academists, the abbe Furetiere, the editors of Trevoux, Savary, Chauvin, Harris, Wolfius, Daviler, and others have done, has been subservient to my purpose. To say nothing of an inferior class of books of this kind, which contributed their share; dictionaries on almost every subject, from medicine and law, down to heraldry and the manage."[58] With the same knowledge of the difficulties and scant rewards of lexicography, with the same frankness and in the same grateful spirit, Johnson in *his* Preface acknowledges *his* sources: Bailey, Ainsworth, Phillips, and especially Junius and Skinner, "the only names which I have forborn to quote when I copied their books; not that I might appropriate their labours or usurp their honours, but that I might spare a perpetual repetition by one general acknowledgment."

Such parallels were almost inevitable between any two intelligent discussions of lexicography in the eighteenth century, and the differences between the relations of Chambers and Johnson to their respective predecessors must not be overlooked; yet the familiarity of nearly all of Johnson's topics and of most of his ideas clearly emerges, even when the difference between a dictionary and an encyclopedia has caused him and Chambers to apply their commonplaces differently. Both men, for example, were more than a little disturbed by the fact of linguistic change and by the current state of the English language. So Johnson writes: "Our language, for almost a century, has, by the concurrence of many causes, been gradually departing from its original *Teutonick* character, and deviating towards a *Gallick* structure and phraseology, from which it ought to be our endeavour to recal it, by making our ancient volumes the ground-work of stile, admitting among the additions of later times, only such as may supply real deficiencies, such as are readily adopted by the genius of our tongue, and incorporate easily with our native idioms." Johnson was not copying Chambers, but the following passage from Chambers will show that he was repeating old ideas which Chambers, making a different application, had repeated before him: "UPON the whole, nothing could be more desirable than an *index expurgatorius*, to clear the language of superfluous words and synonymons; to expunge the modern French and Italian terms in the several arts, where we have Latin and Greek ones; and even the Latin and Greek ones, where we have English or Saxon ones, equal in sound and significancy."[59] Of the "casual and mutable" technical terms which gave the lexicographer so much trouble to gather and to define, Chambers thought no better than Johnson, though what Johnson called "the laborious and mercantile part of the people" were perhaps not responsible for "the modern French and Italian terms in the several arts" to which Chambers objected.

The two men's ideas of the problems of definition again were similar and again were unoriginal. Johnson had no hope of satisfying his critics with his definitions, since he had not always satisfied himself. One difficulty was to explain the simple words: "To interpret a language by itself is very difficult; many words cannot be explained by synonimes, because the idea signified by them has not more than one appellation; nor by paraphrase, because simple ideas cannot be described." Chambers had also drawn the distinction between simple words, which are inexplicable because the simple ideas attached to them cannot be communicated by language but must be had from sensation, and terms, which *can* be defined since they symbolize a combination of simple ideas; and he, too, had been dissatisfied with his efforts at definition. When a word had a number of senses, he had said, the most regular procedure would be to begin by settling its etymology, for "IN strictness, every term should be first given in its literal, or grammatical meaning; especially if it be a term in several arts: as this helps to shew the orderly derivation of the word, from the simple or general idea that gave rise to it, to its last and most complex state.—Yet we have not always kept to this method."[60] Johnson made the same confession: "In every word of extensive use, it was requisite to mark the progress of its meaning, and show by what gradations of intermediate sense it has passed from its primitive to its remote and accidental signification; so that every foregoing explanation should tend to that which follows, and the series be regularly concatenated from the first notion to the last. . . .

"This is specious, but not always practicable."

The troublesome multiplicity of meanings was made worse by sloppy thinking and imprecise speech; but for this neither lexicographer would accept responsibility. As Johnson said, "this uncertainty is not to be imputed to me, who do not form, but register the language; who do not teach men how they should think, but relate how they have hitherto expressed their thoughts." He had given up the old dream that the lexicographer might fix his language; and Chambers, though he regretted that all men did not mean "precisely the same thing, by the same name," was just as willing to excuse the lexicographer: "The Dictionary-writer is not supposed to have any hand in the things he relates; he is no more concerned to make the improvements, or establish the significations, than the historian to atchieve the transactions he relates."[61] The lexicographer as historian is hardly the man to fix "the Use and Acceptation of an infinite Number of Words." He had enough to do to keep his minutes of the language; someone else might call the meeting to order.

To many other plans and prefaces of dictionary-makers, Johnson's may usefully be compared, not in order to establish sources, but to show that many men, at work on different undertakings, were thinking in similar ways—a conclusion which, for the present argument, is more significant than the establishment of a single source would be. Here the prefaces to the dictionaries of the French and Italian academies must naturally be included; if England was to have no academy, individual Englishmen must do an academy's job, and Johnson invites the comparison by his repeated references to the academies, both in his Preface and in his *Plan*. If, then, one reads the prefaces which the Accademia della Crusca and the French Academy provided for editions of their dictionaries published before 1747,[62] one finds some eight or ten topics which they share with Johnson's *Plan* or Preface or with both, though the answers given to the various questions may differ widely. The two academies and Johnson all make a good deal of their patriotic purposes, and each has discovered a golden age for the native language: the fourteenth century for Italian, the seventeenth century for French, from the time of Sidney to the Restoration for English. Change in all three languages is looked upon with suspicion, and the lexicographers of all three would like to prevent, retard, or direct it. The sources of linguistic authority have been considered, and the Englishman and the Italians have included, from writers having authority, illustrative quotations whose importance they emphasize; after some debate, the Frenchmen omitted quotations, since their own pronouncements, made by celebrated orators and poets in the most flourishing century of their language, were sufficiently authoritative in themselves. All three dictionaries have been more or less selective, emphasizing the core of the vocabulary, the words in common use among cultivated speakers and writers, especially those of the golden age. The different senses of the chosen words have been distinguished in all three; something has been done to indicate levels of usage; and consideration has been given to technical questions of organization, spelling, and the like. One gets the feeling, in the course of this comparison, that Johnson was fully as aware of tradition in his *Plan* and Preface as he was in his history and grammar.

The feeling is strengthened when one moves from technical matters, which are better discussed in the evaluation of Johnson's practices in the body of the *Dictionary*, to examine his theories about language. They are theories which many writers had expressed before him. Words, he says, are the signs of ideas, names imposed by man, not by God, and hence arbitrary and governed by custom. On the other hand, some usages remain barbarous and improper, whatever custom may be and whoever may be cited as authority for them, and here etymology may rightly be invoked to determine propriety; for, although every language as a whole is arbitrary, its native structure should not be weakened or distorted by unwise innovation. Language thus appears as a kind of battleground between reason and "general grammar" and the natural instability of man, the creator of language and its corruptor. The battle is inevitably a losing one; some "anomalies" will remain, however much the critic of language may prefer "analogy" —that is, the usual modes of derivation, composition, and inflection. Linguistic change, which is often "corruption," will go on, but the good lexicographer will do his stoic best to direct it and to root out the less firmly planted "improprieties and absurdities"; for the ideal language should be stable, regular, and slow to change.

Why is it that, despite the watchful lexicographer, each living language constantly degenerates? The ultimate cause is the nature of fallen man, but a more immediate cause is that language, inconveniently, is speech; and in speech, corruption begins. In its earliest stages language was not written at all, but "merely oral," a wild and barbarous jargon of words pronounced so carelessly and heard so imperfectly that dialects arose. Since early spelling was very unsettled, it was a long time before writing could exert its benevolent regularizing influence; in the interests of regularization, one should resist the corrupt notion that we should spell as we speak. To Johnson, then, living speech was painfully irregular; yet he saw in linguistic change this much regularity, that it was always cyclic, a sequence of growth, perfection, and decay. The idea of growth toward perfection was not irreconcilable with the belief that linguistic change is inevitably bad, since the traditionalist could always hold that the present was the golden age from which degeneration should not be allowed; or he could maintain, as Johnson did in his Preface, that English had passed its prime and was gradually subsiding into a Gallic babbling. In addition to the corruption inevitable in speech, further causes of this sad state of affairs were the caprice and fashions of an ordered commercial society, the growth of science, the use of figurative expressions, numerous translations, the study of foreign languages, and simple ignorance.

Johnson's fear of translations recalls his Francophobia; it also suggests that he recognized clear structural differences among languages and families of languages, differences which were not obliterated by lexical mixture through loan-words. English, Johnson recognized, was lexically a mixed language, which for known reasons and by known processes had borrowed both phrases and words, especially polysyllabic words, from Latin and Romance, sometimes to the detriment of the native word-hoard. The fact remained that this mixed language, neither "primitive" nor "self-originated" and of ancestry ultimately unknown, was descended from "the Saxon dialect," and as such it was a Teutonic language and cognate with Dutch, German, and the rest. Among its distinguishing characteristics were its limited inflections; its syntax, which was "too inconstant to be reduced to rules"; and its "vague and indeterminate" use of many common words. Johnson would have written a better grammar if English had been a little more like Latin.

This summary is more complete and more systematic than any single statement which Johnson ever made about language, so that it may perhaps impose on his disconnected remarks an order which he never intended. The alternative to such a presentation would be a mere listing of isolated propositions; and orderly summary, as an expository device, will not be misleading unless it is forgotten that Johnson's separate propositions are here related as he himself nowhere explicitly related them. In any case, the same judgment may be passed on his linguistic views as on his grammar: unless one wishes to maintain that, implicit in Johnson's thinking about language, there was an order which gave his single statements a significance that they did not have in isolation or in other systems, then Johnson was not an original thinker about language. Though this large question may be left partially open, the burden of proof must lie with those who would make Johnson both systematic and creative in his system; his individual questions and answers about language are alike traditional. The ancients had asked whether language exists by nature or by convention and had debated the claims of analogy and anomaly. Less remotely, Dante had made the cause of linguistic change the instability of man; and generations of philologists, examining the scriptural account of the Creation and the unfortunate affair of Babel, had searched out other causes of the diversity of speech. The collective lexicography of the French Academy had been devoted to the hygienic fixation of a language, and eighteenth-century Italy was full of Francophobes. From Aristotle to the academicians, parallels to Johnson's beliefs can be cited almost at will, and this without examining the English traditions, in which, for example, Sir John Cheke in the sixteenth century[63] had applied the theory of cyclic change to Latin and to Greek. Any noteworthy originality in Johnson's philosophy of language must lie in his system as a whole, not in its elements; and he made no systematic statement.

At the present stage of the argument this predictable conclusion is almost trivial. What is more important is to note that impressive reasons could be given for what Johnson and his contemporaries thought and tried to do about language, so that ideas and undertakings which today seem nonsensical not only had their justification but were closely linked with those which today seem wise. A good example is the attempt to fix a language—French, English, Italian, or some other. Johnson abandoned the attempt, it is true, but one should remember that he abandoned it in his Preface, after he had been compelled, for some years, to face the facts of linguistic life directly and after he had been preceded in dereliction by writers like Benjamin Martin, who had closed his *Physico-grammatical Essay* with a flat renunciation: "As to the pretence of fixing a standard to the purity and perfection of any language, while the state of the people remains unchanged and unmix'd with others, [it] is utterly vain and impertinent, because no language as depending on arbitrary use and custom, can ever be permanently the same, but will always be in a mutable and fluctuating state; and what is deem'd polite and elegant in one age, may be accounted uncouth and barbarous in another. Of this truth none I think can doubt, as we have such numerous instances of it in the fore-going part of this essay, to which perhaps two or three centuries may add as many more."

Yet the notion so abandoned was not a stupid notion. From Martin's own premise that language depends on convention, one could go on, by a suitable misunderstanding of the term "convention," to replace the language-giving God of Genesis with an enlightened parliament and so arrive at the belief that man could mold a language at his will. According to Wilkins in his *Real Character*, at least one language—the Malayan—seems to have originated by precisely this kind of convention; for it was "occasioned by the concourse of Fishermen from *Pegu*, *Siam*, *Bengala*, and several other Nations, who meeting together at a place convenient for Fishing, and finding that it was by situation exceeding commodious for Traffick from several parts, did agree to settle there a Plantation; and accordingly built the Town of Malacca . . ." and invented Malay.[64]

Once granted this ability to mold a language freely by the exercise of reason, a slight shift or misunderstanding would make a real language seem as pliable as a specially invented, artificial language; and for reshaping real languages there were any number of reasons and predispositions. To the pious, Genesis might offer suggestions: in the beginning, language was God-given; it had perhaps remained unchanged from Adam to Noah; and the most spectacular of linguistic changes had been a divinely inflicted punishment. A little modified, the theory of a divinely given original language could become the theory of cyclic change, with a golden age relegated to the past; and the history of Latin and Greek made both the cyclic theory and the possibility of fixing a language seem plausible. Or one could argue, as Chambers argued, from a doctrine of ideas. Ideas spring from sensation, and the relations among them "are as immutable as the Creator's will." There is, therefore, "no more possibility of seeing the relations of things to each other, differently; than of altering their nature, and overturning the system." The trouble lies in language, for "if all men meant precisely the same thing, by the same name, there would be no room for their differing upon any point, either in philosophy, or any thing else."[65] The lexicographer, as Chambers said, need not be the one to enforce agreement in the use of names. He might play the part of a simple historian of language, providing essential information concerning the actual, not the ideal, use of names to the grand reformer. In some such fashion one could work one's way from the "nonsensical" belief that a language could and should be fixed to the "wise" belief that a good lexicographer should divide and number the different senses of words, if only as a means to establish an artificial, philosophic language. It was William Lloyd, bishop of Worcester, who so distinguished the meanings of English words in the dictionary which was printed at the end of Wilkins' *Real Character;* "it being," as Greenwood said in his *Grammar*, "*the best* English *Dictionary that was ever published.*"[66]

Very little ingenuity, then, is required to show, between eighteenth-century premises and eighteenth-century practices, a good many more potential connections than Johnson ever troubled to develop systematically; and with this reminder that the attempt to place Johnson's ideas and methods in historical perspective is not an impertinent effort to belittle his accomplishment, we may draw to a conclusion with an evaluation of his work in the body of the Dictionary. The conventional verdict, in general, is obviously sound: it took the historical linguistics of the nineteenth century to make a better dictionary than Johnson's. Still, the conventional verdict needs correction in some ways. It puts too much emphasis on the differences between Johnson's and earlier dictionaries, especially those of the academies, rather than on the continuity of the development, where the emphasis should lie; and it is incorrect and misleading both in some of its details and in at least one of its vaguer but most important propositions.

That proposition is to the effect that Johnson's *Dictionary* had some noteworthy influence on the development of English. According to McKnight, whose account of the *Dictionary* is better than the average, Johnson did much to correct, improve, and ascertain the language.[67] According to Starnes and Noyes, who have written the best book so far on the earlier English dictionaries, the language was permanently improved, in many ways, by Johnson's work.[68] W. K. Wimsatt calls the *Dictionary* "a public instrument of the highest authority for shaping the language."[69] Even an outstanding Germanicist like Fernand Mossé seems unnecessarily alarmed when he finds it lucky that Johnson's prohibitions of certain kinds of words and phrases were not observed, so that the language did not lose its idioms.[70] Statements of this sort are more likely to be made by men of letters than by philologists; and linguists, at least in the United States today, too often dismiss them with an impatience which only prolongs misunderstanding. The misunderstanding goes deep and involves such basic matters as the nature of language itself as the most massively resistant, the most nearly self-determining, of human conventions; the relation of speech to writing; the relative importance of what are sometimes called grammar and lexicon; and the aims of humanistic study and teaching.

Perhaps, however, agreement concerning Johnson's alleged influence on the language can be reached without any rash attempt to pronounce upon these larger issues. One can admit that Johnson, as the codifier of a spelling already pretty well established by the printers, enjoyed high orthographic authority, that his preference for distinct preterits and participles may in one small point have affected the English verbal system, that he commented on usage more frequently and more extensively than his predecessors had done,[71] that his dictionary was a model and a source for later lexicographers, and that his general and particular opinions about language were often repeated. One can admit, too, that an understanding of those opinions is a help to the understanding of certain aspects of prose style in the later eighteenth century—a style which, it has often been said, Johnson influenced by both precept and example. But to say that Johnson had considerable influence on prose style is not to say that he had considerable influence on the English language, unless one quietly assumes appropriate definitions of both language and style. Certainly he did not influence the sounds of English, for he did not mark pronunciation. With the one exception already noted, it will hardly be argued that his derivative grammar influenced English morphology; and of English syntax he had almost nothing to say. Even his influence on prose style cannot be very precisely stated until his place in the literary and scholarly traditions of his time has been more accurately fixed. Since in matters of language his ideas were not particularly new, what might seem at first the influence of Johnson may actually be the influence of the whole tradition in which he stands.

With the concession that Johnson probably had some influence, not yet too clearly defined, on the style of English literary prose, and with the statement that a Johnsonian influence on English grammar in the sense of English phonology, morphology, and syntax was virtually impossible, one may turn to the lexicon; those who say that Johnson shaped the language often mean by "language" only the vocabulary. Again it will hardly be argued that the *Dictionary* had much effect on the use of the simplest and commonest words, however fine its distinction and logical its classification of their varied senses may have been; and to assert its strong influence on the great middle range of the English vocabulary is to assert an influence on thought, not only on language, which Johnson himself refused to claim. The indistinctness of thought which, Johnson said, made definition difficult was not corrected by the reading of the definitions which recorded it.

There remain the learned words, the technical terms and Latinisms of Johnson's word-list, which have been so much discussed. These did not influence the diction of the common man; he did not understand them in 1755, and he does not understand them now. Horne Tooke spoke for at least one school of thought when he said: "Nearly one third of this Dictionary is as much the language of the Hottentots as of the English; and it would be no difficult matter so to translate any one of the plainest and most popular numbers of the *Spectator* into the language of that Dictionary, that no mere Englishman, though well read in his own language, would be able to comprehend one sentence of it."[72] Noah Webster agreed with Horne Tooke and helped to set the abiding fashion of drawing up jawbreaking lists of Johnson's sesquipedalian monstrosities,[73] an amusement which is on a par with the endless repetition of Johnson's definitions of words like *cough;* but in fairness to Johnson and for the benefit of those who would find his influence in the learned vocabulary of English literature, a strong qualification must at once be made. That influence may have been real, but attempts to state it precisely are liable to degenerate into elaborate Websterian lists, which seem so impressive that students may not notice how tenuous are their connections with the generalizations drawn from or imposed upon them. The listing game can be played with dozens of English dictionaries besides Johnson's, partly because the English dictionary, through much of the seventeenth century, was primarily a collection of hard words and technical terms, partly because the dictionary, from even earlier times, had been made to serve some of the functions of an encyclopedia.

Full illustration would entail the making of more lists, for which the skeptical may more economically be referred to the dictionaries themselves; but the notorious definition of *cough* may well be cited. Johnson's definition reads thus: "A convulsion of the lungs, vellicated by some sharp serosity. It is pronounced *coff*." The words of Benjamin Martin's definition seem equally philosophic, and there are more of them: "COUGH, a disease affecting the lungs, occasioned by a sharp serous humour vellicating the fibrous coat thereof, and urging it to a discharge by spitting."

Since Martin's definition reads word for word like that of Ephraim Chambers, the stock joke at Johnson's expense is here an exact inversion of the facts: in his definition he compressed and simplified the description current in his time.[74] Johnson did use big words in his prose, and he did put big words into his *Dictionary;* as he says in his Preface, he found them in the dictionaries of others, and the public, on the authority of Chambers,[75] had come to expect them. Horne Tooke and Noah Webster must be taken seriously, but not, after all, too seriously. The word *Hottentot,* which could have been directed against other dictionaries than Johnson's, was one more missile in a critical bombardment of word-lists which was almost conventional. In the sixteenth century, before purely English lexicography had begun, William Turner had damned Thomas Cooper's *Thesaurus* for its inkhorn terms; and in the eighteenth, only a few years before Johnson set to work, Chambers had devoted a long paragraph to berating an unnamed dictionary-writer for such "detestable stuff" as the noun *pugnacity*.[76] As often as not, the accusation was no more than partially justified. Turner was wrong about Cooper, and Starnes and Noyes have shown that even the hard-word lists of the seventeenth-century lexicographers can be matched, to a considerable extent, by citations from contemporary prose.[77] Johnson lists *pugnacity* without examples but without complaint.

Theories spun from Johnson's remarks on the social status of various expressions must be spun with as much caution as theories concerning the influence of his "philosophic words." It is often hard to say whether his strictures were justified by the actual usage of his time, but it is easy to show that many of his objections were as vain as Swift's campaign against *mob*, which Johnson did not condemn. He did condemn *to bang* "beat, thump," *to belabour*, *black-guard*, *to budge*, *to cajole*, *to coax*, *to con* "study, commit to memory," *conundrum*, *to doff*, *doings*, *to dumbfound*, *fuss* sb., *gambler*, *glum*, *ignoramus*, *job* sb., *lead* sb. as in "to take the *lead*," *pat* "fit, convenient," *posse*, *to sconce* "fine," *scrape* "difficulty," *sensible* "reasonable, judicious," *shabby*, *to shail* "walk sideways," *to sham* "trick" and *sham* sb., *shambling* adj., *simpleton*, *slim* "slender," *souse* adv. "with sudden violence," *spick and span*, *squab* adv. "plump and flat," *to squabble*, *stark* adv. as in "*stark* mad," *tiff* sb., *touchy*, *trait*, *to transpire* "to escape from secrecy to notice," *to volunteer*, *width*, etc.[78] An examination of some eight hundred of his comments in the light of the evidence provided by the *OED* reveals that Johnson's condemnation was no death warrant to these and similar expressions, which went their upward, downward, or level ways despite him; and one must conclude that the extent of his influence on the vocabulary of English, as on English grammar, has been overestimated.

The traditional judgment of another aspect of Johnson's work, his etymologizing, is also somewhat distorted. His etymologies have been rendered more notorious than by rights they ought to be, and even the occasional attempts at their defense have usually been halfhearted. So R. W. Chapman wrote in 1948: "Everyone remembers Macaulay's snap verdict: 'Johnson was a wretched etymologist.' He does not tell us who knew any better. Who *should* etymologize, beyond the limits of the obvious, in that pre-Copernican age before philology was born?"[79] That verdict is more just than most, and in a single lecture on *Lexicography*, Chapman could hardly say more; but the defense can be made more persuasive by adding that Johnson was exposed to contagious delusions of which most of his critics now know very little, that he had no time for etymological research and did not set himself up as a professed etymologist, but that he gathered together the best available resources and made better use of them than many alleged professionals.

Apparently few students have taken the trouble to examine the etymological works which were in Johnson's library. It has been easier to repeat his acknowledgment to Skinner and Junius, from his Preface, and the story of how he assured a visitor that he also had a collection of Welsh proverbs, which would help him with his Welsh. As a matter of fact, the number of etymological works among his books was rather large, including not only Junius and Skinner but Bailey, of course, and Camden, John Davies' Welsh dictionary, Hickes's *Thesaurus*, Martinius' Latin etymological dictionary, Ménage, Minsheu, Somner's dictionary of Anglo-Saxon, and G. J. Voss's *Etymologicon linguae Latinae*. For a dictionary-maker, Johnson had a useful collection.

Unfortunately, the largest collection, in the eighteenth century, would have presented him with more chaff than grain. Two main foundations of eighteenth-century etymologizing were the baffling history of the wanderings of the peoples (a shifting picture drawn from the Bible and the accounts of ancient and medieval historians) and the elaborately tabulated "mutations of the letters," which can be traced ultimately to the classical grammarians. The wanderings of the peoples, with which the division of languages into matrices and derivatives was connected, are more than a little confusing. The etymologists rouse admiration both for their learning and for the ingenuity with which they bring into a single story the adventures of Shem, Ham, Japhet, the Homeric heroes, the Phoenicians, Gomer, Odin, Hengest, Horsa, the Scythians, and the Druids. Linguistic patriotism was an irresistible driving force, a flame by which the most diverse languages could be welded together. Benjamin Martin repeats a common theory when he writes: "We are told also by Cluverius and other geographers and historians that the ancient Germans, Gauls, Spaniards, and Britains [*sic*] were all call'd by the name of *Celto-Scythae;* and further that they had all one language and differ'd only in dialect; and many of the learned have thought that this ancient German, Celtic, or as it was most commonly call'd, Teutonic language was an original one, or one of those we have deriv'd from the confusion of tongues at Babel; yea, some have gone farther, and insisted on its being the vernacular tongue of Adam, his family, and descendants."[80] Some had gone farther still; but that way lies the stupidity of patronizing learned men who merely shared the errors of their times.

As for the mutations of the letters, the chief conclusion to be drawn from them is that any letter, and presumably any sound, could become any other, without regard to time, place, or linguistic relationship. The mutations, which may be seen to advantage in Ménage and Skinner, amounted to an exhaustive classification and exemplification of the possible differences in spelling between any two words; and though in theory some mutations were limited to or characteristic of particular languages, in practice they were applied with small restraint. Some likeness of sound or sense provoked a guess at an etymon; the etymon and the word derived from it were then compared, and the differences in their spelling tabulated; and these differences, generalized, became rules for the explanation of other origins. Erudition, close knowledge of texts, and a practical mastery of many languages kept the best scholars within some bounds, but lesser men could and did do fantastic things. The listing of their fanciful etymologies is as cheap a sport as the quotation of Johnson's high-flown definitions; but anyone with a taste for the bizarre might look into the Rev. George William Lemon's *English Etymology*, published at London in 1783, or at Cleland's somewhat earlier *Way to Things by Words, and to Words by Things* (1766), whose contents are sufficiently characterized by the rest of its title: "A Sketch of an Attempt at the Retrieval of the Antient Celtic, or, Primitive Language of Europe. To which is added, A succinct Account of the Sanscort [*sic*], or Learned Language of the Bramins. Also Two Essays, the one On the Origin of the Musical Waits at Christmas. The other On the Real Secret of the Free Masons." Obviously, too much fuss has been made about Johnson's etymologies. Without pretense, he did what he could from the materials at hand. He had the common sense to correct, in his grammar, the etymological extravagance of Wallis and, in his Preface, the less plausible speculations of Junius.[81] He should not be asked for more than he set out to give.

There remain the two features of the body of Johnson's text which are most frequently considered Johnsonian innovations: his use of divided and numbered definitions, in which the different senses of words are analyzed, and his inclusion of quotations illustrating the use of the words defined. The statement of H. B. Wheatley, who in 1885 listed "the three grand characteristics of the book which distinguish it from all other dictionaries that preceded it," may still represent the standard view:

"I. It was the first English dictionary that could in any way be considered as a standard, all its predecessors being mere lists of words in comparison. For a century at least literary men had been sighing for some standard, and Johnson did what Dryden, Waller, Pope, Swift, and others had only talked about.

"II. In this dictionary the meanings of words were, for the first time, fully illustrated by well-selected authorities.

"III. The definitions are full, clear, and above all praise for their happy illustration of the meaning of words. These can never be superseded, and the instances in which Johnson's successors have been able to improve upon his work in this respect are singularly few. That he had no assistance from his predecessors in this most important part of a lexicographer's work will be seen by a casual reference to the earlier dictionaries."[82]

With Wheatley's first point and with his praise of Johnson there can be no quarrel. Difficulty arises, however, with the phrase "for the first time," as Wheatley applies it to Johnson's use of citations from authorities, and with the remark that in definition Johnson had no assistance from his predecessors, as "a casual reference to the earlier dictionaries" is supposed to show. The statement concerning the illustrative quotations is true, if it is limited to English dictionaries; but that limitation is hardly wise in view of Johnson's knowledge of the classics and his announced intention to rival the academies. Illustrative quotations had been given, with more or less skill and in more or less abundance, by the Greek and Latin lexicographers since the sixteenth century, by the Accademia della Crusca and by Altieri for Italian, by Bluteau for Portuguese, Richelet for French, and no doubt by many others; the list is drawn from Johnson's own library. Here Johnson, or Johnson's printer, did not even reach the highest level of practice in his day. Already in the seventeenth century, the academicians della Crusca had taken some care with their examples. For words taken from fourteenth-century authors, they had tried to give citations both from poetry and from prose. For words taken from well-printed books, they had given exact references, and when they cited from manuscripts, they had named the owners. Still they had not escaped the minute faultfinding of Ottonelli, who greatly enjoyed correcting their references and whose book was likewise in Johnson's library.[83] In the eighteenth century, therefore, they took yet greater care. Their dictionary, they said, was better than those of other languages, because it gave numerous examples of the usage of each word—examples whose number had been much increased since the earlier editions. The new quotations had been added with care, in certain specifically stated situations, so that they served much better purposes than mere enlargement. They provided a fuller record of usage ancient and modern, in prose and in poetry, in manuscript and in print. Sometimes the mere examples, without explanations, would clarify meanings. And the examples were carefully presented. Quotations which had been so truncated that they were meaningless or untrue to the author had now been lengthened so that it was a pleasure to read them, and the references had been reviewed and corrected, care being taken that citations from printed books should be from the best editions.[84]

That sort of work, the student of Johnson should admit, could only be done by an academy; the life of a single man would be too short. And it was partly because Johnson did not do that sort of work that he was able to produce a standard dictionary single-handed. He took his quotations where he found them, from books which happened to be in his own collection or which he could borrow from his friends; and either he, his amanuenses, or his printer was often content, not with exact references, but with only authors' names, some of which themselves are wrong. A second Ottonelli would have had good hunting in Johnson's book.

The case is just as clear with Johnson's divided and numbered definitions, for which predecessors can be found in England as well as abroad. Starnes and Noyes have already shown that Martin, in his *Lingua Britannica* of 1749, had used the divided and classified definition and that, for this part of his work, Martin in turn had drawn upon the Latin dictionary of Robert Ainsworth, which Johnson also used, and on the English-French, French-English dictionary of Abel Boyer, which likewise was in Johnson's library.[85] It is possible that Martin, publishing in 1749, took his scheme of definition from Johnson's *Plan* of 1747;[86] but he need not have found it there. He might as well have found it in Lloyd's dictionary at the end of Wilkins' *Real Character*, the dictionary which Greenwood had called the best and which Johnson also certainly knew, as can be gathered from his reference, in his grammar, to Bishop Wilkins' "great work of the philosophical language."[87] Both Martin and Johnson, again, could have found the scheme in the dictionaries of the academies, whose prefaces regularly discuss the divided definition, or, for that matter, in half-a-dozen dictionaries of one language or another, as anyone may see who makes something more than a "casual reference" to the books in Johnson's library. What one lexicographer had joined together, it took a long time for others to put asunder: synonymies of the later eighteenth century were concerned to distinguish words which had been linked in dictionary definitions since the Renaissance;[88] but the eighteenth century was a discriminating age, and when the time and the man came together, Johnson did the work which someone was destined to do. His definitions deserve all the praise which has been given them, and in substance they are largely original with him; but in concept at least, and to some extent in execution, they were far from novel.

At last to summarize what, despite its length, is not a full account but a correction and extension of earlier studies: Johnson's *Dictionary*, a booksellers' project, was what its age demanded—a standard and standardizing dictionary which included a history of the language, a grammar, and an extensive list of words selected with some care, explained by divided and classified definitions, and illustrated with quotations from authorities. Like Johnson's ideas about the nature of language in general and the history and structure of English in particular, his techniques in lexicography do not seem new when they are viewed against the background of earlier work, not in England only, but in Europe at large, the international "republic of letters." To English lexicography, Johnson's original contribution was noteworthy; for European lexicography, he produced another good dictionary, an outstandingly good dictionary, of a modern language. Not all parts of his work are of the same high quality. His grammar and history of the language and his etymologies are mediocre, as one would expect of a man of Johnson's century, training, and temperament when called upon to do single-handed the work of forty men. His influence on the development of the language is dubious at best, and too much has been made of the Latinity of his word-list and definitions. The magnitude of his achievement remains, more clearly seen when he is not judged in unnatural isolation.

II

The Composition and Publication of *The Plan of a Dictionary*

THE story of the composition and publication of *The Plan of a Dictionary of the English Language* begins in 1746 and ends in 1755.[1] Since of no other of his works do we possess such abundant manuscript material, it is a story that provides an unparalleled opportunity to observe Johnson's methods of composing and revising. Also, in scope at least, it is the sort of account which, because of the paucity of evidence, can be written about very few eighteenth-century (or earlier) works. In the present chapter, we attempt to reconstruct the principal events in the production and printing of the pamphlet; in the following chapter, we have concentrated on the series of incidents involving Johnson and Lord Chesterfield.

I

The story begins with the writing of "A Short Scheme for compiling a new Dictionary of the English Language," which is in Johnson's own hand, is reproduced, in facsimile, in Volume II of *The R. B. Adam Library*, and is now a part of the Hyde collection. Both Johnson's known habit of rapid composition and the manuscript itself suggest that the "Scheme" was written only a short time before April

30, 1746, the date that Johnson noted on the last page, presumably as soon as he completed the piece. For a man who had "long" considered the possibility of making a dictionary and who testified repeatedly to his speed in writing,[2] the composition of the nineteen-page "Scheme" was, at most, probably a matter of a few days' work. On the other hand, it is possible that, like "forty-eight of the printed octavo pages of the Life of Savage,"[3] the whole document may have been produced at a single sitting.

Whatever the actual period of composition, a study of the manuscript indicates, first, that Johnson was primarily intent on setting down, rapidly but systematically, his notions about the problems and practices involved in compiling a dictionary of the English language and, second, that he was not making a determined effort to write in his most polished style. The "Scheme" originally consisted of nineteen pages, but part of page 3 and all of pages 8 and 9 are now missing. The remaining sixteen and a half pages—each measuring, with minor variations, 6¼ by 7¾ inches—contain approximately 3,300 words (we estimate that the complete document contained about 3,800 words) arranged in some 41 paragraphs.[4] In these paragraphs, which correspond to the "body" (pars. 7–74) of the printed version of the *Plan*,[5] Johnson considered, successively, such topics as the choice of words for inclusion in his dictionary, spelling, pronunciation, etymology, syntax, definition, "the Distribution of words into their proper classes," and illustrative quotations. That he recorded his thoughts speedily and painlessly and without too much attention to the niceties of writing is evidenced, in varying degrees, by the clean appearance of most of the pages, the probable omission of several words, the heavy reliance on the comma for pointing and the absence of all punctuation marks in a good many spots where one would normally expect them, the few lapses from "correct" or typically Johnsonian syntax, and the small number of revisions relative to the number made during subsequent stages in the composition of the *Plan*.

Specific facts may help to give substance to this generalization about Johnson's method of composition. In the first place, although none of the sixteen and a half pages are completely "fair," only six,[6] at most, can be described as even moderately "foul"; and the appearance of these six, as well as the slightly messy appearance of some of the other pages, is largely the result of a reader's marks, not of the author's repeated changes while engaged in the initial job of writing. In the second place, among the words apparently omitted by Johnson's "rapid" hand[7] (and added later by a reader) are *as*, *be*, *to*, and *can*.[8] In the third place, the unrevised "Scheme" contains approximately 160 commas and 65 periods, but only 1 semicolon. The following passages—the first in the section on etymology, the other in that on definition—reveal Johnson's fairly common tendency (1) to employ the comma as a jack-of-all-marks and also (2) to omit all forms of punctuation:

1. "This search will give occasion to many curious disquisitions, and sometimes perhaps to conjectures which may by those who are unacquainted with this kind of Study appear improbable and capricious, but it may be reasonably imagined that what is so much in the power of Men as Language will very often be capriciously conducted, nor are these disquisitions and conjectures to be considered altogether as wanton Sports of wit or vain shows of Learning, our Language is well known not [to][9] be primitive or selforiginated" (p. 7).[10]

2. "The signification of Adjectives may be often ascertained by uniting them to Substantives as *simple* swain *simple* sheep and sometimes the sense of a Substantive may be elucidated by the epithets annexed to it by good authours as the *boundless ocean* the *open Lawns*" (p. 13).[11]

In the unrevised fair copy of the *Plan* (pp. 19–20, 34), the first passage is divided into three sentences, with periods after *capricious* and *conducted*, commas after *imagined* and *wit*, and a semicolon after *Learning;* while the second adds commas after *Substantives*, *simple*,[12] *swain*,[13] *authours*, and *ocean*, and a semicolon after *sheep*.

In the fourth place, the presence of a few jumbled or decidedly un-Johnsonian passages—clear evidence, it seems to us, of haste in writing—may be illustrated both by *which may by those . . . appear* in quotation 1 above (Johnson first intended that the verb in this clause should be *may be considered* or the like; then he used *may . . . appear*, but he neglected to change *by those* to *to those*) and also by this sentence (from a paragraph on English syntax): "Thus we say who use the present modes of speech The Soldier *died of* his wounds, but we say The Sailor *perished with* Hunger" (p. 10).[14] Both passages were greatly improved in later stages of composition.

Finally, an examination of the revisions in the "Scheme" strengthens our impression that the piece was written quickly, easily, and a bit carelessly. So far as we can tell, all Johnson's revisions involved the addition, deletion, or substitution of one or more words; none, apparently, consisted solely of such details as spelling or punctuation. About half the total of roughly 70 alterations can certainly be labeled "pre-reader," and all except 11 or 12—

which we discuss on pages 55–58—*may* fall in the same group. But it should be noted that some of the changes listed now may actually belong to the "post-reader" group.

The changes which Johnson made before submitting the manuscript to readers consist almost wholly of (1) the substitution of words (largely) or phrases for the originals, (2) the correction of mistakes resulting from haste or carelessness, and (3) the deletion of words (largely) or phrases. They are distributed fairly evenly throughout the document, with thirteen of the sixteen and a half pages each containing, roughly, from two to five. With respect to the first group, frequently—as in the replacement of *properly* by *strictly* on page 15[15]—the revision avoids the repetition of a word used elsewhere in the same sentence; sometimes—as in the substitution of *admits of* for *is not* on page 15[16]—Johnson apparently decided to recast a passage before he had actually written all of his first version of it; occasionally—as in the substitution of *use* for *purpose* on page 18[17]—the replacement seems to be more appropriate to the context than the original; and sometimes—as on pages 1, 2, 10, and 18—the reason for the change cannot be inferred, either because the original is illegible or because Johnson erased the first expression instead of merely crossing it out. In the second group, revisions include such changes as the scoring of superfluous words (e.g., the first of a pair of *the*'s in *the the Poetical sense* on p. 13),[18] altering the form of a word to fit the syntax (e.g., *placing* for *placed* in *by placing with them* on p. 6),[19] and replacing a word which doesn't make sense with one which does (e.g., *in* for *of* in *forms in which it is used* on p. 10).[20] As for the third group, the small number of deletions seem to be prompted mainly by Johnson's desire to avoid repetitious or awkward phrasing (as in his crossing-through of the second *the* in *the sound of the mono-*

syllables on p. 6 and in the deletion of *explaining* in *as in explaining the term Baronet* on p. 11).[21]

After he had written the "Scheme" and had made changes of the sort indicated, Johnson presumably submitted the document to at least one reader and possibly more: the extant manuscript contains the comments of two different persons. We can offer no conjecture about the identity of the more taciturn of the two, who seems, from the location of his remarks, to have been the second reader. But we think that the first, and much more vocal, reader was probably the bull-breeding King of Ashbourne, Johnson's close friend, Dr. John Taylor.[22] Taylor's handwriting is markedly similar to the writing of this first reader, whose comments, especially one about "your Dictionary,"[23] sound as though he were on terms of easy familiarity with the author. Moreover, we know that Johnson had earlier sent Taylor the manuscript of *Irene*[24] and that somewhat later he was to intrust him with the fair copy of the *Plan*. We speculate that Taylor may have spent much of the spring of 1746 in London seeking the office of prebend of Westminster, to which he was appointed on July 11, 1746,[25] and thus may have been readily available as a reader of the "Scheme."

Whether Taylor or someone else, the "first" reader made a total of approximately 40 sets of marks, corrections, and/or comments on the manuscript, most of them inserted between Johnson's lines or in the margins. At least 1 appears on every page except 19, which contains only three lines of text, but there are almost twice as many—roughly 24 to 15—on pages 1–10 as there are on pages 11–18. Approximately 13 suggest various changes in phraseology, ranging from a single word to a much larger part of a sentence, with a line drawn above and across the original to indicate deletion. For example, the reader recommended the substitution of *Phrases* for *Phraseology* in the sentence on page 10 beginning "When the Construction of a word is explained it is necessary to persue it through its train of Phraseology";[26] and in the sentence on pages 6–7 beginning "The care of such minute particulars may be censured as trifling but these particulars have not been," he offered "thought unworthy of attention in more polished Languages & therefore they are more polished" for Johnson's "thought in more polished Languages unworthy of attention."[27] Ten other notes consist of as many terms used to describe the series of topics discussed in the "Scheme" and written at the beginnings of the appropriate paragraphs (e.g., "Words" on p. 1, "Orthography" on p. 4,[28] etc.). Some 7 are concerned—briefly, for the most part—with examples that illustrate general statements in the manuscript. The 2 shortest consist of a single word and an abbreviation: (1) *plough,* which is written next to Johnson's *Plow* on page 6, reveals the reader's doubt about the proper use of *Plow* in connection with the remark that "many words written alike are differently pronounced, as *flow* and *Plow*";[29] (2) *Queer.*[30] queries *to make good a breach* (one of a series of phrases, on pp. 10–11, exemplifying the "train of Phraseology" which, according to Johnson, is to be given for each word in his dictionary[31]) and Pope's "*in* endless errour *hurl'd*"[32] (cited by Johnson on p. 17 as an illustration of "Barbarous and impure Words and expressions," "discovered too frequently in the best authours," which are to be "branded" in his *Dictionary* "with some note of infamy"[33]). The two longest deal, respectively, with the noun *file* and the phrase *dies for thirst* as used in quotations from Shakespeare and Addison.[34] Objecting to Johnson's remark, on page 13, that *file* illustrates the "peculiar sense" given a word by a "great authour,"[35] the reader says, "File is here in its common & natural Sense" (p. 13 verso). And earlier, commenting on the use of *died of* and *dies for thirst* to exemplify Johnson's contention that English syntax "can be only learned" by considering the practice of the "best authours,"[36] he declares, in part, that *died for thirst* "is stronger & more emphatical" than *died of thirst.* "Thirst is not the Distemper but the Cause of it" (p. 10 verso). On the other hand, the second reader of the "Scheme," it may be noted in passing, thought that *died for thirst* was "against Custom."[37] Taken together, these comments of the two readers indicate that, as Johnson implies, both *died of* and *died for* were "acceptable" in the eighteenth century, although individual critics offered what they believed to be weighty arguments for preferring one to the other.

Three additional notes by the first reader resulted from three of Johnson's general statements about his intentions in the *Dictionary*. First of all, Johnson had said: "When the Orthography and Pronunciation are adjusted the *Etymology* or Derivation is next to be considered, and the words are to be placed in their different classes whether simple . . . or compound . . . whether primitive . . . or derivative" (p. 7).[38] Evidently assuming that this remark disclosed Johnson's intention to arrange the words in his *Dictionary* on the basis of their etymologies, the reader argues vigorously, in his longest single note, for a strictly alphabetical arrangement of words. He begins by inquiring, "Is not Fabers [*sic*] Method quite thro', the best?" and then continues: "If the Words are not alphabetically placed, a Man must understand the Language only to find a Derivative, & then he has no Occasion for your Dictionary. This would spoil the Sale of it to Schools & Foreigners. Besides may not the Author & I differ in a Derivation, & if it should so happen, by what Rule can I find the Derivative I want? A Dictionary has no more to do w^{h} Connection & Dependance than a Warehouse book. They are both mere Repertoriums, & if they are not such they are of no Use at all" (p. 7 verso). In his second general note the reader again directs Johnson's attention to the model for a new English dictionary provided, in classical lexicography, by Basilius Faber's *Thesaurus eruditionis scholasticæ* (first published in 1571). Commenting on Johnson's statement, in the section on definition, that it may be "necessary to give the interpretation of the principal words in some other Language[s?]" (p. 12),[39] he says, "Look at Faber's Thesaurus" (p. 12 verso).[40] These references to Faber, together with the second reader's mention of "Stephen[s],"[41] offer additional evidence, it should be pointed out, of the inclusiveness of the lexicographical tradition—Continental as well as English—within which Johnson worked and the nature of which we have discussed in the preceding chapter.[42] In the third of his general notes, prompted by Johnson's remarks (pp. 17–18)[43] about the illustrative quotations to be cited in the *Dictionary*, the reader expresses very precise notions: "All Examples," he declares, "should be compleat Sense & Grammar, (not the Author's whole Sense) for without that a Learner can not judge how, why, in what Sense a word is employed. At the Conclusion of each word there ought to be—Examples 1 of the Elegant Uses of each Word & Phrase in which it is employed 2. Examples of the Abuse of each Word &. w^{h} Cautions how to correct & avoid it" (p. 18 verso).

Finally, the first reader seems, on the basis of a comparison of handwriting, to have supplied several small words (e.g., *as*, *to*, *be*, and *can*)[44] which were omitted by Johnson in writing the "Scheme." And he also presumably inserted the *e* between *b* and *r* in *Gebrish* on page 5.[45]

The comments of the "second" reader can be treated very briefly, for there are only three of them on the manuscript. Like the first reader, the second queries, by means of "Q^{r}.," the quotation from Pope's *Essay on Man*. Like his predecessor, too, he apparently misunderstood the statement about placing words "in their different classes." "Whether," he asks, "Stephen's Method which seems to be meant here will not be more puzzling?" (p. 7 verso). "Stephen[s]" refers, of course, to a member of the famous French family (Stephanus or Estienne)[46] of classical scholars, lexicographers, and printers; and the "Method" which the reader almost certainly had in mind is the modified etymological arrangement[47] followed in Robert Stephanus' *Thesaurus linguæ Latinæ* (1531), published in four volumes at London in 1734–35. But, unlike the other person and as noted already, the second reader was unwilling to approve the phrase *died for thirst;* he wondered, specifically, "Whether *for* is not against Custom? & whether Custom is not ye Chief Rule of Language?" (p. 10 verso).

After at least two critics had read the "Scheme," Johnson made additional changes in the manuscript. One group, numbering approximately 7 alterations, was caused by the first, and only the first, reader's comments; a second, perhaps smaller than the first group, was decided on independently of the comments. Neither group gives any sign of systematic revision.

When he began considering the first reader's suggestions and comments, Johnson marked through those proposed changes which he did not intend to accept; later, however, he failed to strike out some of the alternatives, and evidently he also occasionally changed his mind about adopting them. Thus it is only by consulting the fair copy of the *Plan* that we are able to determine his final reaction to a good many of the reader's suggestions. On the whole, he was not very hospitable to the proposed improvements. He accepted, of course, all the words which he had omitted and which the reader had presumably supplied. But he usually preferred his own writing to that of the reader, and the very few revisions he actually accepted are quite slight (e.g., in the sentence concluding "whether it [the *Dictionary*] should take in the Language of particular professions, which generally derive their terms as their art from other nations" [p. 1], the reader had suggested that *with* be substituted for *as* and *arts* for *art;* Johnson accepted *arts* but crossed through *with*, which appears, however, in the fair-copy version).[48] He also made a few revisions of his own which seem to have been, in part at least, the result of the reader's suggested alterations (e.g., in this sentence, cited earlier,[49] "Thus we say who use the present modes of speech The Soldier *died of* his wounds, but we say The Sailor *perished with* Hunger" [p. 10], the reader had suggested that *who . . . speech* and the second *we say* be deleted, and he had written *died of Hunger* above *perished with Hunger;* Johnson kept *perished with*, but in expanding the "Scheme" he revised the first part of the sentence to read: "Thus, we say, according to the present modes of speech, The Soldier died *of* his Wounds, and the Sailor perished *with* Hunger"[50]). Apparently he was influenced only once by the reader's comments about the examples cited in the "Scheme"; in the fair copy (p. 33) *faculties* (as used in *Macbeth*, Act I, scene 7, ll. 16–18) has replaced *file* as an instance of a word given a "peculiar sense" by a "great Author."[51] And, so far as we can tell, Johnson was not led, by the general remarks, to make any changes in the statements about the various aspects of making a dictionary.

Exclusive of those just noted, the revisions Johnson definitely or probably made in the "Scheme" after its return from the readers number some 4 or 5 (the actual total may be larger, obviously, since it may include some of the changes which, as noted earlier, cannot be classified either as "pre-" or "post-reader"), are limited to five of the first seven pages of the manuscript, and may have been made at different times. Two of these revisions consist of additional passages written on the backs of pages 4 and 7 and designed for insertion on the rectos of the same pages. The latter passage, which is the final paragraph on pronunciation in the printed *Plan*, describes the successful efforts of the French and Italians to fix "the sounds of their letters"[52] (although Johnson subsequently observed in the Grammar that "in general," "words are unable to describe" sounds[53]). The first passage, which appears in the section on the choice of words for the *Dictionary*, argues for the inclusion of the names of plants: "if no plants are to be mentioned," Johnson begins, "the most pleasing part of nature will be excluded, and many beautiful epithets be unexplained."[54] (The sixth edition of the *Dictionary* itself, it may be added parenthetically, was criticized—by Harrison, for example[55]—because of its treatment of plants.) Two other fragmentary changes indicate that Johnson had begun to rewrite, or at least to consider rewriting, the "Scheme." In its final revised form, the first sentence on page 1 reads: "When I first conceived the design of compiling [substituted for *In an attempt to compile*] a new Dictionary of the English Language, [both the original *the first question to be considered is* and the revision *it did not appear* crossed out] by what rule or by what marks of Distinction the *words* are to be chosen?"[56] Similarly, in its final version, the sentence on page 2 listing the causes of "naturalized" English words reads in part: "This naturalization [an *X* followed by *or it* written above the line] is [*either* crossed out] the consequence of frequent use." The presence of the *or it* suggests that Johnson decided to specify another cause of naturalization before mentioning "frequent use," and examination of the fair copy (p. 8) shows that this is precisely what he did. There the corresponding part of the sentence reads: "This Naturalization is produced either by an Admission into common Speech in some tralatitious Signification . . . ; or it is the consequence of frequent use."[57] The last of this group of revisions involved both the addition, on page 4, of the reference to Lord Chesterfield's views on spelling, which is discussed in detail in the next chapter, and the crossing-through of about half the remainder of the same paragraph. Versions of this crossed-out passage and also of the rest of the paragraph subsequently become the last paragraph in the section on orthography.[58]

II

The second major step in the composition of the *Plan* was the expansion of the "Scheme" into a document closely resembling the printed form of the piece. With the "Scheme" evidently close at hand, Johnson presumably wrote another holograph manuscript, beginning with the address to Chesterfield as "one of his Majesty's Principal Secretaries of State" and concluding with one version of the last sentence in the *Plan*. Although the exact date of composition remains uncertain, the document must have been produced after October 29, 1746, since, as we point out in the next chapter, Chesterfield did not become a secretary of state until that time.[59] One may guess that Johnson wrote the expanded piece sometime during the fall of 1746 or the winter of 1746–47.

The manuscript itself is lost. But a clerk's fair copy of the *Plan*—consisting, originally, of 46 pages (of which all except p. 32 are extant) measuring, on the average, 7⅜ by 9 inches—was almost certainly made from this manuscript. Thus we are able, by comparing the "Scheme" and the fair copy (reproduced, like the "Scheme," in Vol. II of *The R. B. Adam Library* and, also like it, now a part of the Hyde collection), to reconstruct the contents of the missing document. Since a detailed study of all the differences between the two manuscripts would enlarge this essay beyond reasonable limits, our attempt at reconstruction is restricted to a sketch of the more important changes. These may be conveniently summarized in the accompanying table. The general pattern shown in the table can be understood, we hope, without reference to the *Adam Library*, although full comprehension of some of the items probably demands an examination of the facsimiles.

One broad conclusion about the lost manuscript may be drawn immediately from these figures: in transforming the "Scheme" into the *Plan*, Johnson, with only one clear exception, built on what he had done already. He kept the basic form of the structure the same, so to speak, but added an entrance and exit and some new rooms. Specifically, he added (1) the introductory and closing remarks addressed to Chesterfield (pars. 1–6, 75–76); (2) the paragraph (9), in the discussion of the principles governing the selection of words for the *Dictionary*, about the moral to be drawn from the reluctant admission of "Terms of Science" into the dictionary of the French Academy; (3) the statements, in the section devoted to orthography, about the

Page No. in "Scheme"	Paragraph No. in "Scheme"	Corresponding Paragraphs in Fair Copy	Paragraphs Added in Fair Copy	Page No. in Fair Copy
....	....	....	1–6	1–5
1	1	7–8	....	5–7
....	....	....	9	7
2	2	10	....	7–8
2	3	11	....	8–9
Half of 3 missing	?4	12	....	9–10
....	....	?13		10
?3–4	?5	14	....	10–11
4 verso	?6 (par. division uncertain)	14	....	....
4	7	15	....	12
4–5	8	16	....	12–13
....	....	....	17–18	13–15
....	8	19	....	15
5–6	9	20	....	15–16
....	9	21	....	16–17
....	9	22	....	17
....	9	23	....	17–18
6–7	9–?10 (par. division uncertain)	24	....	18
7 verso	11	25	....	18–19
7	12	26	....	19
7	13	27	....	19–20
8–9 missing	....	?28–36		20–26
?9–10	14	37	....	26–27
....	14	38	....	27–28
10–11	15	39	....	28–29
11	16	40	....	29
11–12	17	41	....	29–31
12	18	Omitted in fair copy and printed *Plan*	....	....
12	19	42	....	31
....	....	....	43–44	31
....	....	....	45 (from printed *Plan*)	32 (missing)
....	....	....	46 (not in unrevised fair copy)	Added by Johnson on 31 verso
12	20	?47	....	? 32
12	21	?48	....	? 32
12	22	?49	....	? 32
12–13	23	50	....	? 32–33
13	24	50	....	....

Page No. in "Scheme"	Paragraph No. in "Scheme"	Corresponding Paragraphs in Fair Copy	Paragraphs Added in Fair Copy	Page No. in Fair Copy
13	25	51	....	33
....	....	....	52 (contains example in par. 24 of "Scheme")	33
13	26	53	....	33
13	27	54	....	34
14	28	55	....	34
....	....	....	56	35
14	29	57	....	35–36
14–15	30	58	....	36
15	31	59	....	36–37
....	....	....	60	37–38
15–16	32	61–63	....	38–39
16	33	64	....	39
16	34	65	....	39
16	35	66	....	39
16	36	67	....	40
17	37	68	....	40–41
....	....	....	69	41–42
17–18	38	70	....	42
....	....	....	71	42–43
18	39	72	....	43
18	40	73	....	43
18–19	41	74	....	43–44
....	....	....	75–76	44–46

Total length of "Scheme": approximately 3,800 words

Total length of the lost manuscript: approximately 6,925 words

"Contest" "between Etymology and Pronunciation" (par. 17) and also about his decision (par. 18) to "make no Innovations" in spelling "without a reason sufficient to balance the Inconveniencies of Change"; (4) examples (par. 56), in the section on definition, of the varied "characters of words"—those, for instance, used solely "in the sense of praise" or "of disapprobation"—which will be explained in the *Dictionary;* (5) a reply (par. 60), at the conclusion of the discussion of definition, to those persons who may consider "many of these remarks" "trifling"; (6) the announcement (par. 69), at the end of the section on classifying words, of his decision—prompted by Chesterfield's "opinion"—to "interpose my own Judgment" concerning "Questions of purity, or propriety"; and (7) the statement (par. 71), in the section on quotations and "Authorities," that "Mr Pope" had "chosen" "Many of the Authours" to be cited in the *Dictionary*.[60]

Our conclusions about the presence in the lost manuscript of three other groups of paragraphs must be presented with less than perfect assurance, because of the fact that portions of both the "Scheme" and the fair copy are missing. These problem passages, as question marks in the table indicate, are paragraphs (1) 4–5 of the "Scheme" and 13 of the fair copy; (2) 28–36 of the fair copy; and (3) 45 and 47–49 of the fair copy (20–22 of the "Scheme").

Reconstruction of the missing half of page 3 of the "Scheme" is based on several pieces of evidence. For example, the presence of paragraph 4 (which sets forth the necessity of including "the Dialect of every Profession" in the *Dictionary*)[61] can be inferred from the fact that the last sentence of paragraph 3 ends in the middle of a line and that the tops of some of the letters in the next (missing) line have survived the loss of the line itself. Again, the existence of paragraph 5 (which discusses the "Names of Species" to be included in the *Dictionary*)[62] is suggested by the first passage at the beginning of page 4 of the "Scheme": this passage, a part of which obviously completes a sentence beginning on the missing portion of page 3, is very similar to the concluding section of the corresponding paragraph (14) of the fair copy. But paragraph 13 of the fair copy (a single sentence concerned with the means of differentiating English from "foreign" words in the *Dictionary*) remains a problem: it may have appeared in the "Scheme," or it may have been added in the lost manuscript.[63]

Almost no informed guesses can be made concerning the relationship between the contents of the missing pages (8–9) of the "Scheme" and paragraphs 28–36 of the fair copy. It would seem, from the difference between the number of words (roughly 900) in the latter (and the last part of par. 27 and the beginning of 37)[64] and the estimated number (roughly 410–50) on the former, that in writing the lost manuscript Johnson added about 450–500 words to this section of the *Plan*. But we can make no specific inferences about the proportion of these words in new paragraphs or in those already existing in the "Scheme."

The last group of problem passages contains one paragraph (fair copy, 45) which was probably added sometime during the composition of the lost manuscript and three (fair copy, 47–49) which were probably transferred from the "Scheme" (pars. 20–22) to the lost manuscript. In paragraphs 20–22 of the "Scheme," Johnson used the noun *ground* to illustrate how he proposed, in the *Dictionary*, to "sort the several senses"—primitive, consequential, and metaphorical—"of each word" in "the general or popular Language." At some point in writing the second and longer manuscript, he apparently decided to add another illustrative example—as he did elsewhere in the piece—and to place the second example before the paragraphs dealing with *ground*. This time he selected the verb *arrive*. He may have hastily inserted the paragraphs (fair copy, 43–45) which distinguish its senses after he had copied (perhaps in revised form) the three paragraphs ("Scheme," 20–22; fair copy, 47–49) which treat *ground;* or (though this seems unlikely to us) he may have decided on the addition after the clerk had actually begun to copy his manuscript. At any rate, paragraphs 43–44 appear at the bottom of page 31 of the fair copy, and paragraph 46—which was almost certainly added after the fair copy had been prepared[65]—on the verso of the same page. Paragraphs 45 (which illustrates the metaphorical sense of *arrive*), 47–49 (which deal with *ground*), and part of 50 (which distinguishes the poetical sense of words and extends to the top of p. 33 of the fair copy) presumably comprised the contents of the missing page 32. This hypothesis, although it cannot be proved, is supported both by a comparison of the number of words (some 130) in these paragraphs with the estimated number (ranging from 120 to 170) contained on the missing page and also by the text of the printed *Plan*, in which the paragraphing is the same as that suggested in the table.[66]

Exclusive of completely new paragraphs, additions in the lost manuscript involved the expansion of one or more parts of paragraphs in the "Scheme." Occasionally, as the table indicates, one paragraph in the earlier manuscript burgeoned into two in the later; for example, the opening paragraph in the "Scheme"—consisting of a (roughly) 250-word discussion of the choice of words for the *Dictionary*—has become paragraphs 7–8, with a total of some 300 words, in the fair copy.[67] Much more frequently, however, the number of paragraphs remained the same, but the number of words increased (see, for example, the two paragraphs quoted on pp. 65–66).

The other kinds of changes Johnson made in transforming the "Scheme" into the *Plan* proper may be described briefly. He occasionally increased the number of paragraphs simply by breaking up a longer one—for instance, paragraph 9 of the "Scheme," which is devoted to the discussion of pronunciation, becomes paragraphs 20–23 and the beginning of 24 in the fair copy[68]—and this without any notable increase in the number of words. At least once, however, and for no discernible reason,[69] he apparently combined two paragraphs ("Scheme," 23–24, which distinguish the "poetical" and "familiar" senses of words) into one (fair copy, 50) that, so far as we can tell,[70] is very similar to the first version. On the level of sentences, he seems generally, though not always, to have been more concerned than he had been previously with punctuation and phrasing. As suggested by the examples already cited in this essay, his punctuation normally increased in both frequency and weight: he pointed some passages which had been largely unmarked at first, and he substituted periods (usually) and/or semicolons (occasionally) for a good many of the commas employed so ubiquitously in the "Scheme." His alterations in phraseology, resulting, of course, in numerous additions, ranged from the fairly frequent substitution of one or more words for the original to the very infrequent revision of almost a whole paragraph. When placed together, paragraph 7 of the revised "Scheme" and 15 of the unrevised fair copy offer a graphic, but extreme, example of Johnson's combined expansion and rewriting. Paragraph 7 reads: "Besides all such words require that their accents should be settled, and their sounds ascertained and must have their original from some other Language, and to point out that Original is one of the purposes of the Dictionary, in which I should rather wish many Readers to find more than they expect than one to miss that information which he expected to receive." In paragraph 15 of the unrevised fair copy, the passage is transformed thus: "Besides all such words require that the Accents should be settled their sounds ascertained and their etymologies deduced and therefore cannot be properly admitted [*sic;* changed by Johnson to *omitted*] in the Dictionary. And though an explanation of some may be censured as trivial because they are universally known, and of others [*as* added later by Johnson] unnecessary because they will seldom occurr [*sic*] and may in general be thought to belong to Systems of Phylosophy, rather than to a Grammatical Dictionary, yet it seems most eligible to insert it since it is rather to be wished that many Readers should find more than they expect, than that one should miss that Information which he hoped to receive."[71]

Lastly, so far as we can tell, Johnson omitted from the lost manuscript only one sizable passage (par. 18) which appears in the "Scheme." In the section on the definition of words, he had declared: "It may be doubted whether it be not necessary to give the interpretation of the principal words in some other Language[s?], which would much facilitate the use of the Dictionary to foreigners and might perhaps contribute to its sale in other Countries, and would not be without advantages to the English themselves." When he came to this paragraph during the composition of the longer manuscript, however, he apparently decided not to use it. The reasons for his decision can only be guessed at, but perhaps he was struck by the frankly commercial—and inappropriate—tone of the passage and was impressed by the difficulties involved in compiling, at the same time, a new English and bilingual dictionary. At all events, the paragraph did not appear in the expanded version of the "Scheme."

III

The next major phase in the composition of the *Plan* began when Johnson, supposedly as soon as he completed the lost manuscript, gave or sent it to an amanuensis for copying. Since, as will appear shortly, the clerk had great dif ficulty in deciphering several passages, it seems probable that the manuscript was not a model of neatness or legibility. After the amanuensis completed the fair copy, Johnson presumably read it through at least once, making corrections and other changes as he went along, and adding the complimentary close and his signature at the end. The nature and number of his revisions at this time cannot be estimated with any precision. Consequently, in order to avoid unnecessary repetition, we consider all of Johnson's changes (with the exception of a single group) later in this essay.[72] But it should be emphasized that some of the alterations discussed later were almost certainly made before, not after, the fair copy circulated among readers.

The group of revisions to be considered here comprises corrections of over 20 faulty words or passages in the fair copy. Perhaps not all these corrections were made at the same time, but, since apparently none of the glaring mistakes rectified by some of them evoked comments from other persons subsequently, a good many (at least) were clearly made before Johnson submitted the fair copy to anyone else. Some 15 changes resulted from the clerk's inability either to read Johnson's hand or to understand the arrangement of certain passages. They include the substitution of right for wrong words (as, for example, of *decreed* for *derived* on p. 2; of *omitted* for *admitted* on p. 12; and of *denied* for *decreed* on p. 42),[73] the occasional insertion of words in spaces left by the puzzled clerk (as of *Folly* on p. 22),[74] and the replacement of two hopelessly garbled lines with the correct reading. In copying the paragraph, on pages 41–42, concerning Chesterfield's "opinion" that Johnson should "interpose" his "Judgment" with respect to "Questions of purity, or propriety," the amanuensis, perhaps confused by Johnson's interlineations and/or phrases written in the margins, had continued the sentence beginning "And I may hope that since you whose Authority in our Language" as follows: "declare my own opinion, I shall be considered as Exercise is sufficiently known have commissioned me to a kind of vicarious Jurisdiction." Johnson corrected the corrupt passage to read: "is so generally acknowledged, have commissioned me to declare my own Opinion, I shall be considered as exercising a kind of vicarious Jurisdiction."[75] Six corrections add words omitted either by the clerk or by Johnson himself in the manuscript that the clerk copied (e.g., *Corpus* in the phrase *Habeas Corpus* on p. 8 and *it* in *Crescembeni has not thought it unnecessary* on p. 18),[76] while two others apparently delete superfluous words (i.e., *but others* on p. 7 and *should* on p. 31).[77]

After he had made at least one set of revisions on the fair copy, Johnson, as Boswell tells us in the *Life*, sent the manuscript to Dr. Taylor "for his perusal."[78] From Taylor the document proceeded, via the poet William Whitehead and a "noble Lord" (perhaps Whitehead's patron, William Villiers, third Earl of Jersey),[79] to Lord Chesterfield and afterward to at least one other unidentified reader.

Chesterfield's comments on the *Plan*, as well as Johnson's reaction to them, are discussed in detail in the following chapter. The second reader, who sometimes echoes or reinforces Chesterfield, made 11 actual notes on the fair copy; like Chesterfield's comments, these are written on the backs of the pages immediately preceding the pages to which the notes refer. In addition, and exclusive of the signs which direct attention to the notes, the second reader made at least 19 other significant marks or sets of marks (largely red crosses and underlinings) on the manuscript. The largest group of notes (5 in number) relates to illustrative examples cited by Johnson in various sections of the *Plan*. Specifically, 3 comments raise implicit or explicit objections to the use of *Cynosure* as an instance of words "naturalized" "by an Admission into common Speech in some tralatitious[80] Signification" (p. 8), of *gen'rous* and *rev'rend* as examples of "contractions" (p. 17), and of *flexions* (instead of *inflections*) in the discussion of "analogy" (p. 23).[81] Concerning the use of *Cynosure*, the reader declares: "If the author quotes, in his dictionary, this and simialar [*sic*] forms of expression, should he not brand them with some mark of reprobation? for this cynosure of neighbouring eyes is pedantry itself" (p. 7 verso). As for the contractions, he asks: "are generous, reverend, Chancelor &c. ever pronounced accurately as only of two syllables?" (p. 16 verso). And, in support of Chesterfield's note on *flexions*,[82] he thought that Johnson's "own rule of preserving the radical letters" demanded the use of *inflections* (p. 22 verso). The fourth comment in this group denied the propriety of a quotation from Sir John Davies which Johnson cited, in the section on syntax, as a precedent for Addison's use of the phrase *dies for thirst*;[83] to the reader the usage "appears" "improper in both" authors (p. 27 verso). And the fifth suggests that, in the discussion of pronunciation, a quotation from Milton containing *sonorous* be substituted for a passage from Gay containing the same word (p. 16 verso).[84]

Another group of four notes criticizes Johnson's choice of expressions. (1) In the discussion of the selection of words for his dictionary, Johnson had remarked: "Words in Dictionaries must be conjoined with things, as Form and Motion in Mechanics must be united to matter" (p. 6);[85] the reader comments: "This does not seem to me very clearly expressed" (p. 5 verso). (2) Reinforcing Chesterfield's doubt about the use of *tralatitious* in the passage cited above,[86] he declares: "I believe not one reader in a hundred will understand this word" (p. 7 verso). (3) In the section on analogy, Johnson had said that "Speech was not formed by an Analogy from Heaven" (p. 23);[87] the reader comments, "I own I do not understand what is meant by an analogy from heaven" (p. 22 verso). (4) As a part of the discussion of definition, Johnson had wondered whether "under the word *Barometer*, instead of being satisfied with observing that it is a *Contrivance to discover the weight of the air*, it would not be fit to spend a few lines upon its invention construction and principles" (p. 30);[88] the reader inquires, "whether it should not rather be an *instrument?*" (p. 29 verso).

The two remaining notes state the reader's reaction to two of the general statements in the fair copy. First, in response to Johnson's announcement that "Verbs are . . . to be distinguished according to their qualities as Actives from Neuters, the neglect of which has already introduced some Barbarities in our Conversation, which if not obviated by just animadversions, may in time creep into our writings" (p. 25),[89] the reader says: "There is one instance of this almost universal, in conversation at least—He *makes* a good husband—She will *make* a good wife: which therefore ought to be stigmatized" (p. 24 verso).[90] Later, when Johnson remarks, with respect to "Questions of purity, or propriety," that "I was once in doubt whether I should not attribute too much to my self in attempting to divide [*sic*][91] them," but that "I have been since determined" by Chesterfield's "opinion to interpose my own Judgment" (p. 41),[92] the second reader is warm in his praise: "This," he declares, "will be of infinite use, rightly executed: and therefore the Author, I doubt not, will proceed in this part with all the accuracy, as well as all the caution, possible" (p. 40 verso).

Practically all the reader's red markings query various aspects of Johnson's writing in the *Plan*. Most of them indicate objections to specific words or phrases (e.g., to *Blind* in *employment for the Blind* on p. 1,[93] *dread the fascination* on p. 15,[94] *unchangeable* in *unchangeable Stability* on p. 26,[95] *heterogeneous Phrases* on p. 44,[96] etc.); several criticize a series of *which*-clauses (on pp. 7, 8);[97] and one evidently questions the lack of agreement between *no higher qualities* and *than that* on page 1.[98]

A short time, apparently, after he had sent it to Taylor, the fair copy, bearing Chesterfield's and the second reader's comments, was returned to Johnson, who, by his own account, was rather displeased at having the "bloom" taken off the publication of the *Plan*.[99] He presumably read it through at least once more, considering, as he read, the comments of the critics and making, in addition, various changes which were completely independent of the readers' comments. His reactions to Chesterfield's 8 remarks are specified, as noted earlier, in the next chapter. Of the second reader's 20-odd suggestions (both actual notes and significant marks) which are unrelated to Chesterfield's comments, Johnson was influenced in varying degrees by about two-thirds, or about 16. For example, he substituted the word *Instrument* for his own *Contrivance* and the quotation from Milton containing *sonorous* for that from Gay; he rewrote (and expanded) the whole sentence (beginning "Words in Dictionaries") on page 6 which the reader had criticized for its lack of clarity; he noted, in response to the reader's remark about "pedantry itself," that *Cynosure of Neighbouring eyes* is a phrase from Milton;[100] he reduced the number of *which*-clauses used in two different series; and he changed *with no higher qualities than that* to *without any higher quality than that*, *through various dialects* to *through various Tongues* (p. 21),[101] *an Analogy from Heaven* to *an Analogy sent from Heaven*, *awaken to pure diction* to *awaken to the care of purer diction* (p. 44),[102] etc. But he refused to alter, among other things, his use of *gen'rous* (and *rev'rend*) and *dies for thirst* as examples and, on the level of writing, such a phrase as *dread the fascination*.

Besides his certain or probable corrections of the clerk's errors and also his favorable responses to the readers' suggestions, Johnson's revisions in the fair copy of the *Plan* number well over 200. They appear on 44 of the 45 pages, but with greatest frequency on pages 3, 12, and 21, and they include changes in phraseology, punctuation, spelling (probably), and capitalization (apparently) as well as the deletion and addition of several sizable passages. Alterations in phraseology, which account for about four-fifths (approximately 175) of the changes, range from rare shifts in the form of individual words through frequent revision—by substitution, cancellation, or addition—of single words and phrases to the occasional recasting of whole sentences. Taken together, they provide ample material for a separate essay; but here we must content ourselves with a brief, and admittedly inadequate, statement about them. In making some changes, Johnson clearly aimed at greater precision of expression, as in the substitution of *improvement* for *cultivation* in *promote the cultivation of their native Tongues* on page 3;[103] of *The Title which I prefix to my Work* for *A Dictionary* on page 6; and of *Practice* for *Method* in *When a Question of Orthography is dubious, that Method has* on page 14.[104] In others he wanted to avoid repeating the same word, as in the deletion of the *and* between *Law* and *Merchandise* in *and of History, and those of Law and Merchan-*

dise and on page 9, and the substitution of *the Information* for *that Information* in *that one should miss that Information* on page 12.[105] In making still others, he elaborated or qualified or emphasized the meaning of the original expressions; for example, he expanded *and that it might afford me an employment which would make my Life useful, and keep it innocen*[*t*] to read *and was drawn forward by the prospect of employment which though not splendid would be useful, and though it could not make my Life envied would keep it innocent* (p. 2); he altered *But this is a privilege which words are not to expect, they, like their Authour, will be always gaining or losing strength* to *But this is a privilege which Words are scarcely to expect, for, like their Authour, when they are not gaining strength, they are generally losing it* (p. 26); and he changed *had some reason to expect* to *had reason to expect* (p. 3).[106] Sometimes he compressed wordy, awkward expressions into smoother, more pointed phrases, as when he altered *Whether this Opinion . . . be either nearly or remotely derived from truth, whether Reputation be distributed by Equity or Caprice* to *Whether this Opinion . . . had its beginning from Truth and Nature or from accident and prejudice* (p. 2).[107] Occasionally he changed the form of a whole sentence, as when he altered the loose *Besides all such words require that their Accents should be settled, their sounds ascertained, and their etymologies deduced, and therefore cannot be properly omitted in the Dictionary* to the periodic *Besides as such words like others require . . . , they cannot . . .*" (p. 12).[108] And occasionally he increased or reduced the number of sentences in the original passage; for instance, he changed "The great Orthographical Contest has long subsisted between Etymology and Pronunciation; it has been demanded on one hand that men should write as they speak; but it has been shewn that this Conformity neve[r] was attained in any Language, And that it is not more easy to perswade Men to speak than to write in the same manner. It may therefore be asked with equal Propriety why men do not rather speak as they write" to "The great . . . ; but as it has been shewn . . . Men to agree exactly in speaking than in one [*sic*] writing, it may be asked . . . (p. 13).[109]

Johnson made two substantial deletions in the fair copy of the *Plan*. In the section on the choice of words for the *Dictionary*, he canceled the following passage: "How much an assemblage of Trees may deserve an Explanation will appear from an old English Poet who wrote in Latin

—Idæus consurgit apex, vetus incola montis
Silva viret, vernat Abies procera, Cupressus
Flebilis, interpres Laurus, vaga pinus, Oliva
Concilians, Cornus venatrix, Fraxinus audax,
Stat comitis patiens Ulmus, nunquamque senescens
Cantatrix Buxus: paulo proclivius Arvum
Ebria vitis habet."[110]

In its place he inserted the following sentence, which serves as an introduction to the examples demonstrating how both Shakespeare and Milton might have benefited from "a Dictionary of this kind": "The Usefulness of such explications appears from the mistakes which the want of them has occasioned" (p. 11).[111]

Again, in the section on the definition of words, he deleted the following lines, which illustrate his statement that "some words are used in the sense of praise and others in that of disapprobation": "So we generally *ascribe* Good but *impute* Evil. The Authour therefore who informs us that 'those who had judged favourably of him would think that he had crowned the *good*, and those who had entertained prejudices against him, that he had attoned for the *ill imputed* to him,' must be allowed with all his elegance to have deviated at least once from the purity of our tongue" (p. 35).[112] For this mere example, he substituted a passage stressing the importance of usage in determining the "rules" of the English language: "So commonly, though not always, we *exhort* to good actions, we *instigate* to ill we *animate incite* and *encourage* indifferently to good or bad. So we usually *ascribe* good but *impute* evil, yet neither the use of these words nor perhaps of any other in our licentious language is so established as not to be often reversed by the correctest writers. I shall therefore since the rules of Language like those of law arise from precedents often repeated, collect the testimonies on both sides, and endeavour to discover and promulgate the decrees of Custom who has so long possessed whether by right or by usurpation the Sovereignty of words" (p. 34 verso).[113]

Lastly, the only other sizable addition in the fair copy consists of a qualification of Johnson's remark that his "method" of arranging illustrative quotations will amount to a record "of the gradual changes of the Language." "But," he cautioned, "observations so minute and accurate are to be desired rather than expected, and if Use be carefully supplied, Curiosity must sometimes bear its disappointments" (p. 43).[114]

Unlike his revisions which involved the writing of one or more letters, Johnson's changes in punctuation cannot always be distinguished from the marks made by the clerk. Moreover, even when a particular change seems, on the basis of the difference in appearance, to be Johnson's, one cannot always decide whether it is an actual revision or merely a correction of the clerk's mistake. Nevertheless, in spite of the difficulty of determining a good many cases, enough clear evidence exists to prove that, in revising the fair copy, Johnson paid considerably more attention to punctuation than he had given to it in previous stages of the composition. Specifically, he continued the practice, which we have noted earlier,[115] of substituting periods for commas; and, except in the new passages he added in the fair copy, he tended to increase the quantity of his pointing, especially of commas. Finally, unless we assume that all the (roughly) 20 changes are corrections of the clerk's errors, it seems probable that Johnson made at least a few alterations in the spelling and capitalization which he had employed in the manuscript that the clerk transcribed.

After his last revision of the fair copy, Johnson presumably sent the document to the printer's (perhaps the shop of William Strahan), where it served as copy.[116] But, unlike the bookseller Andrew Millar on the more famous occasion connected with the *Dictionary*, he was not able to say, "Thank God."[117] For a comparison of the revised fair copy and the first edition of the printed *Plan* shows that he revised rather extensively while he was reading the proofs of the work. About 100 of the (approximately) 420 differences between the two versions consist of changes in phrasing, for which, with hardly any exceptions, Johnson himself was surely responsible. These variations in phraseology appear on all pages of the first edition except 1 and 20–24 (since p. 32 of the fair copy is missing, it is impossible to determine whether any differences appear on pp. 22–23 of the printed text). As a group, they show Johnson engaged in putting final touches to his prose—correcting obvious mistakes, selecting more appropriate words or phrases, improving rhythms, sharpening parallel constructions, condensing wordy passages—above all, avoiding glaring repetitions. Most of them are limited to the deletion, addition, or substitution of single words; but some involve the revision of phrases (e.g., the substitution, on p. 3, of *obstruct the reception of the work* for *obstruct that* [the reputation] *of the Performance;* and, on p. 4, of *In the first attempt to methodise my ideas* for *In the first entrance upon my undertaking*);[118] and a very few consist of such alterations (made with a minimum of change) as the combination or multiplication of sentences (e.g., *sake. The* to *sake, and* on p. 10; and *safe, and was* to *safe. I was* on p. 2).[119]

The changes in the last sentence of the *Plan*—which evidently caused Johnson much trouble, since he had already drastically altered it (and the preceding sentence) in the fair copy—suggest the extent of the heaviest revision. In the revised fair copy, the sentence reads: "But I do not yet despair of pardon from those who know[ing] [?] the fallibility [*weakness* not struck out] of reason, the Scantiness of knowledge, the uncertainty of memory, and the unsteadiness of attention, can compare the causes of error, with the means of avoiding it, and the immensity of Art, with the faculties of Man, but whatever be the event of my endeavours, I shall not easily regret an attempt which has procured me the honour of appearing thus publickly, as . . ." (pp. 45–46). In the printed version, the passage is altered to read thus: "Yet I do not despair of approbation from those who knowing the uncertainty of conjecture, the scantiness of knowledge, the fallibility of memory, and the unsteadiness of attention, can compare the causes of error with the means of avoiding it, and the extent of art with the capacity of man; and whatever . . . thus publickly . . ." (p. 34).[120]

The largest single group of differences between the fair copy and the printed *Plan*, numbering almost 300 and appearing on every page of the first edition, consists of variations in punctuation; the smallest group, with about 20 members, consists of changes in spelling. With few exceptions, pointing in the printed version is markedly heavier than that in the fair copy; 200 of the changes, for example, signify the addition of as many commas, and a majority of the other differences consist of the substitution of semicolons for commas. One cannot assume, of course, that Johnson was responsible for all these revisions; but since, as we have already pointed out, he tended to punctuate more frequently in successive stages of the composition of the *Plan*, it is almost certain that he was the cause of at least some of them. As for the changes in spelling, little can be inferred about the number—if, indeed, there were any—of Johnson's alterations. The spelling in the printed *Plan* itself is not entirely consistent; for instance, *public* appears on page 3, *publickly* on page 34; *errour* on page 29, *error* on page 34. Perhaps the most one can say, in view of the fact that he certainly made changes in spelling in the fair copy, is that Johnson may have been responsible for some of the similar changes in the printed version.

IV

The last part of our account presumably begins soon after Johnson returned the proofs containing his final revisions to the printer. He may have done this sometime during June or July, 1747, for the publication date was early August of the same year. The pamphlet appeared first in a quarto edition, later in an octavo; and the printing of the former and the publication of the latter comprise the chief topics discussed in the remainder of this chapter.

The general collation of the first edition of the *Plan* is as follows: 4°, π1(=E2) A–D^4 E^2(–E2); [$2 signed], 18 ll., pp. [*2*] 1–34. Contents: π1 title, π1v erratum, pp. 1–34 text.[121] But the edition includes two different settings of signature A and two different states of E1v. As Chapman first pointed out[122] and as even a hasty comparison of the two verifies, signature A of the pamphlet was set once and then completely reset later. Copies of the *Plan* containing the original setting of signature A are labeled "Chesterfield" because this address appears at the head of page 1 "To the Right Honourable *PHILIP DORMER*, Earl of *CHESTERFIELD;* One of his Majesty's Principal Secretaries of State." Copies containing the second setting are called "Non-Chesterfield" because this address does not appear on page 1. To the arguments presented by earlier commentators[123] concerning the priority of the "Chesterfield" setting of signature A may be added the results of a collation of the two settings with the fair copy: the "Chesterfield" setting agrees with the fair copy in five of the six points for which the text of the fair copy provides the opportunity for a valid comparison with the two settings. The accompanying table indicates the specific likenesses and differences between the fair copy and the "Chesterfield" setting of signature A in relation to the chief variations (exclusive of those caused by different lineation[124]) between the "Chesterfield" and "Non-Chesterfield" settings. As for the two states of E1v (p. 34), one—almost certainly the earlier[125]—contains the duplication of the word *the* ("the/the mazes") in ll. 1–2, while the second does not contain this error. So far as we know, no copies of the *Plan* exist which contain the "Chesterfield" setting of signature A *and* the uncorrected state of E1v.[126]

Beginning with Chapman, all commentators have stated that two different grades of paper were used in printing the first edition of the *Plan*. Although most copies, it is said, are printed on ordinary paper, at least three—the Wise (Ashley) copy in the British Museum, the copy in the Library of Congress, and the MacGeorge-Hyde copy—are printed on thick paper.[127] But, thanks to the kindness of Mr. David Foxon, of the Department of Printed Books, British Museum; of Mr. Frederick Goff, of the Rare Books

Fair Copy	Chesterfield	Non-Chesterfield
P. 1: address to Chesterfield	P. 1: address to Chesterfield	P. 1: no address to Chesterfield
P. 1, l. 10: higher quality	P. 1, l. 10: higher quality	P. 1, l. 10: greater quality
P. 2, between ll. 17–18: innocent,	P. 2, l. 19: innocent,	P. 1, l. 19: innocent;
	P. 2, bottom: no press figure	P. 2, bottom: press figure "1"
P. 3, l. 15: suffered (but might be read *suffer'd*)	P. 3, l. 9: suffer'd	P. 3, l. 9: suffered
P. 5, l. 5: elegance or discernment	P. 4, l. 8: elegance or discernment	P. 4, l. 8: elegance and discernment
P. 5, l. 13: of English words,	P. 4, l. 17: of our English idiom;	P. 4, l. 17: of the English idiom;
	P. 4, bottom: no press figure	P. 4, bottom: press figure "2"
P. 5, verso: to become useful	P. 5, l. 7: to as be of no advantage	P. 5, l. 7 as to be of no advantage
P. 6, l. 14: would be useless	P. 5, l. 16: would be all darkess (*sic*)	P. 5, l. 16: would be all darkness
	P. 6, bottom: press figure "3" on some, but not all, copies	P. 6, bottom: no press figure
P. 9, l. 5: necessary	P. 7, ll. 3–4: ne-/nessary	P. 7, ll. 3–4: ne-/cessary
P. 10, l. 14: that,	P. 8, l. 7: that,	P. 8, l. 7: that

Division, Library of Congress; and of Mrs. Donald Hyde, we have learned that the watermark on these three copies is the same (either HN or NH) as that on ordinary-paper copies (including 3 in the British Museum, 3 in the Hyde collection, 2 belonging to Herman Liebert, and 1 in the University of Chicago library). In view of this fact, we conclude that "thick-paper" copies of the pamphlet do not exist.

Once the existence of thick-paper copies ceases to operate as a complicating factor, reconstruction of the probable stages in the printing of the first edition becomes relatively simple.[128] The sheets (with sheet A in the "Chesterfield" setting) of the whole edition were started through the press. During the printing, the redundant expression (the repetition of *reason*) on page 19 was discovered, and the erratum directing its deletion was placed on the verso of the title-page; later the duplication of *the* on page 34 was discovered, and that error was corrected. Then the assembling of sheets began. After the early copies had been sewn and possibly even put on the market, it was decided, probably by Johnson, to remove the address to Chesterfield on page 1 and to correct several small errors in signature A, which was entirely reset as a cancel sheet, since type had been distributed. Johnson probably took the opportunity to make a few more revisions. Specifically, it seems likely that he was at least responsible for the change from *higher* to *greater quality* on page 1 (*greater* seems more appropriate as the characterization of *quality*, and, besides, *higher* is used earlier in the same sentence), from *or discernment* to *and discernment* on page 4 (as Chapman remarks, "Johnson is inviting criticism of his plan from the judicious; a *distinction between* elegant and discerning critics does not seem to have much point"), and from *our English idiom* to *the English idiom* on page 4 (*our* is used twice in the following part of the sentence). The cancel sheet then replaced the "Chesterfield" setting of signature A in all unsewn copies. The fact that no "Chesterfield" copies, apparently,[129] contain the duplication of *the* on page 34 may be explained thus: assuming that sheet E was piled up in the order, or roughly in the order, in which it was printed and that the sheets were assembled from the tops of the various piles, one would expect the "Chesterfield" setting of signature A to be assembled with the corrected state of E1^{v}.

Early in August, 1747—almost five months after newspaper announcements had informed the public that the *Dictionary* was "*now Preparing for the* PRESS, *and in good Forwardness*"[130]—copies presumably of both the "Chesterfield" and the "Non-Chesterfield" settings were offered for sale. By the eighth of that month, Daniel Wray the antiquary had bought one,[131] for an unknown price, from Dodsley, whose *Museum* for August 1 contains an enthusiastic puff, along with quotations from the "Non-Chesterfield" setting. The piece was also noticed in the July–September number of the *Bibliothèque raisonnée des ouvrages des savans*, published across the Channel at Amsterdam.[132]

So far as we know, the period from late 1747 to the end of 1754 contains no notable events which have a bearing on the publication of the *Plan*. The partners in the *Dictionary* probably continued to distribute copies of the pamphlet until the supply was exhausted; in April, 1755, at least one reviewer of the *Dictionary* thought that they had been circulating free copies for several years past.[133] But, in spite of the statements of most commentators to the contrary,[134] they did not publish the octavo edition in 1747 (or during the intervening period).

Toward the end of 1754, however, when the *Dictionary* was almost ready for publication, the booksellers resumed their advertising campaign, which had been largely inactive for almost seven years. In that campaign, the *Plan of a Dictionary* played an active role. It appeared (in the "Non-Chesterfield" setting) in the Appendix to the *Scots Magazine* for 1754[135] and possibly in other places, though we know of none, at about the same time. Then, at the end of February, 1755, fifteen hundred copies were published in an octavo edition (set, without the salutation, from the "Chesterfield" setting) dated 1747, free copies of which, according to newspaper announcements of the approaching publication of the *Dictionary*, were available for the asking.[136] An entry in William Strahan's ledgers proves that the date of publication was actually 1755. In April of that year, Strahan recorded, among other items under the heading "Partners in Johnson's Folio Dictionary," the following:

> Reprinting y^e Plan 2½ Sheets N°. 1500
> £1:5..3 2 6

Below, on the same page, in a list specifying the disposition of 2,341 reams of paper, he noted: "—for the Plan—7½."[137]

The collation of the edition is as follows: 8°, π1(=E4) A–D⁴ E⁴(–E4); [$2 signed], 20 ll., pp. [*2*] 1–37 *38*. Contents: π1 title (verso blank), pp. 1–37 text, p. *38* blank.[138] An examination of 14 copies (largely in microfilm)[139] reveals only one definite variant: in the Cambridge University copy, the press figure "8" appears on page 4 instead of "4." A collation of the octavo and quarto ("Chesterfield" setting) editions reveals only minor variations (restricted almost wholly to spelling and punctuation). None of them indicates that Johnson made any changes in the text of the work. Granted that he was told in advance about the new edition, he may have decided that he had already done all he wanted to do with the *Plan*. He had written the "Scheme" and had revised parts of it both before and after readers commented on it; he had written (and probably revised) the manuscript of the *Plan* proper; he had (almost certainly) revised the fair copy both before and after it circulated among readers; he had revised proofs at least once; and, finally, he had probably made changes in signature A of the first edition during the re-setting of that signature. In 1755 Johnson perhaps felt that the *Plan* should be able to speak for itself to contemporary and later audiences. If so, the present essay helps, in a sense, to prove that he was right.

III

Lord Chesterfield and Dr. Johnson

When so much has been written about Johnson and Chesterfield, perhaps the old formula of academic introduction will not be quite inert: in the events leading up to the "celebrated letter," much remains obscure. The problems of fact are centered in the years 1746–48, the problems of motive in 1754 and 1755; and it may not be unjust to say that, in general, recent accounts have neglected the facts and distorted Johnson's motives.

Both sets of problems have been vigorously dealt with by the distinguished editor of Chesterfield's letters, Professor Bonamy Dobrée. According to Dobrée, Johnson got seriously to work on the *Dictionary* in 1747, when he drafted "a rough prospectus or 'Plan' " which reached Chesterfield unofficially, through intermediaries. Chesterfield "liked the Plan" and received Johnson graciously in an interview which "evidently passed off well"; but "still only the rough draft of the Plan was in existence." It was Dodsley the publisher who grew impatient, hurried Johnson to revise and polish, and suggested the obvious dedication. When the finished *Plan* appeared, "Chesterfield gave Johnson ten pounds," but then, under pressure of business and ill health, simply forgot about him. He had not treated Johnson ungenerously, and there is no truth in Johnson's statement of 1755 that he had waited fruitlessly in Chesterfield's outward rooms or had been repulsed from his door.[1]

Professor Dobrée's account is widely known, in some ways typical, and by no means the worst of many; but it is open to two objections. It is itself only partially true, and it makes Johnson out to be a liar. Its factual inaccuracy begins with its first phrase, for, as we have already shown,[2] Johnson's "rough prospectus" still exists, written out and dated in his own hand; and the date is not 1747, but April 30, 1746. The probabilities are that Chesterfield never saw the *Plan* in this stage of its composition, but he did see it in the second surviving manuscript, the fair copy, which he read and annotated. Dobrée has apparently confused the manuscripts.

When he turns from facts to motives, Dobrée is baffled by his astonishing belief that Johnson, at a decisive moment of his life, invented a preposterous lie and successfully passed it off on people who admired his truthfulness. Johnson tells us himself that his immediate provocation in 1755 was the two papers puffing the *Dictionary* which Chesterfield had contributed to Dodsley's periodical *The World* late in 1754; but Dobrée will not believe him. "It is not easy," he says, "to place a finger on what exactly had annoyed him in Chesterfield."[3] That is untrue. Though the precise facts of 1746–48 may never be fully known, Johnson's motives in the winter of 1754 and 1755 are clear enough. Dobrée's uncertainty results from his own carelessness and from his conviction that Johnson was worse than careless; it is easily resolved when decent respect is paid to Johnson's word and the evidence of Chesterfield's behavior; and one might hesitate to discuss it seriously if more recent writers than Dobrée had not expressed the same bewilderment.[4]

The first step toward clarity is to discuss once more the

two manuscripts, the "Scheme" and the fair copy of the *Plan*, which we have already analyzed in the preceding chapter. Both are listed in *Bibliotheca Boswelliana*, the sale catalogue of the library of James Boswell, Jr., and both are partly described there in terms of Chesterfield's relationship to the *Plan*. The "Scheme," says the maker of the catalogue, "is the original Draft of the 'Plan,' before Dodsley had requested Johnson to inscribe it to Lord Chesterfield. There are some friendly critical observations in another hand."[5] The fair copy, he says later, "is in the hand of an Amanuensis, but with very copious Corrections and Interlineations in Johnson's own hand. . . . There are animadversions on part of it in two distinct hand-writings, one of which I believe to be Chesterfield's."[6]

Whether Boswell himself owned the "Scheme" and the fair copy of the *Plan* or whether James Boswell, Jr., secured them after his father's death is not clear.[7] It seems unlikely that had he possessed the manuscripts, Boswell would have failed to use them in the *Life* to help clarify the relationship between Johnson and Chesterfield. Whatever the reason, Boswell did fail to use them; and, so far as we know, John Wilson Croker was the first biographer who undertook to amplify the account in the *Life* with evidence drawn from the fair copy. His note, dated 1846, is as follows: "Mr. Anderdon [*sic*] purchased at Mr. James Boswell's sale many of his father's MSS., one of which he communicated to me, after my first edition, and which is very curious, and indeed important to the question between Lord Chesterfield and Johnson. It is a draft of the prospectus of the Dictionary carefully written by an amanuensis, but signed in great form by Johnson's own hand. It was evidently that which was laid before Lord Chesterfield. Some useful remarks are made in his lordship's hand, and some in another. Johnson adopted all these suggestions. Amongst them is to be found the opinion . . . that *great* should be pronounced *grate*."[8] Croker's note, though better than Dobrée's, is not impeccable; and later commentators, aside from quoting relevant passages in Johnson's letter and in the *Plan* itself, have relied almost entirely on Boswell and/or Croker for information about Chesterfield's connection with the *Plan*. For example, in his edition of the *Life*, G. B. Hill cites part of Croker's note but omits the statement concerning Chesterfield's pronunciation of *great*.[9] In the revision of Hill's edition, Dr. L. F. Powell remarks that two drafts of the *Plan* are extant—the first holograph, the second the same as that mentioned by Croker—and notes that the second "differs from the form finally printed."[10] And Professor Gulick, one of the most recent writers on the subject, merely states in a footnote that "Mr. Herman Liebert has called attention to the fact that Chesterfield read the *Plan* in MS. . . . and returned it to Johnson with comments in his own hand. This was apparently unknown to Boswell."[11]

As matters stand today, therefore, it would appear, first, that no one has ever fully analyzed the comments which Chesterfield made on the fair copy[12] and, second, that, with a single exception,[13] no one has ever examined the earlier of the surviving manuscripts, the "Scheme," for further evidence connecting him with the *Plan*. With the distinction between the rough draft and the fair copy clearly in mind, we may proceed to such analysis and examination.

"A Short Scheme for compiling a new Dictionary of the English Language," besides providing much evidence about Johnson's methods of composition and response to criticism,[14] contains one sentence which throws some light on his relations with Chesterfield. Writing of spelling, Johnson said at first: "When all the words are selected and arranged the first part of the work to be considered is the ORTHOGRAPHY, which was long very vague and uncertain but is now more settled, and settled with such propriety that it may be generally received [*sic*] at least the Word is always to be ranged according to the Spelling in present Use, though it may be often proper to observe that the present Use is a deviation from the truth, particularly when by the change of a Letter or more, the reason of the meaning becomes less obvious, as in *Farrier* for *Ferrier*."[15] The revised form of this sentence expresses a very different opinion, with a significant addition: "When all the words are selected and arranged the first part of the work to be considered is the ORTHOGRAPHY, which was long very vague and uncertain[,] was at last in many cases settled, and by accident, and in which *your Lordship observes*[16] that there is still great uncertainty among the best writers." In the revision, the "settled propriety" of English spelling has given way to "great uncertainty," and the added phrase *your Lordship observes* indicates the source of the change.

The manuscript of the "Scheme" does not inform us how the lordly observation was communicated to Johnson, and the date on the manuscript, April 30, 1746, does not indicate the precise time at which Johnson revised his sentence. Presumably he dated the "Scheme" when he had finished it and was ready to show it to the booksellers with whom he was negotiating;[17] but, as indicated earlier, revisions in the manuscript were almost certainly made both before and after April 30. The reference to "your Lordship" not only belongs to the post–April 30 group but was also one of the later additions to that group.[18] Regardless of the impossibility of dating the revision precisely, however, we can say immediately that the lord was Chesterfield; for the revised sentence, with the added reference, reappears both in the fair copy and in the printed *Plan*.[19] It is therefore certain that although the "Scheme" is not formally addressed to Chesterfield and nowhere mentions him by name, Johnson determined, probably during its revision, that it should be so addressed and changed his opinion of contemporary English spelling accordingly. The change would not seem negligible to either man. Chesterfield's remark has not been found in his publications up through 1747,[20] but his later statements, in the letters to his son and in the second of the ill-fated essays in *The World*, indicate that he was much troubled by the prevalent cacography;[21] and Johnson returned to the subject, with renewed respect for established use, both in his grammar and in the Preface to the *Dictionary*.

The sentence we have been discussing shows only one of the many changes which Johnson made at various stages in the composition of the finished *Plan* and which are treated in the preceding chapter. The lost manuscript from which the amanuensis made the fair copy of the *Plan* was much longer, it will be recalled, than the "Scheme"; for the fair copy consists of forty-six pages, of which all except page 32 are extant. Unlike the "Scheme," the fair copy is undated, but, since it is addressed to Chesterfield as "one of his Majesty's Principal Secretaries of State," it must have been prepared after October 29, 1746—the date when Chesterfield accepted office.[22] The formal signature and numerous revisions are in Johnson's hand, and the hand of one of the two readers is Chesterfield's. Some of Johnson's revisions, including those which correct the errors of the clerk, were presumably made before the manuscript went to the readers; others were apparently made, independently of the readers' comments, after the manuscript was returned to Johnson; while a third group, with which we are here concerned, were made in direct response to the readers' marks and annotations. Chesterfield was the first reader, as the content and location of some of the other reader's notes make clear; and since the second reader sometimes echoes Chesterfield's comments, it is a fair conclusion that no Johnsonian revision intervened between the two readings.[23]

The two critics together made at least thirty-eight significant marks or comments on the manuscript, a total of eight remarks being Chesterfield's.[24] Two of these eight deal with Johnson's choice of words, one with the choice and spelling of a word, one with spelling only, one with morphology, one with etymology, one with syntax, and one with pronunciation.

1. Johnson had written that "Naturalization" of words into English "is produced . . . by an Admission into common Speech in some tralatitious Signification." Chesterfield asks: "is it *tra*latitious or *trans*latitious?"[25] Johnson changes *tralatitious* to *metaphorical.*[26]

2. ". . . a Dictionary designed . . . for popular use," Johnson had written, ". . . should comprise in some degree the Dialect of every Profession." In response to Chesterfield's question, "can one properly say the *Dialect* of a profession?" Johnson substitutes *Peculiar words* for *Dialect.*[27]

3. Describing inflections in English, Johnson (or the clerk) had begun a sentence, "Our flexions therefore. . . ." Chesterfield comments: "should it not be *inflections?* And is it not surer to spell, *reflection*, *inflection* &ra from *flectare*, than *reflexion*, *inflexion* &ra?"[28] Johnson substitutes *Inflections* for *flexions.*[29]

4. "It is to be remarked," Johnson had said, "that many words written alike are differently pronounced, as *flow*, and

Plow, which may be thus registred *flow—Woe, Plow, Now.*" Chesterfield asks: "is it not plough?" Johnson substitutes *Brow* for *Plow.*[30]

5. Johnson had characterized "the accentuation . . . of Polysyllables" as "one of those capricious Phænomenons which cannot be easily reduced to rules." Chesterfield remarks: "In this word, I think the Greek plural is adopted into our language, and *Phænomena* commonly us'd." Johnson changes *Phænomenons* to *Phænomena.*[31]

6. Discussing the "Etymology of Phrases," Johnson had remarked that some "Expressions are . . . borrowed from other Languages . . . even when we do not . . . seem to borrow their words. Thus to *bring about* or accomplish, appears an English Phrase but in reality our English word *about* has no such import, and it is only the French expression *porter a bout.*" Chesterfield comments: "This is no French expression; *Venir a bout d'une affaire*, is us'd in French, to signify bringing a thing about. [*sic*] but *porter a bout* is never us'd." Johnson's revision reads: ". . . it is only a French expression of which we have an example in the common phrase *venir a bout d'une affaire.*"[32]

7. In illustrating his statement that "Our Syntax . . . is not to be taught by rules but by precedents," Johnson had cited Addison's phrase "dies for thirst"[33]—sometimes labeled a "Solecisn" [*sic*]—and had defended Addison with the argument that it "is not in our power to have recourse to any established Laws of Speech, but we [must remark how] the writers of former Ages have [used the same word,] and must acquit him of impropriety [upon the tes]timony of Davis given in his favour by a similar passage.

> She loaths the Watry Glass wherein she gaz'd
> And Shuns it still although *for Thirst She dye.*"[34]

Chesterfield asks: "is Davis a sufficient Authority."[35] Johnson changes *must acquit him* to *consider whether he can be acquitted.*[36]

8. "Some words," Johnson had said, "have two sounds which may be equally admitted, as being equally defensible by Authority. Thus *great* is differently used:

> For Swift and Him despis'd the farce of State,
> The sober follies of the Wise and *Great.* Pope
>
> As if Misfortune made the Throne her Seat,
> And none could be unhappy but the *Great.* Rowe"

Commenting on the quotation from Rowe, Chesterfield declares, "This is undoubtedly a bad Rhyme, and therefore should not be quoted as an Authority, though found in a good poet. Pope would not have made use of it." After he had written his comment, Chesterfield thought better of his last sentence, which he deleted; Johnson made no revision.[37]

Chesterfield's reputation as a man of wit and sense will not be enhanced by these eight remarks. Confining himself to strictures on particular words and phrases, he gives the *Plan* no general praise or blame; one might conclude that he glanced over the fair copy very hastily. Presumably, however, he had already made his general comments, some of which Johnson mentions in the *Plan*, before the fair copy reached him; and his final approval was to be stated with enthusiasm in *The World*. In any event, Johnson was hardly overwhelmed by the eight objections. Though Croker and later writers have said that he adopted all Chesterfield's suggestions, he certainly did not accept Chesterfield's pointed criticism of Rowe's pronunciation. Here Chesterfield's judgment was balanced against the "equiponderant authority" of other good speakers; Sir William Yonge sent Johnson word, when the *Plan* was published, that only an Irishman would rhyme *great* with *state*.[38]

The comments of the second reader, which have been treated more fully in the preceding chapter,[39] may be briefly discussed again, since, by comparison and contrast, they tell us at least something about Chesterfield's relationship to the *Plan*. Whoever the second reader may have been, he spent more time on his annotations than Chesterfield spent on his. More than once he writes his comments beneath remarks of Chesterfield which they echo or reinforce. When Chesterfield, for example, asks whether it is not surer to spell *inflection* with *ct* than with *x*, the second reader answers the question: "It should seem so according to the author's own rule of preserving the radical letters."[40] Yet the second reader had a mind of his own, and Johnson seems to have respected his opinions about as much as he respected Chesterfield's. Most notably, he worked with an eye on Johnson's larger plans, for one of which, as we have already pointed out, he expressed warm approval. Regarding "Questions of purity, or propriety," Johnson had remarked that "I was once in doubt whether I should not attribute too much to my self in attempting to divide [*sic*][41] them," but that "I have been since determined by your Lordship's opinion to interpose my own Judgment." In this instance, Chesterfield had clearly expressed his general opinion elsewhere than in his annotations, but the second reader writes enthusiastically: "This will be of infinite use, rightly executed: and therefore the Author, I doubt not, will proceed in this part with all the accuracy, as well as all the caution, possible."[42]

Further examination of the manuscripts of the "Scheme"

and *Plan* will tell us little more about the relations between Johnson and Chesterfield. From Johnson's revision of his opinion on contemporary English spelling, we have seen that he determined, before he left off working on the "Scheme," to address himself to Chesterfield, with whom he had had some oral or written communication, direct or indirect, not very long before or after April 30, 1746; the address to Chesterfield in the fair copy has shown that this manuscript was written after October 29 of the same year; and the nature of Chesterfield's annotations, as contrasted with those of the second reader, has helped to establish that Chesterfield had made his general comments before the fair copy reached him. More precise and detailed statements must be based on a chronological survey of other evidence.

Chesterfield's movements and official activities in the crucial years from 1746 to 1748 raise no particular difficulties. After spending the summer of 1745 in England, he took up his duties as viceroy in Ireland, where he remained from August 31, 1745, when he reached Dublin, until April 24, 1746, when he returned to England. On April 30, 1746, he was in Dunstable, hoping to be in London that night; but he was ill and had much to do on his return. In September and October he spent some time at Bath, recovering from "a long and dangerous illness"; and from October 29, O.S., 1746, until February 6, O.S., 1748, he served as "one of his Majesty's Principal Secretaries." In that capacity he had some time for reading, since he complains in December, 1747, that no good pamphlets have lately appeared in England, and about the same time he very flatteringly thanked Warburton for a dedication; but his duties undoubtedly made severe demands on his time and attention. After his resignation, he went at once to Bath, partly for a cure but "chiefly to be out of the way of being talked to, and talked of." He was back in London by March 15, O.S., 1748, busied himself in June with moving to his new house, and went to Cheltenham for a fortnight early in July.[43] In short, nothing in the record of his activities conflicts with Johnson's statements in the "celebrated letter." On the contrary, a busy man in uncertain health, beset with seekers after favors, might very well think little of an obscure and unprepossessing author; and the fact that Johnson dates his futile visits to Chesterfield about the time of Chesterfield's resignation and retreat to Bath increases the credibility of Johnson's story.

So clear a record of Johnson's doings in 1746–48 is hardly possible. At the time, he had no Boswell, and in writing to Chesterfield in February, 1755, he felt no need to go into autobiographical detail. It is clear, however, that before April 30, 1746, the date of the "Scheme," Robert Dodsley had recommended him as the right man to do the *Dictionary*,[44] and that Johnson had entered into negotiations with Dodsley and the other booksellers, who would want from him some statement of his intentions. We have shown already that Johnson went a long way in the composition of the "Scheme" with no thought of dedication to Chesterfield. Very probably he did not entertain that thought until after he had signed his contract on June 18, 1746;[45] for he says in the fair copy of the *Plan* that he had been "content with the Terms . . . Stipulated" until he found that his design had excited Chesterfield's curiosity and attracted his favor.[46] The statement suggests that Johnson heard of Chesterfield's interest indirectly, almost certainly through Dodsley, a known friend of Chesterfield.[47] Since Dodsley was also a partner to Johnson's contract for the *Dictionary*, he would have told Johnson of Chesterfield's interest if he himself had known of it when the contract was signed. Thus the further probability is established that Dodsley's communication with Chesterfield about the *Dictionary* should likewise be dated after June 18, and, in the absence of any recorded correspondence on the subject, we may assume that the communication was oral.[48] Dodsley had no false pride; he knew the financial value of Chesterfield's patronage and was no doubt pleased to find his Lordship willing.

At this point, Johnson must be allowed to tell his own story, as he told it to Boswell in 1777: "Sir, the way in which the Plan of my Dictionary came to be inscribed to Lord Chesterfield, was this: I had neglected to write it by the time appointed. Dodsley suggested a desire to have it addressed to Lord Chesterfield. I laid hold of this as a pretext for delay, that it might be better done, and let Dodsley have his desire. I said to my friend, Dr. Bathurst, "Now if any good comes of my addressing to Lord Chesterfield, it will be ascribed to deep policy, when, in fact, it was only a casual excuse for laziness."[49] To this episode, Dobrée's statement applies: "still only the rough draft of the Plan was in existence," perhaps with the annotations which seem to be in the hand of Taylor, but certainly without Johnson's added phrase *your Lordship observes;* the "Scheme" remained too crude for effective use in the advertising campaign which the booksellers were to launch in the spring of 1747.[50]

Urged on by Dodsley, Johnson set about transforming the "Scheme" into the *Plan*. In this work, done mainly or entirely after October 29, 1746, the first traceable step was the addition of *your Lordship observes*. When the necessary changes proved too extensive to be made on the original manuscript,[51] Johnson made a fresh start. Directly or indirectly, he learned a good deal about Chesterfield's views, including Chesterfield's opinion that in matters of purity and propriety Johnson should offer his own judgments; and he must have completed a manuscript in which Chesterfield was directly addressed when the carelessness of Taylor caused him considerable disappointment.

Again Boswell records the story: "Dr. Taylor told me, that Johnson sent his 'Plan' to him in manuscript, for his perusal; and that when it was lying upon his table, Mr. William Whitehead happened to pay him a visit, and being shewn it, was highly pleased with such parts of it as he had time to read, and begged to take it home with him, which he was allowed to do; that from him it got into the hands of a noble Lord, who carried it to Lord Chesterfield. When Taylor observed this might be an advantage, Johnson replied, 'No, Sir; it would have come out with more bloom, if it had not been seen before by any body.' "[52] Three reasons strongly support the opinion that the manuscript which Taylor speaks of was a manuscript of the *Plan*, almost certainly the fair copy itself, and not the "Scheme." First and most obviously, the fair copy bears Chesterfield's annotations. Second, the manuscript in question must have been addressed to Chesterfield, as the "Scheme" was not; otherwise the taking of the manuscript to Chesterfield would demand explanation. Third, Johnson's remark suggests that he was ready to print. In what must inevitably be an inferential narrative, no better place can be found for Taylor's indiscretion than we have given it; a precise date might be established if a time could be discovered, probably early in 1747, when Taylor, Whitehead, Chesterfield, and the other "noble Lord"[53] were all in London.

Whether or not Johnson had visited Chesterfield before, he would visit him now. On his first visit or visits, at whatever time, he was well received and favorably impressed with Chesterfield's elegance and knowledge; Chesterfield made "great professions" and perhaps accompanied them with his gift of ten pounds.[54] Eager to please, Johnson paid due attention to the suggestions by Chesterfield and the other reader of his fair copy; and after final revision in proof, the quarto edition of the *Plan* was printed by August, 1747. Comment was mainly favorable, though Thomas Birch thought the style was "flatulent," and Daniel Wray the antiquary not only agreed with Birch but had gone so far as to write a "critique" by August 8.[55] Prevailing opinion was against these quibblers. The *Plan* was puffed in Dodsley's *Museum* for August 1, as one might expect; but it was also highly praised in the July–September number of the *Bibliothèque raisonnée des ouvrages des savans*, published at Amsterdam; and in Ireland it shortly evoked the compliment of rival proposals from one John Maxwell, M.A.[56]

Yet Johnson's great bid for favor did not win active patronage from Chesterfield, whom most of all he had hoped to please. Nothing came of the great professions after the ten pounds. If we are not to believe, with Dobrée, that Johnson was a neurotically persistent and strangely successful liar, those painful visits followed when Johnson waited vainly in anterooms or was turned away from Chesterfield's door. Certainly, Chesterfield was under no obligation to pamper every impecunious author who lay in wait for him with a dedication, and his later explanation to Dodsley makes it likely that, at the time, he did not even know of Johnson's disappointment. The facts remain that Chesterfield offered his explanation to Dodsley and sent that unlikely emissary, long Sir Thomas Robinson, to make his ultimate peace with Johnson. He would not have done so if he had not been conscious of some failure. It is safe, then, to take Johnson's word that more than once he called on Chesterfield and was not received; and about the time of Chesterfield's resignation, he decided that he had danced his awkward attendance long enough.

From this date, the facts are clear. Until November, 1754, Johnson and Chesterfield went their separate ways; and if it had not been for Dodsley, who had not abandoned the idea that Chesterfield might still put money in his pocket,[57] their paths might never have crossed again. The fiction of Chesterfield's patronage had been kept up, however, by the distribution of copies of the *Plan*,[58] which was to be reprinted, for free distribution, shortly before the actual publication of the *Dictionary*.[59] In this situation Dodsley was just the man to see that a timely puff might confirm the fiction and make all the difference to his sales. Full of his scheme, he told Chesterfield that the *Dictionary* would soon appear,[60] and the damage was done. Chesterfield "fell a-scribbling," his papers on the *Dictionary* appeared in *The World* for November 28 and December 5, Johnson learned from Dodsley who had written them,[61] and in February his letter lay on Chesterfield's table.[62]

Given these facts, what can now be said of Johnson's motives and of Chesterfield's? Anger at Chesterfield's neglecting him is not in itself enough to explain Johnson's behavior; he had lived with that grievance for seven years without composing any denunciatory letters. Nor were Chesterfield's papers in *The World*, if read outside their context, particularly offensive. The first of them, down to its last two paragraphs, is serious, polished, and no more commonplace than complimentary; the last two paragraphs, like the whole of the second paper, are a little silly and tactlessly condescending, but those who explain Johnson's outburst by Chesterfield's flippancy and want of tact assume that Johnson was even sillier. A more discreet assumption is that Johnson was not silly and that he meant what he said: "I hope it is no very cynical asperity not to confess obligations where no benefit has been received, or to be unwilling that the Publick should consider me as owing that to a Patron, which Providence has enabled me to do for myself."[63] This sentence expresses quite directly the controlled anger of a man who has been placed in an intolerably false position, of a man who was soon to declare, in a Preface perhaps already composed, that his great work had been written, without the "patronage of the great," for "the honour" of his "country." Johnson owed no debt of gratitude to Chesterfield; Chesterfield deserved no credit for the completion of the *Dictionary*. Yet the two papers in *The World*, particularly if they were read, as Chesterfield suggested, in conjunction with the *Plan*, invited precisely the opposite conclusion. Johnson had either to pretend the gratitude which he did not feel and which Chesterfield had not earned, or to block the unjustified inference. His complaint, therefore, was not merely that Chesterfield had done next to nothing for him but that now, at last, Chesterfield was acting as he might properly have acted if he *had* done something for him. If Chesterfield had been a generous patron, he would praise the *Dictionary;* he was praising the *Dictionary;* therefore—. Logical or not, that was the way people would think, and the presumed innocence of Chesterfield's desire to help the likable but imperceptive Dodsley could not avert the penalty for obtuseness. He had stupidly given Johnson the double opportunity to acquit himself of ingratitude and to teach the most zealously elegant gentleman of the age a lesson in manners. Johnson did both.

In Chesterfield's favor it must be said that, after his initial blunder, he recovered himself with resolute dexterity. He had little cause to regret his conduct before November, 1754, and he took the punishment for his meddling papers with good grace: "Dr. Adams mentioned to Mr. Robert Dodsley that he was sorry Johnson had written his letter to Lord Chesterfield. Dodsley, with the true feelings of trade, said 'he was very sorry too; for that he had a property in the Dictionary, to which his Lordship's patronage might have been of consequence.' He then told Dr. Adams, that Lord Chesterfield had shewn him the letter. 'I should have imagined (replied Dr. Adams) that Lord Chesterfield would have concealed it.' 'Poh! (said Dodsley) do you think a letter from Johnson could hurt Lord Chesterfield? Not at all, Sir. It lay upon his table, where any body might see it. He read it to me; said, "this man has great powers," pointed out the severest passages, and observed how well they were expressed.' "[64]

Dodsley's blindness is comical, and it may be that Adams and Boswell, too, underestimated Chesterfield. What Boswell called duplicity may have been fair play, the means which Chesterfield used to set the record as straight as Johnson wanted it; and the evaporation of Johnson's bitterness, after Chesterfield had sent him a message by Sir Thomas Robinson, might indicate Johnson's recognition that Chesterfield had finally done him right. A letter which John Douglas wrote to Lord Hardwicke on October 13, 1783, is relevant here: "This Day I saw Dr Johnson, who said that he should be very ready to trust me with a Copy of his Letter to Lord Chesterfield, particularly as your Lordship wished to see it; but he assured me that it did not exist in writing, in his Possession. I urged the Expectation of the Public to have that masterly Composition, preserved; but, I find, that a Message which long Sir Thomas Robinson brought him from the Noble Lord, before he died, has melted the Heart of the Writer of that epistolary Philippic."[65] Chesterfield had done no more than Johnson intended when he allowed the letter to become, for a few months, the talk of the town; but the public, after some initial hesitation, had decided the question between them in Johnson's favor. Secure in that decision, Johnson refused to advertise his victory. He knew that, in the end, Chesterfield had proved himself generous when generosity was not easy.

One final handful of facts about the initial hesitation of public judgment may prevent the objection that we have been too clever by half. Johnson's *Plan* was widely distributed by the booksellers, was reprinted in the Appendix to the *Scots Magazine* for 1754,[66] and was often quoted in the early reviews of the *Dictionary;* Chesterfield's papers for *The World* were reprinted in the *Gentleman's Magazine*, the *London Magazine*, the *Scots Magazine*, and probably elsewhere.[67] The reprint in the *Scots Magazine* closes with a note stating what was generally known, "that the two papers preceding were written by the Earl of Chesterfield."[68] At least twice, the logical conclusion was drawn, once by a writer in the *Scots Magazine*, who predicted great things for a dictionary "composed by the author of the RAMBLER, and patronized by the Earl of Chesterfield,"[69] and once by Chesterfield's friend Dr. Matthew Maty. In his *Journal britannique* for July–August, 1755, Maty reviewed the *Dictionary* very favorably, but he regretted the absence from it of the excellent *Plan*. The inclusion of the *Plan*, he said, would have spared Johnson the composition of a new preface, which contains only some of the same things, and its omission seemed a device to conceal the patron whom

Johnson had chosen and the obligations which Johnson owed him.[70]

Maty drew precisely the conclusions which the "celebrated letter" had been written to prevent, and Johnson saw no reason to be generous to *him*. He said he would throw "the little black dog" into the Thames.

IV

The Early Editions of the *Dictionary*

BEFORE Johnson's death in December, 1784, five folio editions of the *Dictionary* had been printed for its proprietors; and late in 1785 the publication of the sixth and seventh editions was begun. The sixth edition was in two volumes quarto; the seventh, again in folio but in one volume only. Both were advertised as including Johnson's latest improvements, made in his own hand in the copy of the fourth edition which he had bequeathed to Sir Joshua Reynolds. The Reynolds copy is now in the John Rylands Library. Parts of two other corrected copies, one of the first edition and one of the first and third editions mixed, also exist. The mixed copy, with extensive manuscript notes by Johnson and others, is in the British Museum; and what were described as a collection of Johnson's final corrected proofs of the first edition were sold by Sotheby's in 1927. In the attempt, therefore, to determine where Johnson's considered opinion of any word may be found, at least seven editions must be reckoned with, as well as complete or fragmentary corrected copies of editions 1, 3, and 4.

Much of the history of the first seven "authorized" editions may be conveniently traced in the ledgers and accounts of William and Andrew Strahan, but Johnson had been at work on the *Dictionary* for some time before any

Versification is the arrangement of a certain number of Syllables according to certain Laws.

The feet of our verses are either iambick as alóft creáte, or trochaick as hóly lófty.

~~[illegible]~~ Our iambick measures comprise verses —

— — — — ~~of [illegible] Syllables~~

Here now I may
Think and pray
Before death
Stops my breath
Other joys
~~Are but~~ toys.

of ~~four~~ Syllables

With ravish'd ears
The Monarch hears.

of ~~five~~ Six

In the days of old
Stories plainly told

But when the sun hath clothed the year
Shall three times doubled be
Then shall an end appear
To all our Slavery.

The whole of this manuscript is in the handwriting of Dr Johnson. J. [illegible] 1826 [illegible]

Only Known Surviving Page of the MS of Johnson's *Dictionary* (in the Hyde Collection) reference was made to it in the accounts at the printing-house. The printed *Plan* had been available for over two years when William Strahan, under date of December, 1749, entered a charge in the account of the booksellers J. and P. Knapton for their "5th Share of the first 70 Sheets of Johnston's Dict."[1] This entry not only leaves the year 1748 a blank; the date 1749 is itself problematic, partly because the sum involved, £29:12:0, is deleted, and partly because, elsewhere in the ledger, the first charge against the partners in the *Dictionary* is dated December, 1750.[2] The ledger leaves no doubt, however, of the size of the impression, 2,000 copies; and certainly the 1750 date is not too early: Andrew Millar, another of the proprietors, made the payment for his fifth share of the seventy sheets on December 20 of that year.[3] Indeed, if the letters of Thomas Birch can be believed, Strahan may have had good reason for his partially deleted entry. By August, 1748, Birch writes, Johnson's amanuenses had almost finished transcribing his authorities; by September, 1749, some part of the *Dictionary* was "almost ready for the Press"; and by October 20, 1750, as many as 120 sheets (the first three letters of the alphabet) had actually been printed off.[4] These statements find some confirmation in the fact that Strahan's second charge against the partners is for just fifty sheets; but Strahan does not date his second charge until May, 1752, and by the end of that month only Millar and Dodsley had made the two payments, totaling £45:12:0, for sheets 1–120.[5]

The gap between December, 1750, and May, 1752, may be partially filled by reference to Johnson's correspondence. It was not a happy time. Before Johnson the poet awaked as Johnson the lexicographer, he had apparently thought that he could finish the *Dictionary* within three years; and as the three years stretched almost into nine, he found that the £1,575 for which he had contracted were hardly enough to maintain himself and pay the expenses of his work.[6] Even if Birch was right that 120 sheets had been printed by October 20, 1750, Johnson's progress remained slower than he had expected. He did not begin his second volume until April, 1753,[7] and in these "deplorable Circumstances"[8] the clash of interests led him into a quarrel with the booksellers.

The most direct evidence bearing on this quarrel is a letter of Johnson's, dated November 1, 1751.[9] Disappointed at the slowness of his work, the proprietors, it would seem, had threatened to cut off his payments and had requested a meeting to discuss outstanding differences. Johnson refused the meeting and made a counter-threat. He asked Strahan, who had been acting as mediator, to inform the "Gentlemen Partners" that he would *not* see them until the first volume was in the press and that they might hasten or retard that accomplishment by withdrawing or not withdrawing their last message. He was, in short, prepared to strike. These facts are undoubtedly reflected, with more or less distortion, in a bit of gossip which was current shortly after Johnson's death. In his poverty, the story goes, he had asked for an increase in his agreed pay, and when the proprietors' refusal was accompanied by the threat of a "suit in equity," he stuck by his decision to do no more work until some adjustment was made. Since the success of the whole undertaking depended on Johnson's good will and industry, the proprietors, it is said, eventually gave in, on the agreement that henceforth Johnson should be paid one guinea for each sheet of copy.[10] The dispute was settled with no permanent ill feeling; and from the beginning of 1753 at the latest, the *Dictionary* moved more rapidly toward completion.

Strahan's ledgers provide the next significant date in its progress. Under October, 1753, he charges the partners £190 for another 100 sheets; that is, £38 for each fifth share in the printing of sheets 121–220.[11] That *at least* 220 sheets had actually been printed by this time is proved by the fact that Millar, Hitch, and Dodsley all made their third payment by October 19;[12] and although it is questionable to argue that because Johnson had turned in well *over* 220 sheets by April, Strahan had printed over 220 by October, there is some evidence which points to precisely that conclusion. That evidence is a series of puzzling entries, not in the account of the partners as a group, but in the individual account of Hitch. Dating the entries October 4, 1753, Strahan charges Hitch for three sets of 100 sheets each, which would bring the total to 420 sheets.[13] It is hard to decide whether or not so much of the *Dictionary* had really been printed so early; for the surviving accounts seem not to record, for this time, any payments corresponding to the last two of these three charges. Johnson, moreover, was now supplying "copy faster than the printers called for it,"[14] and whereas the bulk of his own work was done by July or August, 1754, some at least of the printing was not actually finished until early in 1755.[15] On the other hand, if Johnson was ahead of the printer, the printer was ahead of the booksellers in their payments for the printing: Strahan enters his charge for the printing of the whole *Dictionary* at a time when the booksellers had paid only for the 420 sheets in question.[16] Baretti, indeed, said in a letter of April 15, 1754, that the *Dictionary* had already been printed even then.[17] A conservative conclusion would be that when Strahan charged Hitch for printing sheets 121–420, he had received from Johnson the copy for all of Volume I and much of Volume II and had begun the printing of the second volume.

In the summer, presumably, of 1754, Johnson wrote his history of the language, his grammar, and his Preface and put the finishing touches to his work.[18] Though publication, now, was not far off, one last delay was probably caused by his desire to write himself M.A. on the title-page. Binding and lettering could not be done without the title-pages, and the degree was not conferred until February 20, 1755.[19] The advertising which began shortly thereafter, seems to reflect this final difficulty. As early as February 27, and throughout March, the *Dictionary* was announced for publication in the latter month; but it was not until the very end of March that publication was definitely set for April 15.[20] Meanwhile, perhaps around February 28, when the advertisement said nothing of the *Plan*, or March 1, when it was offered free, that now somewhat embarrassing address to Chesterfield became available in a reprint of 1,500 copies;[21] and Johnson's "frigid tranquillity," which did not moderate the heat of the "celebrated letter," undoubtedly thawed somewhat as April 15 drew near. The booksellers kept cool. They had risked an investment of at least £3,000, and they set for the *Dictionary* the high price of £4:10:0. They did not lower it for over thirty years.

What did the prosperous buyers of the first edition get for their money? In the words of the Marquis Nicolini, then president of the Accademia della Crusca, "a very noble Work," which "would be a perpetual Monument of Fame to the Author, an Honour to his own Country in particular, and a general Benefit to the Republic of Letters throughout all Europe."[22] The judgment is no more eloquent than fair; yet the incongruity here forced by fitting a courtly answer to a gross question presides over the making of Johnson's *Dictionary*. The ill-kempt and melancholy genius, assiduously cultivating in words the elegance which his person and surroundings lacked; an association of booksellers, one of them a footman who had abandoned livery for literature, promoting an enterprise which royal and noble patronage had not supported; the author struggling with debt, disease, and grief for his wife's death while printer and publisher were thriving; the book itself embodying the triumph of desperate industry over admitted laziness—that is the picture; and it is made yet more grotesque by the probability that no little of Johnson's effort was simply wasted. The proof sheets—if they are proof sheets—which compose the first of the three extant corrected copies show that many of his improvements in the first edition were never made in print. Whenever it may have been formulated, his considered opinion of numerous words, it will shortly appear, remained in manuscript.

On this question the second and third editions of the *Dictionary* have little bearing. No corrected copy of the second edition is known, and its printed text is of no great importance. There are some revisions in the Preface, different from those which Johnson made for the fourth edition of 1773,[23] and there are some in the word-list proper, apparently different from those in the "proof sheets" of the first edition; but the second edition is essentially a reprint of the first, and the third, printed in 1765, is essentially a reprint of the second. The circumstances, however, in which the second edition was printed and published require some comment.[24]

Most probably it was intended to safeguard a heavy investment. Since not many readers could afford to spend ninety shillings on a single book, the proprietors may well have decided, even before the first edition appeared, that unless it was a failure, they would shortly publish a second edition in weekly numbers, which would appeal to less opulent purchasers. Their decision may also have been prompted or reinforced, or their action hastened, by the knowledge that Scott's revision of Bailey's *Universal Dictionary* was soon to appear.[25] Some such hypothesis, whatever the possible influence of the Scott-Bailey, is necessary to avoid the odd conclusion that by the end of May, 1755, the phenomenal success of Johnson's first edition of 2,000 copies had stimulated its proprietors to produce a second but that after the first edition had been quickly exhausted, the second satisfied the lagging demand for the next ten years. It is more likely that the sale of the two editions overlapped. The first sold well,[26] as Johnson's supremacy was at once acknowledged; but, together, the two editions were more than a market almost glutted with dictionaries could quickly absorb.[27] A number of facts combine to support this hypothesis, which coincides with Boswell's statement that although the booksellers were eventually "considerable gainers" by the *Dictionary*, they were not at first quite sure of any great profit.[28]

The advertisements for the second edition provide the most convenient summary of its history. In the *London Evening-Post* for May 27–29, 1755, and in the *Public Advertiser* for May 29 and June 2 it was stated that there would soon be published proposals for reprinting the *Dictionary* "In Weekly Numbers, at Six-pence each," and in the *Evening-Post* for June 5–7 the actual appearance of the proposals was announced. About the same time, advertisements in a number of papers specified the conditions for the reprint.[29] For sixpence weekly, subscribers could obtain the *Dictionary* in 165 numbers containing three and four sheets alternately, while for a shilling a week they could get it twice as quickly in numbers containing seven sheets each. Publication began, as scheduled, on June 14, and the weekly numbers were regularly announced until mid-December, when subscriptions were still being asked and proposals and earlier numbers still offered.[30] The continuation of these appeals well into 1756 makes one suspect that the demand was not overwhelming,[31] and there is stronger ground for suspicion in the advertisements that marked the end of the *Dictionary*'s serial publication. Repeatedly it was declared that the *Dictionary* was "now finish'd" and that the sale of weekly numbers must be terminated. One such advertisement appeared in the *Evening-Post* for January 13–15, 1757, when subscribers were desired to complete their sets "before Lady-Day next"; but in the same paper for March 7–9, 1758, the deadline was set for the following March 25; and after another year the *Post* for March 22–24 could still say that May 1, 1759, would end the sale of odd numbers. Subscriptions for the sixpenny numbers must therefore have been accepted for six or eight months after the first number had been issued.

The size of the second edition is hard to determine. Strahan's ledgers show clearly that the first edition was of 2,000 copies, the third of 1,024,[32] the fourth of 1,250,[33] and the fifth of 1,000;[34] but his charges for the second edition, entered under date of June, 1755, are not so transparent.[35] Of the first 38 sheets of the *Dictionary*, Strahan charges for 2,298 copies; of the next 174 sheets, 1,274 copies; and of the last 367 sheets, only 768 copies. He charges, that is, for more copies of the first sheets than of the last—a not uncommon practice, it would seem, in the printing of serial publications;[36] and from the sheets for which he charged, only 768 complete sets of the *Dictionary* could be made up.[37] There would still remain, when these sets had been completed, 1,530 copies of the first 38 sheets and 506 copies of the next 174. Perhaps the discrepancy may be explained by the booksellers' expectation that considerably more people would begin buying weekly numbers than would actually complete their sets of the work; but whatever the answer to the riddle may be, it is clear that the second edition could not have been much larger than the first and may have been much smaller. A reasonable guess might be that between three and four thousand copies of the folio *Dictionary* supplied the demand for the first ten years after its publication. It was not unsuccessful, therefore; but the dates 1755 and 1756 on the title-pages of its first two editions should not be misinterpreted to mean that so large and costly a book had emerged as a best seller. That fate was reserved for the octavo abridgment, which appeared, from 1756 to 1786, in eight editions of 5,000 copies each.[38]

Unlike the second and third folios, the fourth edition of the "great Dictionary" was considerably revised. Johnson gives one account of the revision in his "Advertisement" to that edition: ". . . finding my Dictionary about to be reprinted [he says] I have endeavoured, by a revisal, to make it less reprehensible. I will not deny that I found many parts requiring emendation, and many more capable of improvement. Many faults I have corrected, some superfluities I have taken away, and some deficiencies I have supplied. I have methodised some parts that were disordered, and illuminated some that were obscure. Yet the changes or additions bear a very small proportion to the whole. The critic will now have less to object, but the student who has bought any of the former copies, needs not repent; he will not, without nice collation, perceive how they differ, and usefulness seldom depends upon little things."

A briefer but more personal statement, along with scattered references which help to date the progress of the work, may be found in Johnson's letters. In March, 1772, Boswell had found him at work on the revision,[39] and a year later, in February, 1773, he wrote to Boswell: "A new edition of my great Dictionary is printed, from a copy which I was persuaded to revise; but having made no preparation, I was able to do very little. Some superfluities I have expunged, and some faults I have corrected, and here and there have scattered a remark; but the main fabrick of the work remains as it was. I had looked very little into it since I wrote it, and, I think, I found it full as often better, as worse, than I expected."[40]

Other letters show Johnson busy with his revision in August, 1771, and again in the summer of 1772; in October, 1772, he sent the *Dictionary* to the press.[41] When Strahan estimated his own wealth on January 1, 1773, and happily decided that he was now worth £38,000, he listed the printing of the *Dictionary* among his still unfinished work;[42] but the suggestion in Johnson's letter to Boswell, that the job was done by the end of February, is confirmed by another entry in the ledgers. Under date of March, 1773, Strahan enters his charges for printing the *third* edition of the folio dictionary, with "extraordinary Corrections . . . throughout."[43] That he calls the fourth edition the third is as puzzling as the booksellers' statement, in 1774, that they had paid Johnson £300 for "Improvements in the third Edition."[44] Their remark, like Strahan's, might be taken to mean that the fourth edition was printed from the third; but at least its Preface seems to have been printed from the first,[45] the two earlier corrected copies are also wholly or partly of the first edition, and Johnson writes to Boswell as if his one revision was based on a single copy. Yet this line of reasoning also leads to difficulty, not only because one of the corrected copies is described as first-edition proofs; for neither Strahan nor the booksellers explain why many of Johnson's corrections were never printed in any edition. From such a maze, the way out is hard to find.

The improvements that *were* made in the fourth edition are quite various.[46] Some are simply mechanical changes, such as the restoration of the alphabetical order of entries or the chronological order of quotations when it had somehow become confused; and some merely continue a process of abbreviating references and quotations which may be noted already in the second edition. On the other hand, if some definitions, quotations, references, and even whole entries are shortened or omitted altogether, new definitions, new entries, and (in particular) new quotations are sometimes added. Not infrequently, the discrimination of further meanings, the more precise statement of senses previously recognized, or the more consistent indication of the relations among the given definitions entails additional rearrangement. A few changes are made in the Preface; there are some additions to the grammar; and occasional remarks on the etymology or usage of particular words are added in the body of the text. If some glaring blunders remain and a few others creep in, they need no "more apology than the nature of the work will furnish"; and Johnson was hardly responsible for the failure to include all his corrections even in his revised edition.

The most striking evidence of that failure is in the invaluable sheets of the first edition which Sotheby's sold on November 28, 1927. Described in the sale catalogue, the only available source of information concerning them, as an incomplete set of "the final proofs submitted to the author,"[47] they were bought by Maggs for £3,250 and are now in the possession of Col. Richard Gimbel of Philadelphia and New Haven. Title-pages, Preface, grammar, and history of the language are wanting, along with the latter part of the second volume; the body of the *Dictionary*, however, is complete from *A* to *Pumper*, with the exception of the entries *Abide–Abolish*, *H–Hygroscope*, *Mactation–Mythology*, and *Oary–Pack*. "Inserted opposite the words to which they apply are about 1,630 slips containing illustrative" quotations. These were "mostly copied by Johnson's amanuenses," only "a few" being "wholly or partly in his own hand"; but the "numerous corrections and additions in the margins include an appreciable number written by Johnson himself." A facsimile of the single page *Abolishable–Above*, which is included in Sotheby's catalogue, shows two attached quotation slips and almost twenty corrections in the printed text.

The history of these sheets before November, 1927, is completely obscure. Lot 474 in "a Selected Portion of the Library at Keele Hall, Newcastle, Staffordshire; the property of Colonel Ralph Sneyd," they had been at Keele since at least the latter part of the nineteenth century, when they were mentioned in the reports of the Historical Manuscripts Commission;[48] but Keele Hall had been the home of the Sneyds for over three hundred years, and inquiries of all the obvious sources have produced no information how or how early the sheets came there. A few possible clues might just be mentioned. First, Reade's *Gleanings*, his *Reades of Blackwood Hill*, and Mary Alden Hopkins' *Dr. Johnson's Lichfield* have made it certain that Johnson knew the Sneyds and the Sneyds knew him.[49] Second, the Sneyd library also contained one of the few known copies of Johnson's own sale catalogue. Third, in the Johnson catalogue, Lot 644 was "13, of Dr. Johnson's dictionary with MSS. notes," and Lot *649 was "Six of Dr. Johnson's dictionary, and a parcel of reviews and magazines." If these lots were neither nineteen octavos nor nineteen unmanageable folios, but nineteen convenient fascicles of the folio, then one could guess at a reason why the corrected copy in the British Museum was purchased in six parts, each containing one or more letters of the alphabet, and why the three main gaps in the Sneyd copy are complete letters. The guess would not be disproved, moreover, by the appearance of the two lots under the heading "Octavo et infra," for the headings are inaccurately applied; Lot 647, "Gwinn's London & Westminster improved" (1766) is itself a quarto. Perhaps the reigning Sneyd made a notable purchase.[50]

Luckily, the Sotheby catalogue, especially the facsimile, tells a good deal more about the content of the sheets than about their history. Of the corrections shown on the page *Abolishable–Above*, some are very slight: the italicizing of a word here and there, the correction of a reading in a quotation from Shakespeare, rearrangement of some quotations to place them in chronological order, minor changes in the phrasing of definitions, and the like. Other changes are more significant. The booksellers and the printer have sometimes been blamed for the shortening of quotations and of references which marks the second and later editions of the *Dictionary;* but in the Sotheby facsimile, Johnson himself may be seen deleting two lines of a long quotation and removing, from a reference to *Paradise Lost*, not only the number of book and line but even the very title. No less than six references are shortened on this one page. More constructively, Johnson alters several definitions, such, for example, as sense 2 of the adjective *abortive*. In the printed text, this definition reads: "Figuratively, that which fails for want of time"; in the right-hand margin, Johnson has added the further explanation: "that which comes forth into view or practice before its time." The facsimile shows smaller changes in four other definitions.

Most striking of all is the correction implied and partially indicated by one of the two attached slips, for it bears on the questions when Johnson corrected the Sneyd copy and whether or not it consists of proofs. The slip, which belongs to the verb *abide*, should follow leaf B2 verso and precede C1; but since C1 (*Abide–Abolish*) is missing, the slip appears with the facsimile of C2 recto. On it, in the hand of an amanuensis, is an illustrative quotation from "*Hall*"; and across the top of the slip Johnson has written: "5 To endure without resistance or contradiction." Apparently, the slip was intended to supply a fifth sense of the active verb *abide*. The importance of all this is that in the first edition, where there *is* no active verb *abide*, all the senses of the word are listed under *abide*, verb neuter; the slip looks like part of a wholesale correction of this blunder, which is indeed set right in the second edition. There, what had been the first four senses under the single entry *abide*, verb neuter, hold their place; but senses 5–9 under the single entry become senses 1–5 under the newly introduced *active* verb *abide*, though not in that order. The old neuter sense 5 becomes the new active sense 4, the neuter 6 becomes the active 5, 7 becomes 1, 8 becomes 3, and 9 becomes 2. Surprisingly enough, neither the definition nor the quotation on the slip in the Sneyd copy was used in the second edition, and, though they *are* used in the fourth edition, they are used wrongly. The definition is altered so that it reads "To endure without offence, anger, or contradiction," and it stands, with the quotation from Hall, as a new fifth sense of the neuter verb, despite the fact that the quotation clearly illustrates an active usage. The fourth edition also restores the senses of the active verb to the order which they had held under the neuter in the first edition.

The rich confusion of the data here is not the least part of their significance, even after the statement has been simplified for the sake of clarity; beyond assent to the adjective in Johnson's own phrase, "muddling work," generalizations are hard to make. The extensive revision of leaf C1 in the second edition, which normally makes few changes from the first, must somehow be related to the absence of that leaf from the Sneyd copy, but no conclusions can be drawn from this presumption. In the entry *Abide*, as in the Preface, the first edition obviously served as copy for the fourth, and more strenuous collation might show that this was generally the case; but the best preliminary test, while it shows that the references to quotations in the fourth edition very frequently cannot be derived from the shorter references in the second and third but must go back to the first, still does not give uniform results throughout the *Dictionary*. In this connection it is perhaps safe to say only that the accuracy of one part of Sotheby's description would not exclude the inaccuracy of the other: though the Sneyd sheets are of the first edition, they are not necessarily proofs, for Johnson might have corrected them at some time after his work on the corresponding proof sheets had been done. Finally, the use of the slip for *Abide* in the fourth edition is more notable than typical. The fourth edition ignores most of the changes shown in the Sotheby facsimile and makes others not indicated there, including some that conflict with those which *are* indicated;[51] and collation of the facsimile with all editions through the seventh and with H. J. Todd's edition of 1818 confirms the one unshakable generalization: few of the changes which Johnson made in the Sneyd copy were ever printed. It is hard to suggest a reason while the sheets themselves are not accessible, and the tentative explanation in Sotheby's catalogue can be quoted only with reservations. "The printers, exasperated, as is well known, by Johnson's dilatoriness in dealing with proofs, may well have gone to press without awaiting the return of these." The essential conclusion is that most of Johnson's corrections, whenever they were made, were persistently ignored. The purchasers who laid down their £4:10:0 from 1755 to 1785 did get indeed "a noble Work," but some or all of them did not get quite the work which Johnson had intended.

Much that has been said of the Sneyd copy may be said also of the corrected copy in the British Museum, whose examination will lead through similar uncertainties to the same clear, though limited, conclusion.[52] Though bound by the Museum in three volumes, the Museum copy is really only an imperfect Volume I; and the missing sheets, not quite accurately recorded in the Museum catalogue, seem to fall at the ends of the second, third, and last of the six parts in which the copy was purchased. Johnsonian corrections are largely or wholly confined to the second part (that is, to sheets 2N through 3U1, the letter *B* as far as *Bystander*, with the last page of the letter *A*), whose independence from the other five parts is fully established by a variety of evidence. Most obviously, the paper of the interleaves in Part 2 is different; the edges of the pages are rough, brown, and brittle from much thumbing; and an obliging worm has left a distinctive pattern of wormholes which begin with sheet 2N and end with 3U1. Somewhat less obviously, the hand of the amanuensis on the interleaves of Part 2 does not appear in the other parts; and the non-Johnsonian hands in the other parts, one of them very similar to the hand of Johnson's Shakespearean colleague George Steevens, do not appear in Part 2. Outside of Part 2, again, there are no quite certain specimens of Johnson's own hand, though it may have been he who wrote a word or two in the margins (not on the interleaves) alongside the entries *Galleass* and *Giant*. To clench the matter, collation shows that sheets 2N through 3U1 are first-edition sheets, while the other sheets are of the third edition.[53]

Neither the physical characteristics of the Museum copy nor the content of its non-Johnsonian annotations allows a decision when the six parts first came together or when and why the non-Johnsonian annotations were made. In Part 2, it is plain that the amanuensis first did his work, copying out numerous quotations, supplying a few new definitions, making one or two comments on Scots dialect, etc.; he wrote only on the interleaves. Johnson then went through the amanuensis' work, deleted much of it, altered much, and marked for insertion what he wanted to be used. He also made many corrections and additions on the printed pages, quite independently of anything which the amanuensis had done. Conclusions valid for Part 2, however, cannot by any means be automatically transferred to the other parts, and vice versa. Some of the non-Johnsonian annotations seem to have been made with an eye to possible use in a revision; others relieve the barrenness of the philologic desert by the critical zest with which they compare Johnson's interpretations of Shakespeare in the *Dictionary* and in his edition and by their strain of fine contempt for Warburtonian audacities; and though most of them deal in one way or another with Shakespearean quotations, their date or dates, purpose or purposes, and relation or relations to Johnson's own endeavors are no clearer than the identity of their makers. One can hardly go beyond the mere possibility that, unlike such annotated copies of the *Dictionary* as those of Malone and Dyer, none of the six parts of the copy under discussion is negligible in the study of the early editions, since all six may have belonged at some time or other to Johnson's working library.

The relation between the Sneyd and Museum copies is also problematic. According to Sotheby's catalogue of the Sneyd sale, the annotations in the two are similar, and the additional quotations transcribed on the interleaves of the Museum copy are only a selection from the 1,630 slips attached to the Sneyd sheets; but if the comment provokes speculation, it supplies no premises for a conclusion, particularly since Sotheby's cataloguer, like everyone else for the past century, accepted the Museum's description of its copy as a third edition. One last hope for clarity proves equally delusive. The Museum copy was bought for the Museum by E. Pickering on December 20, 1853, at the sale of the library of John Hugh Smyth Pigott, of Brockley Hall in Somerset,[54] and the description of Lot 711 in Smyth Pigott's sale reveals a distressing uniformity in the hypotheses of auctioneers:

> JOHNSON (Dr. Sam.) DICTIONARY OF THE ENGLISH LANGUAGE, vol. I, containing letters A to I, in six parts
>
> MOST INTERESTING COPY, INTERLEAVED, AND WITH NUMEROUS ADDITIONS IN MANUSCRIPT IN THE AUTOGRAPH OF THE JUSTLY CELEBRATED AUTHOR · 1765
>
> *** As these appear to have been the proof sheets sent to the printer, and might on collation be not quite complete, they are sold as they now are.

Two sets of proof sheets are a little hard to bear.

In the Museum copy, therefore, the problem of the date and immediate purpose of *Johnson's* annotations is much the same as in the Sneyd copy, and though only a comparison of the two copies, if ever it becomes possible, may furnish final answers, still the second part of the Museum copy is large enough in itself to provide a sound basis for tentative discussion. Again the evidence completely justifies the conclusion that few of the changes which Johnson made were ever printed. For example, on the last page of the letter *A*, some fifteen changes are made; at least nine of them are ignored by the subsequent editions, including the fourth. This is not surprising when the changes are minor, as many of them *are* on this page from *A;* yet at the foot of the page Johnson added an entire new entry for the word *azured*, and though the illustrative quotation finds its way into later editions, the entry itself does not. Elsewhere in the Museum copy he adds new etymologies for the verb *bamboozle* and the noun *bavaroy*, "a cloak"; a new seventh sense for the noun *base;* a new entry for the "inseparable particle" *be-*; new comments on the currency of the words *behest* and *blazon;* etc. These additions likewise remain unprinted.

Occasionally, it is true, a characteristic note in the Museum copy *is* printed in the fourth edition. Thus the adjective *campaniform*, which Johnson adds to the definition of *bell-fashioned*, is not in edition 3 but is in 4. Now and then a slight difference between a note in the Museum copy and its first printed form in the fourth edition shows that still another stage in Johnson's work must be assumed (revises are not suggested). To the second definition, for instance, of *besot*, "To make to doat," Johnson adds the qualification, "with *on* before the object"; and the fourth edition prints, "To make to doat, with *on*. Not much used." Sometimes, when one change is made in the Museum copy and a *very* different one in the fourth edition, a long interval between the two stages in the work is suggested; but even then the Museum note might be considered as a first attempt which Johnson himself thought better of. A case in point might be the noun *birdcage*, which the first three editions enter without definition. The definition added in the Museum copy, "A small enclosure commonly made of wire or twigs woven into lattice to confine birds," is not the same as that which was finally printed, "An inclosure with interstitial spaces made of wire or wicker in which birds are kept."

These explicable instances, however, are the exceptions, not the rule. The usual case is that a perfectly reasonable change in the Museum copy is altogether neglected. To take care of "His big manly voice . . . ," Johnson added an eighth definition of *big*, "Loud sounding[;] not exile; not slender"; but the definition was not printed, and the labor of the amanuensis in copying the quotation which it explained was wasted. This sort of thing happens over and over; and, as with the Sneyd copy, any explanation must also account for the converse relationship, in which the fourth edition makes changes which are not suggested by the Museum copy. Everywhere there are difficulties. If Johnson annotated either copy or both copies in 1771 or 1772, then, within those two years, there were at least two separate and, it would seem, needlessly toilsome stages in his revision for the fourth edition. To lessen or avoid this embarrassment, one might assume that Johnson made one or both sets of his annotations *before* the seventies. It then follows from his letter to Boswell that he made them before April, 1755 (a supposition strengthened by the fact that 10U1 verso in the Sneyd copy is blank); but the proof-sheet theory likewise has odd consequences. First, unless the letter *B* is as out of place in the Sneyd copy as its Museum counterpart, or unless one corrected copy is assigned to the seventies, there are two sets of proof; second, if the Sneyd copy is corrected proof, then over a period of years Johnson punished himself for stubborn dilatoriness by resolutely wasting his labor; and, third, since Strahan in April, 1755, records a payment of £132:11:0 for "Alterations and Additions" in the first edition of the *Dictionary*,[55] the proof sheets must have been extensively corrected, but (with the exception noted) the Sneyd and Museum copies seem not to differ from the first edition as it was finally published. It might seem more probable that at least the Sneyd copy consists of sheets of the first edition, in its final form, which were given to Johnson as the printing proceeded—a guess which would not contradict the description in the "Catalogue of the Library at Keele Hall, 1862": "first ed. proof copy with the authors Ms. corrections A-Pum."[56] If, therefore, the proof-sheet theory be at last abandoned but the date in the fifties maintained for either or both corrected copies, the whole story must be rewritten on the assumptions that, late in 1754 or early in 1755, Johnson revised some of his earlier sheets for a prospective second edition while the later sheets were still being printed; that for some reason, perhaps forced haste to meet the competition of Scott-Bailey, the revision was not made in the second edition as published; and that Johnson, in his letter to Boswell, treated this early revision as part of the writing of the *Dictionary* and not as preparation for the fourth edition, even though the fourth edition was to include some items from it. The failure of explanation highlights the fact which needs to be explained: a good deal of Johnson's work came to nothing.

From so much fruitless speculation, it is a relief to turn

to the last chapter in the history of the *Dictionary*'s early editions and to find it not only appropriately grotesque but almost clear. The fifth edition, the last to be printed in Johnson's lifetime, is an unimportant reprint of the fourth. Entered in Strahan's ledgers under date of October, 1783, it was published in 1784 and was still being advertised as a new publication in October, 1785.[57] At the old price of £4:10:0 bound, the thousand copies would bring in a tidy profit; and as their copyright in the *Dictionary* expired, the proprietors had no intention of letting a good thing go. Though the sale of the folio had never approached that of the octavo abridgment, still the folio had become one of the more valuable of eighteenth-century literary properties. Its success in the face of sharp competition appears from the prices which shares in it had brought. In 1765, for example, a share of one-fortieth had brought £27:5:0, and in 1783 a share of one-hundredth had sold for 11 guineas. Really precise comparisons would have to include the dates of reprints as well, but the value of the folio is at least roughly indicated by the fact that these prices are higher than some which were paid at about the same times for such dictionaries as Johnson's octavo itself, Bailey's octavo—a great competitor—or Ainsworth's famous Latin dictionary; they are higher, too, than some contemporary prices for literary works like *Paradise Lost*, *Clarissa*, or the *Rambler*.[58] If Johnson had put little money in his own pocket, he had contributed significantly to the wealth of others.

This happy state of affairs was rudely disturbed in the autumn of 1785. In quick succession, while the proprietors' advertisement for the fifth edition at £4:10:0 was still running, two "unauthorized" cheap reprints were announced: one by "Mr. Harrison," publisher of the "Sacred Classicks" and "other esteem'd periodical Works," the other by John Fielding, of 23, Paternoster Row.[59] Fielding was reprinting the folio *Dictionary* in two volumes quarto, consisting of forty-eight weekly numbers, the first of which was published late in October; at a shilling a number, he was careful to announce, his elegant and convenient volumes, with all their advantages, would be two guineas cheaper than the proprietors' edition.[60] Harrison's reprint, in one large volume folio, consisted of one hundred sixpenny numbers, the first of them appearing on October 22; he was as free with his claims as Fielding, and much more objectionable.[61]

Such outrage was more than self-conscious virtue could endure. The proprietors, led by the redoubtable Longman, rallied to the cause of righteousness and property. Harrison had given them an opening by choosing to reprint the first and not the fourth edition, and although Fielding claimed that he was printing from the folio edition as revised and corrected by the author, Longman still managed to produce an effective answer. On November 19, it was announced, the proprietors would publish the first of eighty-four sixpenny numbers of a sixth edition, in two volumes quarto; and a seventh edition, like Harrison's in one large volume folio, would similarly begin to appear on December 10. Both folio and quartos would be printed from Johnson's own corrected copy of the fourth edition, which Sir Joshua Reynolds, to whom it had been bequeathed, had generously made available.[62] Sir Joshua discussed materials for the new edition in a letter of October 23 to Andrew Strahan, who had succeeded to his father's business;[63] and Strahan got quickly to work on the printing, paying extra wages to his men for "Nightwork and Sunday" and saving money, where he could, by overrunning from one edition to the other.[64] By the end of the year, four new and cheaper editions of the *Dictionary* were appearing serially, and the old fifth was still on sale at the classic price of £4:10:0.

Whatever the mental anguish on Paternoster Row, the public benefited from the outburst of free competition. For the first time in England, the *Dictionary* was reprinted in quarto as well as folio, and its price, fixed for thirty years, was halved in a single month. Collectors had a choice of engraved heads of the learned author, and Johnson had, in the competing editions, a monument outside St. Paul's. But it is impossible to attribute these benefits entirely to the high-minded purity of publishing endeavor: the battle of the books was not a chivalrous encounter. Fielding first made, and then abandoned, the suspicious claim that he had in his possession "many original papers respecting Dr. Johnson," on which the life of the author in his edition would be based.[65] Harrison, who also promised an elaborate life and produced a poor one, virulently condemned his competitors as oppressive dullards and "scandalous monopolizers"; recklessly he boasted that he would include in *his* edition not only the corrections in the Reynolds copy but "all the Alterations, Corrections, and Additions" which Johnson had *ever* made.[66] The proprietors, on their part, though they had some cause for pride and some for anger, were not above an altruistic pose:

". . . what could not be accomplished [they said] by Royal munificence, or under the auspices of the Nobility, was reserved for certain Booksellers, who had the peculiar felicity of enabling Dr. Johnson to perform a work, not less advantageous to the interests of literature, than astonishing when considered as the laborious production of one Man.

"To render this inestimable work, so necessary in the present age of refinement, more accessible to all ranks of men, it is proposed to publish a correct, elegant, and cheap Edition, printed from a Copy in which there are many additions and corrections, written by the Author's own hand, and bequeathed by him to Sir Joshua Reynolds, who has, with a liberality which distinguishes his character, indulged the Proprietors with the use of it, that the publick may not be deprived of the last improvements of so consummate a Lexicographer as Dr. Johnson."[67]

So fine a fit of generosity came on a little late.

The conduct of the proprietors, indeed, is rather puzzling. Perhaps they did not know that other corrected copies were in existence and that many of Johnson's improvements had long been withheld from the public, for they seem to have said nothing of his unprinted corrections in any edition but the fourth. Even in 1818, H. J. Todd did not list Johnson's among the annotated copies which he had used in revising the *Dictionary*.[68] It may be that they were not accessible, and, since there is some truth in the proprietors' claim that, without their backing, Johnson's great work could never have been done, one hesitates in adverse judgment; yet a final fact is inescapable. The corrections in the Reynolds copy are numerous enough to invalidate the statement that, for Johnson's considered opinion of *any* word, the fourth edition must be consulted; but they are not numerous enough to bear the weight of the advertising campaign which the proprietors based on them. The writer in the *Morning Chronicle, and London Advertiser* for December 24, 1785, who found in the sixth edition of the *Dictionary* evidence of "a regular revision by the learned author before his death," was taxing his imagination. Johnson made over two hundred notes in the Reynolds copy, but he made them casually. Some are very minute; a few merely rectify errors which had been introduced in the fourth edition; and one can often turn twenty or thirty pages at a time without finding a single stroke of Johnson's pen.[69]

This lightly corrected copy of the fourth edition passed through the hands of Sir Joshua, of "his Niece the Marchioness of Thomond," and of "George John Earl Spencer" before it found a permanent home in the Rylands Library.[70] Unlike the other corrected copies, it contains no slips or interleaves, and a few of the corrections in its margins were slightly trimmed when it was bound or rebound at some time after Johnson had made his notes. The notes are confined almost entirely to the word-list. There are none in the Preface or history of the language, none to speak of in the grammar, a good many in the letter *A*, and at least one in every other letter except *W*, *X*, *Y*, and *Z*. Perhaps there is some connection between the facts that the last Johnsonian note is in the entry *Umbo*, and that the entries from *Unconcocted* through *Uncover* and from *Undismayed* through *Uneasily* are defaced by heavy underlining in red ink. These two sets of entries, omitted by mistake from the first five octavo editions (1756–73), were supplied from the Reynolds copy in the sixth octavo edition of 1778, which shows an error caused by a mistake in the underlining. One might risk the wild guess that perhaps the last sheets of the Reynolds copy were lying about the printing-house while Johnson was making his chance corrections on earlier pages.

Another note confirms the proprietors' advertisement that Sir Joshua had made his book available for their use. Johnson had recommended that the entry *stiptick* be shifted from *sti-* to *sty-*; and at the proper place for the latter spelling, another hand has written, "Bring the art. Stiptic, here." Further confirmation, if it were necessary, could be found in one or two distinctively mutilated quotations which Johnson had hastily jotted down in the margins of the Reynolds copy and which reappear, in their mutilated form, in the sixth and seventh editions.[71] Since some of Johnson's more minute or obscure changes were overlooked or neglected, however, it is possible that his notes were first transcribed from the Reynolds copy into a copy of edition 5.[72] This hypothesis, that the sixth and seventh editions were actually printed from the fifth, would explain both the cleanness of the Reynolds copy and the occasional agreement of the fifth, sixth, and seventh editions in obvious errors which do not appear in the fourth.[73] Such agreements are all the more significant since a corrector for the press did take some independent and fairly intelligent care that the sixth and seventh editions should be accurately printed.[74]

Johnson's notes in the Reynolds copy are various and unsystematic, but apparently independent of those in the Museum's corrected sheets. The entries corresponding to the facsimile page in the Sotheby catalogue of the Sneyd library are not annotated. Though the Reynolds corrections touch every feature of the *Dictionary*—spelling, accentuation, etymology, definitions, illustrative quotations, and comments on usage—only a few have any particular significance. It is notable that Johnson still was shortening his references and quotations, especially technical quotations, and perhaps it is not mere fancy to discover in one or two of his changes a peculiarly Johnsonian quality. A certain mellowing with age might thus be detected in a deletion from the second sense of the noun *mushroom*. In the fourth edition, the definition had read: "An upstart; a wretch risen from the dunghill; a director of a company." In the Reynolds copy, Johnson marked out "a director of a company."

From the sixth and seventh editions, apparently, to the present day, no further attempt has been made to introduce Johnsonian corrections into the text of the *Dictionary*. The established opinion that the fourth edition is the best printed authority for Johnson's considered judgments of English words is therefore largely true, although it overlooks the more than two hundred instances where the sixth and seventh editions incorporate his last revisions from the Reynolds copy. The weakness of the established opinion is that it ignores the existence of the other two corrected copies. Some of the guesses which have here been made about them may be quite wrong, but they certainly contain hundreds, perhaps thousands, of Johnsonian notes which it is almost unthinkable that Johnson himself suppressed. The two hundredth anniversary of the *Dictionary* would be signalized by an act of notable generosity if the Sneyd copy were at last made available for scholarly examination.[75]

V

Johnson's *Dictionary* & Lexicographical Tradition: II

TO DENY that Johnson invented English lexicography is not to affirm that he had no influence on its subsequent development; and although the English language would be much the same today had Johnson never lived, his *Dictionary* was long the dominant model for men who hoped to shape the language, to record its changes, or to prevent them. Like the extravagant praise of respectful imitators, the violence itself with which such men as Tooke and Richardson rejected the work is testimony to its power.

From its first appearance, the *Dictionary* provoked extreme judgments. Gadfly Thomas Edwards easily persuaded himself that the drudge who had demolished his reformed spellings was by no means harmless.[1] In the spring of 1753, Johnson's comments on *The Trial of the Letter Y* had reached Edwards through Samuel Richardson, and two years later Edwards rejoiced that his politely formidable critic had written a book. On February 3, 1755, Edwards wrote to Daniel Wray: "I shall long to see Johnson's performance, if I have it, I will get some blank leaves inserted after every Letter, for I doubt there will be need for some corrections; and indeed I think the work so much above the powers of any one man, that I was surprised to hear there was one so hardy as to undertake it: Not to add that, considering his circumstances, he must have hurried it over too fast."[2] In the following May and June, the predictable verdict was vigorously delivered. Johnson had included too many quotations, often from writers "of no authority." He had stuffed the *Dictionary* with long, encyclopedic articles from Miller and Chambers, and at the same time had contrived to make it "a vehicle for Jacobite and High-flying tenets by giving many examples from the party pamphlets of Swift, from South's Sermons and other authors in that way of thinking. . . . But what most offends me is his crouding his work with those monstrous words from the things called Dictionaries such as adespotick amnicolist androtomy &c words, if they may be called words, merely coined to fill up their books and which never were used by any who pretended to talk or write English."[3] Three-quarters of a century later, when the ideal of a standard and standardizing dictionary had begun to give way to the demand for an impartial, scientific record, the selectivity of a word-list would be a less positive requirement; but Edwards knew his own small mind extremely well. Johnson's *Dictionary* was not what he wanted: ". . . in it's present condition it is, as most books lately published seem to be, nothing but a Bookseller's Jobb."[4]

Other readers awaited and received the *Dictionary* with equally strong prepossessions in its favor. In the *Scots Magazine* for February, 1755, one "A. Y.," identified in a penciled note in the Bodley copy as Jerome Stone, expressed the hope that Johnson knew enough Welsh and Irish to do justice to the Celtic element in English; but however that might be, A. Y. went on in a way that would have left Johnson balanced between pleasure and vexation, "An English dictionary composed by the author of the RAMBLER, and patronized by the Earl of Chesterfield, that living standard of true British eloquence, must certainly be a masterpiece."[5] A better-informed reader than A. Y., when he actually had his first glance at sheets of the *Dictionary*, felt that the public's high expectations had been justified. Thomas Birch, who had followed the progress of the work since 1747, wrote Johnson on April 3, 1755: "The part of your Dictionary which you have favoured me with the sight of has given me such an idea of the whole, that I most sincerely congratulate the publick upon the acquisition of a work long wanted, and now executed with an industry, accuracy, and judgement, equal to the importance of the subject." For his "substantial service to the present age and to posterity," Birch concluded, Johnson deserved "the approbation and thanks of every well-wisher to the honour of the English language."[6]

Except for Johnson himself,[7] early critics of the *Dictionary*, like Birch and Edwards, were not usually distinguished for the moderation of their praise or blame. Sometimes the *Dictionary* was condemned as worthless; more often it was acknowledged as supreme; and a balanced estimate is almost as easily constructed as discovered. At least the topics, however, for such an estimate and the favorable inclination of the majority of the critics are immediately obvious in the mass of conflicting opinions. Among those topics, Johnson's word-list continued to be prominent. Only unusual smugness distinguishes Horace Walpole from the many other dabblers who shared the dislike of Thomas Edwards for the "neological dictionary." "I cannot imagine," Walpole is quoted as saying, "that Dr. Johnson's reputation will be very lasting. His dictionary is a surprising work for one man, but sufficient examples in foreign countries show that the task is too much for one man, and that a society should alone pretend to publish a standard dictionary. In Johnson's Dictionary I can hardly find anything I look for. It is full of words nowhere else to be ſound, and wants numerous words occurring in good authors."[8] Time has taken a less malicious revenge on less toplofty judges, such as J. C. Adelung, who estimated Johnson's word-list on the basis of his own comparable experience as a lexicographer: "with respect to terms of science, and written language, his work is very complete; but it is defective in social language, in the language of civil life, and in the terms of arts and manufactures."[9] This "modern" view was stated even before the old idea of Johnson's as the standard dictionary had lost its force. As late as 1807, the popular opinion was clearly different: ". . . although he has swelled the English vocabulary, perhaps, a *little* beyond its necessary bounds, he seems, by a general, though tacit, consent, to have fixed its *standard*."[10]

In spelling, though the familiar claim that Johnson had "fixed the external form of the language" will not bear precise scrutiny, his authority was even more generally recognized than it was in matters of diction. As James Jermyn wrote of his own lexicographical efforts in 1848: "From the *Orthography* of the last edition of Dr. Johnson's established work, no variation will, of course, be expected."[11] Unfortunately, the great man had not done so much for pronunciation, while his etymologies were generally decried by men whose own efforts were little short of capital crimes. On this subject, Joseph Ritson was his usual wasplike self: "Dr. Johnson is . . . very imperfectly acquainted with the nature and derivation of the English language (and, in that respect, his dictionary, how valuable soever it may be on account of the explanation and use of English words, is beneath contempt; there being scarcely ten words properly deduced in the whole work)."[12] Eighteenth-century ideas of the "proper deduction of words" may be represented by the remarks of another critic of Johnson's etymologizing, William Drake. The mania for Celtic antiquities[13] had bred strange notions about the history of English; and in 1789, in a series of by no means unlearned papers, Drake was arguing that the true original of English had been Gothic: "I must own a zeal for the antiquity of our language makes me observe, with some sort of indignation, our great philologer Johnson deriving our *lesson* from the French *leçon*. This was pidling upon the surface, when he should have dug deep for the true etymon; for words like truth require much opening to come at their original. An English dictionary, indeed, which is not supported upon a Gothic foundation as to its derivations, is—'monstrum horrendum cui lumen ademptum.' "[14] At the bottom of the well which he had dug for truth, Drake found a water-beastie of his own. Referring his readers to the fourth chapter of Mark in the Gothic Bible, he declared that "this verb, *Laisgan*, and the substantive *Laisana*, in the next verse, are the undoubted parents of the English to *lesson*, and a *lesson*."[15] Even so, Drake was probably a better etymologist than most of those who shared his indignation at Johnson's efforts, which remained a favorite object of public condescension. "The slenderness of Dr. Johnson's philological attainments," the world was assured in 1839, "and his black ignorance of that particular philology which the case particularly required—the philology of the northern languages, are as much matters of record, and as undeniable as, in the opposite scale, are his logical skill, his curious felicity of distinction, and his masculine vigour of definition."[16]

Both sides of the scale, in this quotation, were weighted with good, solid commonplaces. Wilkes, Kenrick, and others had made a great noise about a few definitions like that of *pension*, and occasional hardy eccentrics had dismissed *all* of Johnson's explanations as quite worthless: "the radical defect of Johnson's Dictionary is the imperfect or the erroneous explanation of the meaning of the words that are there admitted. These explanations are in almost every case so obscure, or so indefinite, as to convey no accurate idea to the mind of the ignorant person who consults the Dictionary for information."[17] Most readers, however, did not take the eccentrics seriously in their attacks on Johnson's definitions, which were commonly accepted as models "for energy of language, vigour of understanding, and rectitude of mind";[18] and Thomas Edwards' complaints against the quotations which illustrated the definitions, though repeated more than once, were likewise unsustained by the popular verdict. Joseph E. Worcester was in the main line of tradition when, in 1860, he made Johnson's quotations one basis for the praise with which he closed the first century of the *Dictionary*'s existence: "The publication of this Dictionary formed a greater era in the history of the language than that of any other work. No other dictionary has had so much influence in fixing the external form of the language, and ascertaining and settling the meaning and proper use of words. Johnson was the first to introduce into English lexicography the method of illustrating the different significations of words by examples from the best writers; and his Dictionary, from the time of its first publication, has been, far more than any other, regarded as a standard for the language."[19]

Worcester's praise certainly represents the first century of opinion concerning Johnson more nearly than Tooke's or Richardson's or Webster's criticisms could do, though their criticisms must at least be mentioned in any undistorted account; but none of the four men was a perfectly fit spokesman for the *new* ideals which, already in 1860, were guiding the first steps toward the *Oxford English Dictionary*. Talk of a standard dictionary, of fixing the form of the language and settling the proper use of words, was not in keeping with the spirit of the age of evolutionary science. Benjamin Martin and (after some hesitation) Johnson, too, had rejected the dream that the grammarian and lexicographer could make his language changeless and immortal;[20] and the disciples of Johnson who had claimed for the master more than the master had claimed for himself, had not escaped ridicule. "It is believed by some, that Dr. Johnson's *admirable* Dictionary is the most capital monument of human genius; that the studies of Archimedes and Newton are but like a feather in the scale with this amazing work; that he has given our language a stability, which, without him, it had never known; that he has performed alone, what, in other nations, whole academies fail to perform; and that as the fruit of *his* learning and sagacity, our compositions will be classical and immortal. This may be true; but. . . ."[21] In 1860, a damnifying conclusion could have been supplied much more convincingly than it had been in 1782. With their collections of obsolete, provincial, and slang terms, lexicographers and glossarists long ago had demonstrated the power of other interests than the interest in correctness, in the present, national, and reputable; and there were some men in England and many in Denmark and Germany who could explain the principles of the young science of historical linguistics. Such men, on occasion, were openly scornful of the philologers and etymologists who had lived before the great days of Bopp and Grimm or (what was worse) who had neglected to read them. Even milder scholars, with a lingering fondness for the fantasies of Tooke, were calling not only for a new dictionary but for a new *kind* of dictionary. "A Dictionary . . . is an inventory of the language. . . . It is no task of the maker of it to select the *good* words of a language. . . . He is an historian of it, not a critic."[22] The wheel had spun quite round since Thomas Edwards wrote to Daniel Wray. If Johnson had dominated English lexicography to 1830 and had at least shared its dominion since, Trench's famous papers marked the beginning of an era which was not his. To the familiar topics which had composed the framework of earlier discussions of the *Dictionary*, there had now to be added the explanation that Johnson's ideal of a standard which might at least retard linguistic change was not the scientific ideal which permeated modern lexicography; and the note of condescension began to be heard in the conventional tributes. What Johnson had tried to do he had done better than anyone else; but no one would ever attempt precisely the same task again, and the influence of the *Dictionary* had entered its long decline.

II

The leadership in English lexicography for three-quarters of a century was not won, retained, or surrendered without a struggle. Faced by numerous and persistent rivals, Johnson and his publishers prepared the way for his *Dictionary* with an extensive advertising campaign and kept the work before the public with a long series of editions and revisions, Johnson's own and those of others. To the same end, the friendly and unfriendly compilers of supplements contributed willy-nilly.

The publication of the *Plan*, with its proud announcement of the patronage of Chesterfield, created immediate interest in the projected new dictionary and provoked immediate rivalry. No doubt earlier advertisements had attracted some attention. In the *General Advertiser* and the *Daily Advertiser* for March 20, 1747, and in the *Daily Advertiser* and the *London Evening-Post* at intervals from then until September, the public was informed that Samuel Johnson was preparing for the press an English dictionary, in two volumes folio, and had brought the work to a state of "great forwardness"; but readers of newspapers were accustomed to the discrepancy between magniloquent announcement and insignificant performance. Johnson's carefully written *Plan* was a different matter. The preliminary puff in Dodsley's *Museum* for August 1 repeated that Johnson had "employed a great deal of Time upon the Work" and that it had Chesterfield's approval. "The great Importance and general Usefulness of such a Body of Language, appeared so clearly to the noble Person to whom this Plan is addressed, that he signified a Willingness of becoming its Patron."[23] Such an introduction, backed by the names of highly respected booksellers, was an assurance that here was a serious undertaking by a competent scholar; and a considerable flurry of discussion, correspondence, and debate ensued, in England, Ireland, and across the Channel.

The *Bibliothèque raisonnée des ouvrages des savans* for July–September included a flattering notice of the *Plan*.[24] Though lexicography, the notice said, was rather a task for societies than for individuals, in London one Johnson had been working for some time on a complete English dictionary. Encouraged by Chesterfield and equipped with all the knowledge and skill essential for success, Johnson had stated his intentions in a letter distinguished by precision and detail, purity and elegance; and if execution and intention were commensurate, his dictionary would be a book worth waiting for.

In England, as we have seen,[25] Johnson's friends and acquaintances were writing about the *Plan* from the time of its publication in the first week of August. On Saturday, August 1, Birch wrote to Yorke that he had been promised a quick opportunity to read the pamphlet, and a week later both Birch and Wray were expressing their opinions of it.[26] Neither man was particularly favorable. Both thought the style too high; and, although Birch found the performance "ingenious," Wray had "some Objections," which he went so far as to write down. (His correspondence with Thomas Edwards on the appearance of the *Dictionary* in 1755 affords a substitute for his critique of the *Plan*, which we have not located, and makes the expected contrast with the more generous criticism of Birch.) On August 13, 1747, Birch wrote with some enthusiasm to Lord Orrery in Ireland, saying that "Mr. Sam. Johnson," the author of *London*, had "now undertaken a work long wished for, and almost despaired of, an English Dictionary," which would be an excellent book if it matched the quality of his *Plan;* and the *Plan* continued to be a subject of discussion between Birch and Orrery, who also spoke well of it, for over a year.[27] The expectation was general that the work would be completed fairly soon. Although Birch told Orrery in September, 1748, that the *Dictionary* was not likely to appear for two or three years,[28] he had written Yorke in the previous August that the amanuenses had almost finished transcribing the authorities; and in September, 1749, he assured Mrs. Yorke that the *Dictionary* was "almost ready for the Press."[29] At that same time, according to the catalogue of a sale at Sotheby's on June 7, 1855, Joseph Ames made the same statement to Sir Peter Thomson.[30]

Johnson's failure to publish as expected was dangerous in two ways: it cooled the interest of his disappointed friends and gave his rivals the opportunity to forestall him. By October 20, 1750, Birch could report only that Johnson had "printed off the three first Letters of his English Dictionary,"[31] which had been monotonously described as still "in great forwardness" in the *Gentleman's Magazine* for February, 1749;[32] but as early as October, 1747, Strahan had entered his charges for printing all of Benjamin Martin's competing dictionary;[33] for Martin, whatever the size and quality of his work and whatever his possible debt to Johnson's *Plan*, had got on with his job. In the end Martin managed a second edition of his *Lingua Britannica reformata*, nicely timed in 1754, before Johnson produced his first.[34] Johnson, moreover, had no certainty, in 1747 and 1748, that other competitors might not prove troublesome. Strange noises were coming out of Ireland, where the Rev. Mr. John Maxwell was promising lexicographical wonders; and if Maxwell's proposals seemed sufficiently ridiculous, he had still succeeded in getting himself talked about.[35] With the redoubtable Bailey long since established in public favor, with Martin's and other small dictionaries already on the market, and with Maxwell threatening, Johnson's procrastination must have been dispiriting to the booksellers.

The timing of Martin's second edition may testify to the interest which the approaching completion of Johnson's work at last revived. By the summer of 1754, Johnson was corresponding with friends about the publication of the *Dictionary* and about the university degree which would reward his labors and increase the sale of his product. In the next ten months or so, he exchanged letters on these topics with Birch, Thomas Warton, Charles Burney, Edmund Hector, and Bennet Langton; and meanwhile Chesterfield's papers in the *World* for November 28 and December 5 gave Johnson his chance to address the Noble Lord once more. Chesterfield's effusions, reprinted as they were in the *Gentleman's Magazine*, the *London Magazine*, and the *Scots Magazine*, made almost as much noise as Johnson's reply; the *Scots Magazine* also reprinted the *Plan*.[36] By February 20, when Johnson received his degree, the time had come for direct advertising.

The advertising, which began toward the end of February, included the reprinting and free distribution of the *Plan*,[37] and the reviews seem to have been arranged with care suggestive of the twentieth century. They appeared, at various times in 1755 and 1756, in the *Bibliothèque des savans*,[38] the *Bibliothèque des sciences et des beaux arts*, the *Edinburgh Review*,[39] the *Gentleman's Magazine*, the *Göttingische Anzeigen von gelehrten Sachen*, the *Journal britannique*,[40] the *Journal étranger*, the *London Magazine*, the Limerick *Magazine of Magazines*, the *Monthly Review*, and the *Scots Magazine*, which reprinted the notice from the *Monthly* in April, 1755, and the review from the *Edinburgh* in November. Praise for the *Dictionary* was loud, general, and not altogether undiscriminating: Adam Smith was the *Edinburgh* reviewer, and the reviewer in the *Monthly* was careful enough to see and correct a misprint in Johnson's Preface which has either escaped or baffled his modern editors.[41]

The Rev. Mr. Maxwell, of course, took a different view. From his Irish fastness, where a few more years' work, he hoped, would see him through four folio volumes, he announced that Johnson had been wrong in beginning his collection of authorities as late as Sidney; that Johnson had omitted Scots words, English provincialisms, obsolete terms, terms from natural history, phrases and idioms, and proverbs; that Johnson had not successfully explained the "particles"; and that Johnson was no etymologist.[42] Maxwell made just one mistake. He published his own fantastic "specimen," which must effectually have removed him as a serious competitor from the field of lexicography.

Compared to the forces now deployed in support of Johnson, Maxwell's attack was puny. Chesterfield's papers in the *World* had rightly offended Johnson, but not by damaging the prospects of his *Dictionary;* and Garrick's opinion, which carried some weight at home and abroad, had been neatly stated in his verses for the *Public Advertiser*, whence they were reprinted in the *Gentleman's*, *London*, and *Scots* magazines.[43] In France and Italy, other friends of Johnson were active, seeking and winning the approval of the academies. On June 12, 1755, the French Academy received a gift of his *Dictionary*, which it promised to repay with a new edition of its own masterpiece as soon as the new edition should appear. "Aujourd'hui Mr de Cosne, chargé des affaires du Roi de la Grande Bretagne, a remis à M^r le Secretaire, un Dictionnaire anglois en deux volumes in folio, dont Mr Johnson, auteur de cet ouvrage, fait présent à l'Académie. M^r le Secretaire l'a prié d'assurer Mr Johnson que la Compagnie étoit fort sensible à cette marque d'attention qu'elle recevoit de sa part, et qu'elle lui en donneroit une preuve en lui envoyant la nouvelle édition de son Dictionnaire, aussitôt qu'elle paroitroit."[44] Probably the one-man academy was not greatly disturbed that he had to wait a long time for the promise to be kept. His French counterpart at last got around to arranging for the presentation copies of its new edition, but not until November 26, 1761. "Il en sera envoyé un exemplaire à l'Académie de la Crusca, et un à Mr Jonson [*sic*], en reconnoissance des Dictionnaires présentés de leur part à l'Académie."[45] The thanks of the Accademia della Crusca for its gift copy from Johnson had been reported much earlier, in the *Public Advertiser* for October 10, 1755. "Mr. Johnson's Dictionary has been presented to the Academy della Crusca by the Right Hon. the Earl of Cork, attended by Sir Horace Mann, the English Minister. The Marquis Nicolini, their President, who has been long in England, and speaks the Language very well, waited upon his Lordship some Days afterwards with the Thanks of the Academy to Mr. Johnson for so valuable an Addition to their Library, and was pleased to say, it was a very noble Work, would be a perpetual Monument of Fame to the Author, an Honour to his own Country in particular, and a general Benefit to the Republic of Letters throughout all Europe."

To Johnson's unquestioned achievement, therefore, skilful publicity should be added in accounting for his apparent victory in the publishing battle in which he and his booksellers shortly found themselves engaged. Throughout the eighteenth century, the most serious rival of his *Dictionary* was that of Nathan Bailey in its various forms, and it was one of these that challenged the Johnson in the summer of 1755.[46] The *Public Advertiser* for May 29 not only announced the imminent publication of proposals for Johnson's second edition, in weekly numbers; it also announced similar proposals for *A New Universal Etymological English Dictionary*, originally Bailey's, and now revised by Joseph Nicol Scott. On June 3 the *Advertiser* reported the actual publication of the Scott-Bailey proposals; a day or two later the Johnson proposals were out; and for some time thereafter competing advertisements for the two dictionaries appeared in a number of journals—the *Public Advertiser*, the *London Evening-Post*, *Jackson's Oxford*

Journal, the *London Gazette*, etc. Strahan's ledgers record the printing of fifty such advertisements of the Johnson for country papers, as well as 5,000 folio proposals, 24,000 quarto proposals, and "250 Folio Titles to Stick up."[47] By the end of June, the first numbers of both dictionaries were in the hands of their subscribers.

As Benjamin Martin may have used Johnson's *Plan* in compiling *his* dictionary, so the Scott-Bailey also drew upon its rival, but more obviously and extensively. "A glance at any page . . . ," says Gove, "will reveal that line after line is rankly plagiarized"—and plagiarized from Johnson.[48] To be sure, indignation at a lexicographer's raids on his predecessors is a little utopian; but, like Johnson's book, the Scott-Bailey included a preface, a grammar, and a history of the language; it marked the accentuation of words and traced their etymologies; it offered divided definitions with illustrative quotations; and it filled out this familiar pattern with Johnson's own materials. Johnson's proprietors were hardly more flattered than vexed by such interested discipleship.

For some weeks after the end of June, 1755, the successive numbers of the *New Universal* and of Johnson's *Dictionary* were regularly announced, with the Scott-Bailey advertisements continuing after the first octavo edition of the Johnson, published on January 5, 1756, had taken the spotlight from the second edition of Johnson's folio.[49] Though the sale of neither folio dictionary seems to have been spectacular, further advertisements show clearly that Johnson's was the more successful; for the Scott-Bailey met outright disaster. On October 6, 1759, in *Jackson's Oxford Journal*, a second *New Universal English Dictionary* was announced. Compiled by William Rider and printed by W. Griffin for I. Pottinger,[50] this second *New Universal* was to be a single folio volume, the first of whose sixty numbers would appear on October 27. In the advertisement, predecessors were as usual attacked ("... we are sorry to say that, in general, we have found them very inaccurate ..."), and vast improvements were as usual promised ("... we have supplied their Deficiencies, corrected their Errors, and enlarged, as well as improved, their several Plans"). Such noble accomplishments at once provoked the envious machinations of the wicked. Complaining, in *Lloyd's Evening Post* for October 15–17, that "the Publication of this Work, has induced the Proprietors of old Dictionaries to draw forth all their little Artillery upon the Occasion," Pottinger noted and described particularly the proposed "Re-publication of a certain Dictionary" which had been printed in 1755 and which was about to be offered once more to the public as if it were a new book, although its proprietors were well known to "have many hundred Copies ... fast asleep in their Warehouses." Conceivably, Pottinger was not quite unmindful of Johnson's folio, since it was advertised afresh in both March and December of 1759;[51] but the chief object of his scorn was different. As he predicted, his unscrupulous competitors also announced their first number for October 27, and the detailed correspondence between prediction and announcement makes the identity of the white elephant unmistakable: it was the old Scott-Bailey.[52]

The further history of this unfortunate venture is of no immediate concern. In the end, its proprietors took "seventeen years to dispose of" their original "hopefully printed" sheets,[53] and whether the Rider *New Universal* was much more successful is rather dubious. Each such failure of a competitor strengthened the position of the Johnson, which continued to receive sometimes extravagant and not always disinterested praise. Thus the *London Chronicle*'s premature puff of the *Shakespeare* commends the *Rambler*, and then the *Dictionary*. "Add to this that *Monumentum Ære perennius* which he hath erected in Honour of his native Tongue; we mean his Dictionary, in which he hath supplied the Want of an Academy of Belles Lettres, and performed Wonders towards fixing our Grammar, and ascertaining the determinate Meaning of Words, which are known to be in their own Nature of a very unstable and fluctuating Quality. To his Labours it may hereafter be owing that our Drydens, our Addisons, and our Popes shall not become as obsolete and unintelligible as Chaucer."[54] The lapse of some eight years before the market justified a third edition (1765) of the *monumentum ære perennius* should not be forgotten, though it probably indicates the scarcity of readers with four pounds ten to spare, rather than any failure of the *Dictionary* to establish its predominance over its numerous competitors. The fourth folio edition, revised, appeared in 1773; a quarto edition in Dublin in 1775; and in 1784 a fifth edition, folio, which brought to well over 7,000 the total number of copies printed. It was followed the next year by the four competing posthumous editions and in 1786 by the eighth edition of the octavo abridgment, which thus reached its fortieth thousand.[55]

Editions of the *Dictionary* between those of 1785 and 1786 and that of H. J. Todd require little comment; the tenth unabridged edition appeared in 1810, and the fourteenth edition of the octavo in 1815. To understand the full influence of the work, however, it will be necessary to say something of the various supplements which appeared in the first decades of the nineteenth century and of Todd's edition and Latham's, completed, respectively, in 1818 and

1870. Of the compilers of supplements, one, the Rev. Mr. Jonathan Boucher, almost equaled Johnson in his dislike for the nation of savages. When some sixteen years in the colonies had convinced him of the obduracy of the savage breast and the degeneracy of the savage speech, Boucher returned home to nurse his wrath and a *Glossary of Archaic and Provincial Words*.[56] Before he could complete the two quarto volumes which he had proposed in 1801, he was gathered to his fathers, leaving friends to publish his work from *A* to *Blade* in two instalments, the first in 1807 (*A Supplement to Dr. Johnson's Dictionary of the English Language: or, a Glossary*, etc.), and the second in 1832, when the title linked the names of Dr. Johnson and the savage Dr. Webster. Times were changing.

Unlike Boucher, the compiler of a second *Supplement to Johnson's Dictionary*, George Mason, was utterly scornful of the work which in 1801 he undertook to correct and extend. As a writer in the *Eclectic Review* pointed out,[57] Boucher's collection might serve, among other things, "to explain the phraseology of many valuable authors of ancient times" and "to discover the sources, and . . . elucidate the history, of our very complicated and mutable language"; but Boucher intended no attack on Johnson, whose purposes in making a standard dictionary were not the same. "That a Supplement of this kind should be requisite to Dr. Johnson's Dictionary, implies by no means a censure on that work. Its proper department was different. Instead of blaming him for omitting many provincial and obsolete terms which Bailey had inserted, we conceive that he might with advantage have excluded more."[58] Mason did intend an attack. It was not enough for him to indicate by his work, as Boucher did, that a lexicographer might have other purposes than the establishment of a standard; he damned the supposed standard itself, saying that Johnson's *Dictionary* was full of blunders, including misinterpretations of the cited authorities, false definitions of technical and especially of legal terms, and infamous etymologies. "This muddiness of intellect sadly besmears and defaces almost every page of the composition; yet is the *plan* of our author's Dictionary really commendable, and (as far as that plan has been duly completed) the work itself in high estimation."[59]

Mason's remarks, if they are good for nothing else, are at least evidence that it was fashionable, for whatever reason, to add words to Johnson's word-list and that the *Dictionary* continued in high esteem. The comments of John Seager, whose *Supplement* appeared in 1819, indicate that Seager not only shared the general good opinion of Johnson's work but sided with Johnson against his critics Tooke and Richardson on a basic theoretical question. After spending fifteen or sixteen years in "improving" Johnson, Seager wrote in his "Advertisement," he first heard of Todd's revision, which he feared would anticipate his own notes. "Upon examination I found this to be indeed the case with respect to many of them; but the remainder was sufficient, both to show that our best English Dictionary was still far from perfection, and . . . to justify . . . the present publication."[60] "The present publication," Seager continued, made Todd's Johnson more nearly perfect (Seager had forgotten Johnson's jibe in the *Plan*) by adding "elegant and expressive" modern words, omitted senses, citations where none had been given or where more might be useful, etc.; but few changes had been made in the etymologies. After all, etymology does not determine meanings, as some critics (presumably Tooke and Richardson) would have it do. "*The true meaning of any word can be acquired only by vigilant induction;* by inference drawn from the consideration of assembled examples of its use; *and comparison of the best authors.* I am sensible of the absurdity of *that criticism which would make us appeal from the authority of Swift and Addison to the woods of Germany.*"[61] Unfortunately, Richardson never became so sensible.

Of the other supplements to Johnson, only one more need be mentioned. When Richard Paul Jodrell published his *Philology on the English Language* in 1820, he had worked three and a half years collecting words of two classes: "words omitted by Johnson in all the several editions, published in his life," and "words inserted by Johnson, but not illustrated by him with authority to sanction the usage" or else somehow erroneously treated.[62] The nature of Jodrell's 17,500 words leaves the reader wondering why he wasted so much time. To collect large numbers of "hard words," technical terms, and compounds which Johnson had omitted was only to demonstrate the obvious: that Johnson had not pretended to universality and that both language and linguistic tastes and interests had changed since Johnson died; but Jodrell was the sort of man who could value himself on placing his entry-words in the middle of the column, not flush with the margin. He and the other supplement-makers might be thought to justify a remark in the *Monthly Review* for 1828: "UPON the merits of Johnson's Dictionary, that prodigy of labour, both mental and corporeal, it is totally unnecessary to descant at the present day. . . . After all the changes that have occurred since his death in our literature; after philologist has been pursuing philologist over the beaten track of our language, we find, after all, that we cannot better consult our own advantage than to recur to his dictionary just as he left it to the world."[63]

That judgment might seem a little unfair to His Majesty's Chaplain in Ordinary, the Rev. Henry John Todd, whose first revised edition of Johnson was completed, in four volumes quarto, in 1818, and whose second is dated 1827; but Todd not only did not know or did not use Johnson's own corrected copies of the *Dictionary*[64]—he was himself a supplement-maker at heart. "After all, what the present editor has done he considers but as dust in the balance, when weighed against the work of Dr. Johnson."[65] The dust is much like what Boucher, Mason, Seager, and Jodrell had brought or were bringing together; in fact, Todd used Boucher, whom he praised, and even Mason when Mason was usable. As one would expect, Todd made some additions to Johnson's grammar and history of the language, extended Johnson's word-list with obsolete and local terms and with derivatives and compounds, improved the etymologies, added quotations where they were lacking and corrected some of those which had been given, but left the famous definitions pretty much unchanged. Todd's learning, modesty, and industry did not save his labors from a most unflattering description in 1873, when they were called neither good Johnson nor good dictionary;[66] and other critics after mid-century were equally severe. For some, Todd had superimposed his own defects on those of Johnson, especially by his failure to strengthen the department of scientific terminology.[67] For others, he had multiplied technical terms beyond necessity. "There is scarcely a page in Johnson which does not contain some word that has no business there; and yet Todd not only admits all these words, but adds to them; while Webster brings them in by hundreds and thousands at a time; each doing his best to crowd and deform his pages with them, and all the while triumphantly calling upon the world to observe how vast an advantage he has gained over his predecessors."[68] For Richardson, finally, even in 1815, Todd was damned before his work appeared; for he had chosen to follow Johnson's example—and thereby to produce "one uniform and consistent mass of ignorance and absurdity."[69]

Richardson's judgment was hardly representative of common opinion in the earlier part of the century. He was Tooke's disciple and Todd's competitor. Todd's revision did go into a second edition, and Alexander Chalmers, following the pattern set by Johnson's octavo, did make an abridgment, which, with Walker's pronunciations added, enjoyed some popularity.[70] On the other hand, the dictionaries of Richardson and Webster claimed their share of the market, and by the 1850's many students were ready to follow Trench in calling all of them deficient. Robert Gordon Latham built an altar to a dying god when, in 1864, he published the first part of his *Dictionary of the English Language . . . Founded on That of Johnson as Edited by Todd.*[71] Latham, too, produced the inevitable abridgment, in 1876; and some reviewers felt that, by the correction of many errors and the addition of much that was new, he had won the right to consider his *Dictionary* "as virtually a new book."[72] Still, he had remained generally faithful to Johnson's spirit and plan. Though his revision might be as valuable and instructive as a modernized Johnson could be, with better etymologies, more words, and more quotations,[73] it remained a modernized Johnson; and in 1876 the first fascicle of the *OED* was less than ten years away. The genius and industry of Johnson, the skill of his enterprising publishers, and the patience and care of his editors and revisers had, after all, accomplished no small feat in prolonging the life of his *Dictionary* into the age of the Grimms, Littré, and Murray.

III

A detailed account of the influence of Johnson's *Dictionary* would be a history of English lexicography since 1755. It would, indeed, be more; for the historian would have also to consider possible influences on general literature and demonstrable influences on the dictionaries of other European languages, ancient and modern. The present statement, confined almost entirely to English lexicography, is by no means so ambitious. Instead of a genuine history, we have written at worst a fragmentary chronicle and at best a tentative historical outline in which some few of many causes have been briefly traced.

Johnson's influence on dictionaries of other languages than English must be dismissed in a few scattered notes. It can be seen, in western Europe, from Sweden to Portugal, and it operated from 1755 until well into the nineteenth century. Noah Webster suggests its extent when he speaks indignantly of an alleged Johnsonian blunder which had been "received . . . into the Latin dictionaries of Ainsworth and Entick; into the Dutch dictionary of Willcocks, the German of Fahrenkruger . . . the French of Boyer and the Italian of Montucci."[74]

To justify, first, the geographical extremes of our summary statement, the Portuguese and English dictionary of Anthony Vieyra may be cited. In a note to the Portuguese readers, dated London, July 25, 1773, Vieyra refers to Johnson's *Dictionary;* and his definition of *pension* shows that he had used it.[75] Earlier and more impressive evidence from Sweden is afforded by the English and Swedish dictionary of Jacob Serenius, the friend and correspondent of Edward Lye. Writing to Lye on March 5, 1757, Serenius was enthusiastic about Johnson's work. "Nothing will be perfect, much less a Dictionary. But if any thing comes near perfection, it is that of your Johnsons work, Im astonished at that gentlemans labour which is enough for Two Mens life."[76] Serenius says much the same thing "To the English Reader" in his dictionary itself, but with an important and typical qualification. He has, he says, stressed English etymology. "I have been incouraged to this by correspondence with the said worthy gentleman [Edward Lye], and in a manner excited by the late English lexicographer Mr. *Johnson*, that prodigy of laboriousness and sagacity, who in the preface to his excellent Dictionary complains of a *scanty knowledge in the northern literature:* as if there could not be made much progress in the English etymology, for want of hands to bear it out of its true native soil. I must own that the judicious Author is aright."[77] Like the Germans, the Scandinavians, who were almost compelled to learn German, French, and English if they hoped to escape provincialism, were perhaps unusually conscious of the eighteenth-century Englishman's linguistic limitations; but such consciousness did not prevent their long-continued use of Johnson's work. The ninth edition of Johnson was used by Sven Brisman in 1801 in his *Engelskt och Svenskt Hand-Lexicon.*[78]

In Germany the record of the use of Johnson by lexicographers and other scholars is continuous from 1756, when the *Göttingische Anzeigen* recommended his work to the compilers of English-German dictionaries,[79] to at least 1876, when *Meyers Konversations-Lexikon* described the *Dictionary* as the foundation of all similar works up to that time.[80] Thus in Leipzig in 1763, John B. Rogler published a third edition of Christian Ludwig's *Dictionary, English, German, and French,* "Revised, corrected and augmented with more than 12000 words taken out of Samuel Johnson's English dictionary and others."[81] Klopstock, in 1774, made the familiar comparison between Johnson and the academies. "Die Crusca, die französische Academie, Johnson haben Wörterbücher ihrer Sprachen geschrieben. Der einzelne Mann hat's besser, als die Gesellschaften gemacht. . . . Johnson hat mehr, und tiefer in seiner Sprache untersucht, als jemals ein andrer in der seinigen."[82] Goethe wrote verses in a copy of the first volume of the 1785 quarto *Dictionary;*[83] "the Dictionary is said to have been published by Campe, of Hamburg," in two volumes octavo in 1799;[84] the "Vorrede" in the first volume of J. H. Hilpert's *Dictionary of the English and German Languages* (Carlsruhe and London, 1828) announces that that work was based on Todd's Johnson, though with some misgivings, especially about the etymologies; the *English Dictionary* of T. S. Williams, which was published at Hamburg in 1833 as a students' guide to the use of prepositions, was "principally extracted from the larger Dictionaries of Webster and Johnson";[85] etc.

More important, however, than any other of these German users of Johnson's work was J. C. Adelung, whose *Neues grammatisch-kritisches Wörterbuch der englischen Sprache für die Deutschen* appeared in two octavo volumes at Leipzig in 1783–96 and was described as "aus dem grössern englischen Werke des Hrn. Samuel Johnson nach dessen vierten Ausgabe gezogen, und . . . vermehrt."[86] Adelung, who was sometimes considered a kind of German Johnson,[87] also compiled a *Grammatisch-kritisches Wörterbuch der hochdeutschen Mundart* (1774–86), so that his opinions of Johnson in the last of the *Three Philological Essays* translated by Willich have more than the usual weight of authority behind them. Generally, he praised Johnson as a "critical grammarian" and a definer of words but found some fault with his word-list, his alleged excess of illustrative quotations, and especially his etymologies. Even Johnson's definitions were not perfect, since he had sometimes "confounded the various applications of one and the same meaning, with the different significations themselves."[88] In turning these definitions into German, it is said, Adelung sometimes improved them by collapsing Johnson's unnecessary distinctions into single, broader concepts.[89]

The remaining instances of Johnson's influence on dictionaries of foreign languages unite to remind the student once again of the most troublesome feature of lexicographic history, the complexity of the relations among compilers who copy one another as a matter of course; for in these instances the influence of Johnson may often be seen in later editions of works from which he himself had taken methods or materials. The simplest case involves abridgments of Ainsworth's Latin *Thesaurus*. In the *London Evening-Post* for February 19–21, 1756, there was announced for speedy publication a new double dictionary of English and Latin. The compiler, William Young, who is described on the title-page as editor of Ainsworth, certainly published within the year; for 1756 is the date of a detailed, pettish, denunciatory review, entitled *An Examination of a Late English-Latin and Latin-English Dictionary*. This was undoubtedly written by one Nath. Thomas, "Late Assistant of Harrow-School" but a most un-Harrovian character. Thomas was advertised, in August, 1756, as himself the maker of an abridgment of Ainsworth, in which "Care has been taken to compare the English Part with Mr. *Johnson's* celebrated Dictionary of the English Language";[90] and throughout his ensuing controversy with Young, Thomas made his use of Johnson a selling point. In his *Examination*, he praises Johnson and repeatedly cites "the justly celebrated . . . Dictionary" as an unassailable authority; on the title-page of his *Abridgement*, he once more acknowledges his debt; and he makes assurance triply sure by a statement in the Preface to the latter work: "We acknowledge ourselves not a little indebted to the celebrated Mr. *Johnson*, whose admirable treasure of the *English* language we confess to have used with freedom, and we hope with improvement."[91] The line of influence from Ainsworth to Johnson thus leads back again to Ainsworth abridged.

French and Italian lexicographers provide more significant examples of the reciprocal influence of English and other traditions. The rather numerous French-language reviews of the *Plan* and the finished *Dictionary* make one expect that the *Dictionary*'s widespread influence will be found in out-of-the-way places; and that expectation is not disappointed. For example, both prefaces in the French-Italian and Italian-French dictionary of Francesco Alberti (1772) echo Johnson's *Plan*,[92] and Johnson's *Dictionary* provided materials for the new edition of Boyer's French-English and English-French work, published at Lyons in 1768.[93] Amusingly, in the Boyer the complaint is made that, without an English academy, it is difficult to choose among the vast number of words, not all of them equally "pure" or current, which Johnson has included;[94] but within the next ten years not only had F. Bottarelli repeated the stale coupling of Johnson and the academies on the title-page of his dictionary (Italian, French, and English);[95] in 1778 the French Academy had also been set to work, like so many reluctant schoolboys with a bullying master, on a dictionary allegedly modeled after Johnson's.

The master was, of course, Voltaire, who in the very month of his death could still dominate his fellow-academicians. On May 7, 1778, he proposed that the Academy's dictionary should be remade. "He spoke for a very long time, and with great warmth, upon the utility of compiling a new dictionary, nearly upon the same plan with that of Della Crusca, and with Johnson's Dictionary. He urged the matter so forcibly, that in spite of the opposition made by the greater number of the members, it was agreed to undertake this great work. M. de Voltaire immediately entered the resolution with his own hand, in the register of the Academy, stating at large the motives which had given rise to it. He did more, he would not permit the assembly to separate without dividing among them the letters of the alphabet; he himself took A as being the most copious."[96] Voltaire's plan was that the new dictionary should contain etymologies, the conjugation of rare irregular verbs, the various meanings of each word with examples from the best authors, picturesque and forceful old expressions which deserved revival, etc.; it would thus serve as a pleasant and instructive combination of grammar, rhetoric, and poetic. Some further discussion was devoted to the project, which occupied the Academy several times before the month was out; but Voltaire was already ill, and on May 30 he died. He and his colleagues, nonetheless, had paid Johnson a much higher compliment than the mere gift of a copy of their dictionary. As Ainsworth and Boyer had influenced Johnson, and Johnson in turn had influenced later editions of their works, so Johnson had learned from the Academy, and at least some members of the Academy, it would appear, had learned from him.

Italians also have not been wanting who thought that the Accademia della Crusca could learn from Johnson. In Vincenzo Monti's *Proposta di alcune correzioni ed aggiunte al Vocabolario della Crusca*, some fifty pages are devoted to a comparison of the *Vocabolario* with the dictionaries of Johnson and the Spanish Academy.[97] Here the *Vocabolario* is damned, while Johnson is highly praised. With its principles founded on the nature of things, on the discipline of general grammar, on the particular character of the English language, and on common use, his is the most philosophical of all dictionaries of living languages.[98] Klopstock, in short, was right; and Baretti, for these critics, had been a true prophet when in 1754 he wrote of "an English Dictionary . . . which will put our Crusca and the French Dictionary of the Academy and all other dictionaries that have hitherto appeared into the shade, for the excellence of the method used in compiling it."[99]

Because his knowledge of Johnson's *Dictionary* was obtained thus early and because his own dictionaries continued so long in use, Baretti may be cited as a strong final example of the influence of Johnson on the lexicography of foreign languages. To say nothing of Johnson's contributions to his prefaces,[100] Baretti took from Johnson considerable material both for his dictionary of English and Italian and for his dictionary of English and Spanish. Hitch and Hawes published his *Dictionary of the English and Italian Languages* in two volumes in 1760. Each volume contained a short grammar, an Italian one for the English readers and an English one for the Italians, the latter being modeled on "that of Mr. Samuel Johnson prefixed to his English Dictionary." The sixth edition (London, 1820) still quotes Baretti's acknowledgment of Johnson as one of his "faithful guides, in the grammatical labyrinth."[101] Similarly, in *A Dictionary, Spanish and English, and English and Spanish,* Baretti first surveys the existing dictionaries in the two languages and then goes on: "Delpino's edition being sold, and a new one wanted, the present compiler has corrected and enlarged it. This he has performed chiefly by the help of Johnson's Dictionary with regard to the English part, and of the Spanish Academicians with regard to the Spanish. . . . As to the orthography, he has adhered to Johnson and the academicians, without the least deviation."[102] For this dictionary, which was published in 1778, Baretti had begun his work about 1773; it, too, is said to have been quite successful and the basis for later Spanish dictionaries in England.[103]

If Johnson's recognized supremacy over other English dictionaries extended his influence in lexicography throughout western Europe for so many years, it must be expected that within England his influence on histories of the language, on glossaries, grammars, synonymies, dictionaries, and theories concerning them, was all-pervasive. So indeed that influence was; but it is not easy to state with concise clarity, for a good deal of the statement must deal with compilers who undertook tasks which Johnson had refused or neglected. Though his book is not easily comparable with theirs, his influence may be suggested in the very fact that they assumed his work as done. Further complications arise from Johnson's debts to his own predecessors, from his failure to state any systematic theory of language, and from the relative inferiority of his history and grammar to the body of the *Dictionary:* the maintenance of a common tradition must not be mistaken for the individual influence of Johnson, and to some extent the separate parts of his work demand to be treated separately, with statements concerning his theories sometimes drawn largely from his practice.

The glossarists who in the century after the publication of the *Dictionary* collected obsolete or provincial words were among the workers in areas which Johnson had not extensively cultivated. He had done more for the collectors of old words than he had for the dialectologists, since as an editor of Shakespeare he shared the interest in the interpretation of early texts. Indeed, a paragraph in the *Proposals* for his *Shakespeare* shows clear realization of the need for a kind of inquiry which was incidentally to provide extensive materials for the historical lexicographer of the nineteenth century: "Every age has its modes of speech, and its cast of thought; which, though easily explained when there are many books to be compared with each other, become sometimes unintelligible and always difficult, when there are no parallel passages that may conduce to their illustration. Shakespeare is the first considerable author of sublime or familiar dialogue in our language. Of the books which he read, and from which he formed his style, some, perhaps, have perished, and the rest are neglected. His imitations are, therefore, unnoted, his allusions are undiscovered, and many beauties . . . are lost with the objects to which they were united."[104] Plainly, Johnson perfectly understood the need which Capell, Tyrwhitt, Farmer, Percy, Steevens, Malone, and a crowd of others set out to fill; but he himself did less to fill it than exacting critics might have hoped. His *Dictionary*, for example, and his *Shakespeare* sometimes contradicted each other; from the *Dictionary*, some words current within the time limits which he had set himself were altogether omitted; and on occasion his relatively limited knowledge of Old and Middle English caused him to misinterpret words which were included. Probably Johnson's greatest influence on the developing lexicography of Old, Middle, and Early Modern English lay not in the provision of data but in the illustration of a method. As Robert Nares wrote in 1822, "to complete the rational view and knowledge of our language" there were still necessary both a "Chaucerian" and a "Saxon" dictionary, "with all the examples at length." "Our illustrious countryman, Johnson, has shown us, that no Dictionary can be satisfactory without a copious selection of examples, and has given us the most convenient form; his plan and method have, therefore, been followed here [in Nares' *Glossary*], as far as seemed necessary in a work less scientific. The Chaucerian and the Saxon Dictionaries, whenever formed, ought surely to adopt a similar arrangement."[105] Nares even saw, in the suggested "period dictionaries," a means to render Johnson more consistent with himself. Johnson had included a good many obsolete words, and Todd had increased the number, seeking completeness; so that foreigners "may sometimes be puzzled to decide what words are actually in use. . . . The separation of the Dictionaries, as here suggested, would make all clear"; and it might "then, perhaps, be advisable to throw out from Johnson's Dictionary, all the words not actually classical in the language at that time; so as to make it a standard of correct phraseology."[106]

A dictionary in part designed as "a standard of correct phraseology" was certainly no fit repository for large numbers of provincialisms; yet in the century of the *Dictionary*'s most active life it was becoming clear that the study of English dialects was essential to a full view of the language and an understanding of its history. To the more timorous, moreover, among the Scots, the Americans, and other dwellers in outer darkness, lists of Scotticisms and American corruptions of English purity had a certain snob appeal. Volumes of provincialisms might be collected, therefore, either to teach what was right by showing what was wrong, so that purists might avoid the trace of "corruption to which every language widely diffused must always be exposed,"[107] or to "do a useful thing towards the history of the language,"[108] so that antiquarians and local patriots, readers of early texts and mere lovers of knowledge for itself, might also be gratified. Whichever their purpose, the collectors often felt called upon to relate their work somehow to Johnson's *Dictionary*.

Both groups, like the collectors of old words, could draw some materials from Johnson, especially Todd's Johnson when it became available, and could profit from the example of Johnson's method. Thus John Jamieson, in his Scottish dictionary, tried "to give the oldest printed or MS. authorities" for "every word, or particular sense of a word"; and he paid tribute to his "worthy friend and colleague, the Reverend H. J. Todd, in the large and useful additions he has made to Dr. Johnson's English Dictionary. He has, with great propriety, paid far more attention to the etymology of the language than his celebrated precursor had done."[109] The purists, moreover, could invoke Johnsonian curses on those who were so corrupt as to babble a dialect of Scotland or New England. It is regrettable, John Pickering wrote in his *Vocabulary* of Americanisms, that "we [Americans] have in several instances deviated from the standard of the language, as *spoken and written in England* at the present day"; for "as a general rule . . . we should undoubtedly avoid all those words which are noticed by English authors of reputation, as expressions with which *they are unacquainted.*"[110] Pickering took care to avoid not only sin but the appearance of sin. Undoubtedly, he had collected low American phrases, but he damned them as low and said he could not bear them. "It should . . . be recollected, that I was not making a *dictionary* of our language, but a *glossary of provincialisms;* that many words would be admitted into such a work . . . which would be rejected from a dictionary."[111] In the dictionary way, the world already had Todd and Johnson, whom Pickering was fond of citing as authorities.

The historically minded and locally patriotic among the collectors of provincialisms were not so humble. That excellent hater of all things American, "Mr. Boucher, in the Prospectus of his Thesaurus of Archaical Terms," entered the mildest possible objection to Johnson's word-list. "However valuable in other respects Dr. Johnson's Dictionary confessedly is, his warmest admirers cannot deny it to be still incomplete, as leaving unexplained many good and significant words, only because they happen to have fallen into disuse; notwithstanding their being yet spoken by a large portion of the community, and still found in authors on whose works the nation has long rested no ordinary portion of its high literary fame."[112] Samuel Pegge, whose *Anecdotes of the English Language* was published posthumously in 1803, was not so gentle. He accused Johnson flatly of ignorance, saying that he "was scarcely at all aware of the authenticity of ancient dialectical words, and therefore seldom gives them any place in his dictionary."[113] Noah Webster, the linguistic patriot, went further and set the American eagle to screaming at a great rate. Questioning the very foundations of Johnson's authority, he declared that since living languages were *not* condemned to the inevitable cycle of growth, perfection, and decay, the attempt to fix them was impertinent, stupid, and futile. The lexicographer should leave "analogy, custom and habit . . . to guide men in the use of words," which it was his business to record and not to judge; and although most supposed Americanisms were actually "authorized by English usage," necessary or convenient neologisms would in any event require no English license.[114] Even if the milder dialectologists would have been repelled by Webster's violence, their work by its very nature emphasized the limitations of the Johnsonian tradition.

Like the glossarists, the makers of synonymies were extending the field of lexicography as Johnson had left it. Some concern with synonyms, it is true, may be noted among lexicographers in England long before the eighteenth century. The sixteenth-century ideal of "copie of wordes" produced great heapings-up of synonymous terms in some of the Latin-English dictionaries, and in 1668 the nature and organization of Wilkins' *Real Character* made it certain that Lloyd's dictionary, its companion piece, would offer elaborate word-cycles of synonyms, antonyms, and words otherwise formally or semantically related. A patient and reasonably intelligent reader of Wilkins and Lloyd, if he were interested (for example) in the word *corruption*, would find in its definition the carefully discriminated words *defiling*, *destroying*, *infection*, *decay*, *putrefaction*, *unholiness*, *viciousness*, *unchastity*, *bribery*, etc.; and for each of these, in turn, he would find a long list of further synonyms, antonyms, and related words.[115] Wilkins and Lloyd, however, had perversely contrived to make the riches of their book inaccessible to the ordinary man; and for a long time in the following century, dictionary-makers paid little attention to synonyms. The article "Dictionary" in the *Encyclopædia Britannica* of 1773 criticizes even

Johnson, by precept and example, because he has not carried out his plan and fully and clearly exhibited "the nice distinctions that take place between words which are nearly synonymous."

In this situation, given the century's keen interest in language, it was inevitable that attempts should be made to fill up the gap.[116] The first of them, the Rev. Dr. John Trusler's *Difference between Words Esteemed Synonymous*, was of no great importance except for its relatively early date—1766. As Trusler points out, many of the words which he distinguished had been used by Johnson as definiens and definiendum. "Should any one imagine, because some words which are here classed as passing for synonymous, do not immediately strike the mind as such; that labouring at a distinction was unnecessary and useless; if he cannot recollect a passage where he has seen, or call to mind that he has at any time heard them indiscriminately used, let him cast his eye over the folio edition of Johnson's dictionary, and he will instantly discover that these endeavours, though perhaps inadequate to the task, have not been wholly fruitless."[117]

In 1774, another clergyman, the Rev. James Barclay, introduced synonymy into general English lexicography in another undistinguished work, his *Complete and Universal English Dictionary*. Addressing himself to "such *English* Readers as are supposed to be unlettered, and not so happy as to have had the Benefits and Advantages of a very liberal Education,"[118] Barclay promised everything from etymology to a history of the prophets and apostles;[119] and his baits were taken eagerly, for in 1865 Wheatley declared that the *Complete Dictionary* had "served the lower orders, for nearly a century, as a Dictionary of Universal Information."[120] "The *Synonimous* part of our Dictionary," Barclay said, in which "the DIFFERENCES between WORDS esteemed SYNONIMOUS" were pointed out and the reader advised concerning the choice among them, "we modestly assert to be entirely new."[121] If the assertion had been more modest still, decorum would have been better observed. The correspondences between Barclay's work and the earlier but equally insignificant compilation of the Rev. Frederick Barlow, the *Complete English Dictionary* of 1772, are too close for coincidence. Both obviously owed a considerable debt to Johnson, and Barclay's treatment of synonyms, as might be expected, was derived from Trusler. Even so, "the 300 entries offering such material are inconspicuous in this bulky volume of 1,000 pages."[122]

The influence of Johnson, obviously present in these humble early stages of English synonymy, continued in later treatments. His personality was as important as his *Dictionary* in the *British Synonymy* (1794) of Mrs. Piozzi, who had no need to borrow words from anyone; but the Rev. Benjamin Dawson wrote his *Philologia Anglicana* "with Johnson's *Dictionary* open before him."[123] In 1797 Dawson had brought out his *Prolepsis philologiae Anglicanae*, in which he discussed "the nature of synonyms" and definition and "the duties of the lexicographer"; and in 1799 his *Philologia,* in five hundred pages, carried him from *A* to *Adornment.* Described by a reviewer as "the first number of an annotated edition of Johnson," the *Philologia* reprints about half its quotations from the *Dictionary* and includes long defenses of Dawson's disagreements with Johnson. "Synonymy becomes most prominent, however, in the notes, which . . . act as the sounding board for Dawson's theories, and devote much space to discriminations between words used, as Dawson claims, too casually by Johnson."[124] An equally close relation to

Johnson is suggested by the title-page of William Perry's *Synonymous, Etymological, and Pronouncing English Dictionary* of 1805, which describes itself as "Extracted from the Labours of the late DR. SAMUEL JOHNSON; Being an attempt to Synonymize his Folio Dictionary of the English Language";[125] and some connection with Johnson, though it may amount only to a disavowal of his method of definition or a claim to have made an independent collection of quotations, may be traced also in William Taylor's *English Synonyms Discriminated* (1813) and George Crabb's *English Synonymes* (1816),[126] which has since "enjoyed continuous popularity on both sides of the Atlantic."[127]

Despite these early efforts, "synonymy . . . did not actually establish itself as a recognized and systematic department of the English dictionary until the middle of the nineteenth century."[128] Another attempt to extend the field of English lexicography was more immediately successful. Although, as Worcester said, "but little attention was bestowed upon orthoepy, by English lexicographers, till after the first publication of Johnson's Dictionary,"[129] before 1800 the marking of pronunciation had reached approximately the same stage as that which is found in "modern commercial dictionaries."[130] To this rapid development Johnson contributed little, since he had contented himself, in an already old-fashioned way, with a mere indication of the syllable which bore the primary stress; but the orthoëpists were nonetheless mindful of his work and careful to state their position with respect to it. More significantly, the pattern was early established of combining Johnson's with a pronouncing dictionary, so that here again his influence was extended, in some form, beyond the limits of his own undertaking.

Perhaps the earliest writer to refer to Johnson as an authority on English pronunciation was the grammarian Peyton, in *Les vrais principes de la langue angloise* (London, 1756); he directed advanced students to the *Dictionary*, especially for information about stress.[131] Similarly unimportant references may be found at intervals throughout the century, as when *A Spelling-Dictionary of the English Language* (12th ed.; Dublin, 1769) is said on its title-page to be "Revised and Accented By Dr. Johnson's New Dictionary,"[132] and when Alexander Bicknell in his *Grammatical Wreath* (London, 1790) makes Johnson's grammar his chief authority in "the Use and Sounds of the Letters."[133]

A more important work, with a more notable relationship to Johnson, was William Kenrick's *New Dictionary of the English Language*, which was published by William Johnston, Longman, Cadell, and the Rivingtons in 1773. Johnson had good reason for the irritation with which he remarked, not altogether accurately, that Kenrick "had borrowed all his dictionary from him."[134] In 1765, Kenrick had done a savage *Review of Dr. Johnson's New Edition of Shakespeare*. In an advertisement at the end of the *Review*, he had promised, for early 1766, "A Ramble through the Idler's Dictionary," exposing "several thousand" blunders in that work; and though the "Ramble" never appeared, Kenrick repeated, in his *Defence* of the *Review*, that he had made a large collection of Johnson's errors, which other dictionary-writers, at home and abroad, had copied with servile stupidity.[135] After all this, Kenrick was adding injury to insult when he blandly observed, on page viii of his own *Dictionary*, that "with respect to the etymology, explanation of words, and illustration of idiom and phraseology," he had "generally followed the celebrated dictionary of the learned Dr. Johnson."

Examination of Kenrick's work confirms his statement: he had followed Johnson so mechanically that such definitions as those of *cough* and *network* were unchanged and both *windward* and *leeward* were still explained as "towards the wind." Even this was not the limit of Kenrick's impertinence. Since the vast majority of his definitions were copied from Johnson, it had been impracticable and unnecessary to acknowledge each separate borrowing separately under each entry; but to the definitions of *pension* and *pensioner*, Kenrick maliciously added the reference, "*Johnson*." He was equally malicious in his treatment of *Whig* and *Tory*. "The tories," he wrote, "are advocates for ecclesiastical tyranny and arbitrary power; whereas the whigs entertain more popular and republican principles"; and under *Whig* he invented his personal etymology: "Johnson deduces it, after bishop Burnet, from the whiggs or whiggamors, horsedrivers in Scotland. I conceive however, from the known principles of this party, that it may be derived from *wiga*, Sax. signifying a hero, a man of intrepidity, and independency."

It is doubtful that Johnson, in denying Kenrick all originality, was fighting fire with fire. Kenrick had stated that he had given the pronunciation of words "according to the present Practice of polished Speakers in the Metropolis" and that he had given it "in a Manner perfectly simple, and principally new."[136] He had indicated the vocalic nuclei by small superscript numerals, referring to a table of key words; he had at least partially noted the incidence of consonantal phonemes by the use of italic type; and, in addition, he had used two accents—the acute, "sharp and quick," when the accented syllable ended in a consonant, and the grave, "flat and slow," when the accented syllable ended in a vowel. In all this, Kenrick had made a very definite contribution to the description of English pronunciation; but for Johnson the whole subject was apparently of slight importance. Sounds, he said, could not be described in words, and in any case "defect in such minute observations will be more easily excused, than superfluity."[137] If he had intended a real blast at Kenrick, he might have noted, as John Walker later did, that Kenrick had "rendered his Dictionary extremely imperfect, by entirely omitting a great number of words of doubtful and difficult pronunciation—those very words for which a Dictionary of this kind would be consulted."[138]

A slight departure from chronology provides an interesting contrast to Kenrick in Robert Nares, "one of the first editors of the 'British Critic' " and still another of the innumerable eighteenth-century clergymen who hunted words at least as avidly as they sought to save lost souls.[139] His *Elements of Orthoepy*, published in 1784, is described by Worcester as "a judicious and valuable work, though not in the form of a dictionary."[140] To Johnson, Nares was almost painfully respectful, praising him even where others had traditionally blamed. "Etymology . . . ," Nares wrote, "probably will not soon be more completely understood than it is by him";[141] and for English spelling, Johnson had left nothing more to do. "At length, what many had wished, and many had attempted in vain, what seemed indeed to demand the united efforts of a number, the diligence and acuteness of a single man performed. The English Dictionary appeared; and, as the weight of truth and reason is irresistible, its authority has nearly fixed the external form of our language; and from its decisions few appeals have yet been made . . . it is earnestly to be hoped that no author will henceforth, on slight grounds, be tempted to innovate."[142] Nares then spends almost a hundred pages listing and discussing "words . . . in writing which the public practice," despite the weight of truth and reason, "still differs from what the Lexicographer proposes, or still appears to be fluctuating."[143]

Of the two most notable orthoëpists of the eighteenth century, one shortly preceded Nares, and the other shortly followed him. Both borrowed heavily from Johnson, and the work of both was later combined with his in various forms. The first of the two, Thomas Sheridan, began his dictionary in 1760, published his scheme in 1762, and in 1780 printed *A General Dictionary of the English Language*,[144] which "commanded much more attention, as a pronouncing dictionary, than any other of the kind that preceded it."[145] The second of the famous pair, John Walker, likewise saw many years elapse between the publication of his prospectus, *A General Idea of a Pronouncing Dictionary* (1774), and the appearance of his chief work, *A Critical Pronouncing Dictionary and Expositor of the English Language* (1791).[146] His masterpiece, however, "superseded all other previous works of the same nature,"[147] including Sheridan's. Seventy years later, Worcester could still write: "In modern English literature, Walker holds a similar rank, as an orthoepist, to that of Johnson as a lexicographer."[148]

Thomas Sheridan had hoped to do for English pronunciation what Chesterfield had suggested that Johnson do for the language as a whole: "one main object" of his *Dictionary*, according to its title-page, was "to establish a plain and permanent standard of Pronunciation."[149] The definition of the standard, as one might expect, involved an appeal to the cyclic theory of linguistic change. In "the Augustan age of England . . . the reign of Queen Anne," English had been "spoken in its highest state of perfection"; and Sheridan had been fortunate enough to learn this perfect speech in the form in which it had been used by Swift himself.[150] For Sheridan, this happy circumstance made him a competent judge of pure and elegant pronunciation, whereas his critics most unkindly noted that his permanent standard was rather too Hibernian. No doubt he was on safer ground in depending, for spelling and the definition of words, on Johnson's *Dictionary*, to which he gave at least a qualified indorsement. "Nothing worthy the name of a grammar has hitherto appeared; and it is not many years since a dictionary of any value was produced; which, though it must be allowed to have been an Herculean labour, when considered as the work of one man, yet still is capable of great improvement."[151] A Johnson improved by the addition of Sheridan's and Walker's pronunciations was a fairly common product around 1800, as appears, for example, from the *Union Dictionary*, published in that year. The union consisted of "the orthography and explanatory matter selected from Dr. Johnson, the pronunciation adjusted according to Mr. Walker, with the addition of Mr. Sheridan's pronunciation of *Those Words wherein these two eminent Orthoëpists differ*."[152]

With or without Sheridan, great strength was in the union of Johnson and Walker, a combination which held its ground for many years against all rivals. As a matter of fact, Walker's *Dictionary* was itself such a combination, "in reality a transcript of Johnson's, with the addition of the current pronunciation affixed to each word, and the omission of the etymologies and authorities."[153] It need not be repeated that Walker had ample precedent for copying so freely, but perhaps it should be said that he was unusually generous in acknowledging his debt. "With respect to the explanation of words," he said, he had nearly always been careful to follow Johnson, the great authority on "the orthography and construction of our Language"; and when he felt constrained to criticize the Lexicographer, he did it with almost reverent apologies.[154] Walker in turn was treated with similar respect by many of his successors. In America, "even after the publication of Webster's *American Dictionary* in 1828, the combination of Johnson, Todd, Chalmers, and Walker was . . . esteemed invincible";[155] and a half-dozen dictionaries could be cited which show the continued power of Walker's name in England well after the middle of the nineteenth century.[156] Some of Johnson's theories of pronunciation and accentuations of particular words remained familiar as much because Walker cited or discussed them as because they were Johnson's.

As a linguistic theorist, indeed, as a historian of the language, and as a grammarian, Johnson can hardly claim high rank. His derivative grammar, especially, represents an opportunity missed. No doubt a long list of following grammars might be compiled which in some way would show the influence of Johnson's, or at least of other parts of his *Dictionary:* John and James Gough, *A Practical Grammar of the English Tongue* (2d ed.; Dublin, 1760); Joseph Priestly, *The Rudiments of English Grammar* (London, 1761; 3d ed., 1772); Robert Lowth, *A Short Introduction to English Grammar* (London, 1762); Thomas Berry, *Vraie méthode pour apprendre ... l'anglois* (Paris, 1766);[157] Wells Egelsham, *A Short Sketch of English Grammar* (London, 1781); Alexander Bicknell, *The Grammatical Wreath* (London, 1790);[158] Lindley Murray, *English Grammar* (York, 1795); the grammars in the Scott-Bailey *Dictionary* of 1755 and in Baretti's English and Italian of 1760; etc. No doubt, too, some of Johnson's particular grammatical doctrines, such as his insistence on a "conjunctive mode" in English, were important in shaping the schoolroom mythology;[159] and very possibly he invented some new prescriptions and proscriptions with which to frighten the linguistically timid.[160] Such evidence still remains insufficient to alter the verdict which Priestly reached and courteously announced in the Preface to his *Rudiments:* "I must not conclude this preface, without making my acknowledgements to Mr. *Johnson*, whose admirable dictionary has been of the greatest use to me in the study of our language. It is pity he had not formed as just, and as extensive an idea of English grammar."[161] The inferiority of Johnson the grammarian to Johnson the lexicographer was to become almost a commonplace.

As Priestley said, moreover, the weakness of Johnson's grammar was cause for real regret; for Johnson might have commanded public attention at the very moment when the study of English was becoming scholastically respectable. A few quotations from the *Monthly Review* will show the temper of the times. Whereas in 1762 a review of the *Rudiments* complains that "the study of our own Tongue has hitherto been most shamefully neglected in our public schools . . . ,"[162] just six years later a review of the *Rudiments . . . with Notes and Observations* begins very much more happily: "It is with pleasure that we have observed the regard which has, of late years, been paid to the cultivation of our native tongue."[163] By 1775, the notice of Thomas Joel's *Easy Introduction to English Grammar* is actually snappish: "The multiplication of grammars within this few years is become burdensome, and we are tired of perusing them."[164] And snappishness has given way to resignation and even to pity for the multitudinous grammarian in a review of 1787: "Works of this kind have so increased on us for years past, that it seems almost wonderful if the Authors reap any advantage from their publications."[165] In this impressive change, Johnson might have been the acknowledged leader, but almost wilfully he let the chance escape him.

As we have suggested,[166] Lowth early noted the chief weakness of Johnson's grammar: "*The Construction of this Language is so easy and obvious, that our Grammarians have thought it hardly worth while to give us any thing like a regular and systematical Syntax. The last* English *Grammar that hath been presented to the public, and by the Person best qualified to have given us a perfect one, comprises the whole Syntax in ten lines. The reason, which he assigns for being so very concise in this part is, 'because our Language has so little inflection, that its Construction neither requires nor admits many rules.'* "[167] Other grammarians, for many years, kept up the attack on Johnson's vulgar error. For example, in 1767 James Buchanan remarked that English "is not so simple in its Construction, as too many, from Inattention, have imagined it to be";[168] and in 1792 Caleb Alexander called the notion "popular but erroneous" that English "is not capable of being reduced to syntactical rules."[169] Johnson's blunder, moreover, did not result from haste; his neglect of syntax follows logically from the familiar statement in the *Plan:* "The syntax of this language is too inconstant to be reduced to rules, and can be only learned by the distinct consideration of particular words as they are used by the best authors. . . . Our syntax, therefore, is not to be taught by general rules, but by special precedents."[170] Johnson failed, then, as a grammarian largely because he did not produce a satisfactory syntax, and his syntax was inadequate because his considered ideas of syntactic analysis and of the structure of English stood in his way. It was Lowth who took the opportunity which Johnson had refused, and thus won for himself a position as a grammarian comparable to that of Johnson as a lexicographer.

Few men, if any, in the 1750's, could have distinguished themselves as linguistic historians, and Johnson lacked both the methods and the materials which would have been necessary for a good history of English. His methods (those of his age) may be judged from his statement in the Preface to the *Dictionary* that in etymology "little regard" need be shown to the vowels. "This uncertainty is most frequent in the vowels, which are so capriciously pronounced, and so differently modified, by accident or affectation, not only in every province, but in every mouth, that to them, as is well known to etymologists, little regard is to be shown in the deduction of one language from another."[171] With such ideas of linguistic structure and linguistic change, Johnson would have had no great success in the analysis of even the best materials; and his rather abject dependence on Junius and Skinner is a reminder that his own knowledge, in Germanic matters, was quite limited. For his history, he was almost driven to the conventional pattern of a relatively unanalyzed series of quotations.

Most of his contemporaries, of course, were in no position to criticize him; and the history, if it was not regarded as a masterpiece, was certainly not generally considered a disgrace to the nation. His illustrative texts were often reproduced,[172] and his few comments not infrequently repeated. The Scott-Bailey *Dictionary* of 1755, the *Encyclopédie*, and, as late as 1807, the *Encyclopaedia Perthensis* all copied from Johnson's history;[173] and George Ellis and the Abbé Denina both remark on his discussion of Chaucer's vocabulary.[174] Ellis, however, is somewhat less than favorable in his comments. Though he praises the "full refutation of Skinner's very absurd charge" against Chaucer, he condemns "the severe and unnecessary censure on Dryden" and the inconclusiveness of Johnson's final opinion. "With respect to Chaucer's language, it is impossible not to feel some disappointment at the cautious and doubtful opinion, delivered by the author of our national dictionary, and delivered in an introduction to that truly noble monument of his genius."[175] If the history had been anyone's but Johnson's, one suspects, Ellis would not have spoken his mind with such restraint.

Restraint has not been the distinguishing characteristic of those who have criticized Johnson's linguistic theories, in the eighteenth century or later. The *Plan* and Preface, the chief relevant documents, have been much read, widely quoted, and highly praised; but they have been just as vigorously damned. "That whole preface," wrote the author of the *Deformities of Dr. Samuel Johnson*, "is a piece of the most profound nonsense, which ever insulted the common sense of the world."[176] If either extreme is justified, it is certainly the praise; but other possible views of Johnson in the Preface might be that no commonplace mind could give such strength and dignity to commonplaces, or even that a crowd of sleepy commonplaces, like dead metaphors, can jostle one another into embarrassing liveliness. There is nothing surprising in the topics which Johnson discusses; he manipulates the expected concepts; and the innocent reader is sometimes left wondering how the same mind can entertain all of Johnson's propositions. The techniques of the historian of "unit ideas" might, in these circumstances, be applied with some success, when it would appear that Johnson's indorsement gave redoubled strength to ideas already sanctioned by long traditions and that, on the other hand, traditions were checked or deflected by his equally powerful rejection. Instances are the belief that the lexicographer can retard or direct the changes in the language which he records and the opposed belief that such functions are best reserved for the beneficent authority of an academy. In any case, as the example of the grammar would suggest, Johnson's successors sometimes reacted so violently to his doctrines that the history of his ideas and the history of his influence on general dictionaries of the English language, especially those of Richardson and Webster, cannot be clearly separated.

"Of the numerous dictionaries of the English Language which are used in the United States," Webster wrote in 1806, "Bailey's and Johnson's are those which are considered as containing the most original materials; and Johnson's in particular is the fund from which modern compilers have selected the substance of their works."[177] Forty years later, Worcester said much the same thing about the *Dictionary:* "It has formed substantially the basis of many smaller works, and, as Walker remarks, it 'has been deemed lawful plunder by every subsequent lexicographer.' "[178] Between Johnson and Richardson, then, Bailey, of course, continued to have some following, and "many other dictionaries appeared which . . . were in the main Johnson's Dictionary, or abridgments of it, in a new dress"; but clearly nothing was done which could claim to be a *general* improvement on Johnson.[179] The typical products of the time were the glossaries, synonymies, and pronouncing dictionaries; the new edition of Johnson by Todd; the supplements by Boucher, Mason, Seager, and Jodrell; and the many small or middle-sized compilations for which Johnson was a primary source.

Enough has already been said to indicate the character of these works, and further enumeration and description would grow tedious. In Johnson's *Dictionary*, any hack could find, among other things, the greater part of a satisfactory word-list, authoritative spellings, etymologies no worse than the average of the day, the best definitions of English words that had yet been written, and a large collection of illustrative quotations. What was so easily available was freely used, and definitions and quotations from the Johnson still appear in scholarly and commercial dictionaries of the twentieth century. It is an understatement, however, to say that a history of hack lexicographers and their uninhibited transcriptions would be a history in which neither Johnson's nor any other ideas played much part. The transcribers transcribed, with few ideas beyond the turning of a moderately honest penny; and the innovations which Richardson was to make in English lexicography must be explained by reference to a very different man, the Philosopher of Purley, John Horne Tooke.

Tooke may be safely described as one of the most systematically frantic etymologists who ever lived. By pure reasoning a priori he reached certain conclusions about language, which he then attempted to support—naturally with complete success—by the appeal to etymology.[180] In founding his theory, Tooke rejected any elaborate analysis of the operations of the mind. "The business of the mind, as far as it concerns Language . . . extends no further than to receive impressions, that is, to have Sensations or Feelings. What are called its operations, are merely the operations of Language."[181] All necessary words must therefore be the names of the mind's impressions, or else such names with some additional characteristic which is unspecified but necessary for communication. As simply as this, Tooke reduces the parts of speech to two: the noun, "the *simple* or *complex*, the *particular* or *general sign* or *name* of *one* or *more Ideas*," and the verb, which is also a noun, but something more than a noun: "The Verb is QUOD *loquimur;* the *Noun*, DE QUO."[182] It would be a mistake, however, to assume that in a modern language *all* words are *necessary* words and hence the signs of ideas. If "the first aim of Language was to *communicate* our thoughts," the second was "to do it with *despatch*"; and "the errors of Grammarians have arisen from supposing all words to be *immediately* either the signs of things or the signs of ideas: whereas in fact many words are merely *abbreviations* employed for despatch, and are the signs of other words."[183] Aside from the nouns and verbs, then, the so-called "parts of speech" are not parts of speech at all but substitutes or abbreviations which have been introduced in the progress of language from its original "rude and tedious" state.[184]

It becomes apparent, however, that if "the original Mother-tongue" had no abbreviations, but only necessary words, nouns and verbs must be etymologically discoverable in all other word-classes and even in prefixes, suffixes, and inflectional endings. Tooke is quite equal to this embarrassing occasion. Instead of questioning the premises which had led him so far away from facts, he devised methods by which facts might be evaded. If only enough liberty could be taken with the sounds of prepositions, conjunctions, adjectives, etc., some resemblance could always be found between any given word and some Old English noun or verb; and Tooke found reasons for taking such liberty. "*Abbreviation and Corruption are always busiest with the words which are most frequently in use.* Letters, like soldiers, being very apt to desert and drop off in a long march, and especially if their passage happens to lie near the confines of an enemy's country."[185] The etymologist simply should not trouble his head with petty objections. "The difference between a T and a D is so very small, that an Etymologist knows by the *practice* of languages, and an Anatomist by the *reason* of that practice, that in the derivation of words it is scarce worth regarding."[186] As to the supposed fact that the "particles" are indeclinable, they are really not indeclinable at all, but the surviving forms of older paradigms, which appear indeclinable simply because they have been isolated by the loss of the other members of their sets.[187] Tooke proceeds to illustrate his theories with page after page of midsummer madness, in which the statement that *loud* is the past participle of *to low* (or "bel-low") is relatively restrained.[188]

Given Tooke's theories, etymology becomes a matter of the first importance, the means of passing from substitutes or abbreviations to the words for which they stand. How else should one know that "our corrupted IF has always the signification of the English Imperative *Give;* and no other," or that *the* is the imperative of a verb meaning "to get or take"?[189] For lack of such knowledge, Johnson had made a sad muddle of his *Dictionary*. Not knowing that *from* "is simply the Anglo-Saxon and Gothic noun Frum," and therefore "means merely BEGINNING, and nothing else," he had "numbered up *twenty* different meanings of this Preposition" and had "accompanied each with instances sufficiently numerous, as proofs. . . . And yet in all his instances (which . . . are above *seventy*) FROM continues to retain invariably one and the same single meaning."[190] Such were the sins of Johnson, who had attempted to collect the meanings of words from usage, not from etymology, and who therefore deceived his readers with "fraud, and cant, and folly."

In Tooke's denunciation of Johnson, Charles Richardson vigorously joined. To be sure, Richardson had used Johnson in compiling his own *Dictionary*, as he was careful to say: "In my endeavours to collect and settle the vocabulary, I have enjoyed and availed myself of the large store of materials accumulated by Johnson and his editor Mr. Todd."[191] Even the method of Richardson's work had been in part determined by Johnson's *Plan*, which Richardson considered imperfect but still superior to Johnson's execution of it. Johnson had promised "to sort the several senses of each word, and to exhibit first its natural and primitive signification," then "its consequential meaning," and then "its metaphorical sense";[192] but in his Preface he had characterized this undertaking as "specious, but not always practicable" and had weakly referred his reader to the examples for "the solution of all difficulties."[193] As Richardson said, "neither did he himself at that time attempt, nor has any other person since attempted, to construct a work upon the plan prescribed,"[194] so that Richardson was doing, in a way, what Johnson had promised but had not performed.

To a lexicographer, however, such obligations are no restraint on his criticism of his predecessors and benefactors. At various times, Richardson spent some hundreds of pages celebrating the glories of Horne Tooke and damning Johnson. "No man," he wrote, "can possibly succeed in compiling a truly valuable Dictionary of the English Language, unless he entirely desert the steps of Johnson, and pursue the path which Tooke has pointed out";[195] and, what is worse, Johnson's reputation has deterred the competitors who might have exposed and corrected the faults of his wholly unsuccessful book.[196] Richardson boldly proceeds with the exposure. Johnson's principles and practice of etymology are absurd, and, since he allowed himself "no remoter research into our language than the age of Elizabeth," it was quite impossible for him to trace the semantic history of words from their "primitive signification."[197] Johnson did not search out and state true etymological meanings. Instead, he supplied a collection of merely approximate synonyms and of "exemplary passages which can only assist a reader to infer the meaning of a word by induction," so that his famous definitions are "loose, vague, and various" and his heaped-up illustrations simply ridiculous.[198] Tooke's condemnation of such work was perfectly just.

So violent an attack on Johnson invites close inspection of Richardson's own accomplishment. On its publication, the *New Dictionary* was received quite well.[199] One reviewer called it "the most complete dictionary ever published, as regards the etymology and primitive meaning of words, the successive growth of their secondary significations, the gradual advance and changes of the language, the vast body of quotations from all our authors, both ancient and modern, and in consequence, the skeleton history of the English language which it indirectly presents."[200] Dean Trench went further and said that Richardson's "is the only English dictionary in which etymology assumes the dignity of a science"[201]—an extravagance which should have caused the Dean acute embarrassment. The statement, however, that Richardson understood and exemplified the essentials of the historical method in lexicography has become traditional, and not without some reason. Abandoning a rigorous alphabetical order, he placed after each word that he explained "its immediate derivatives," and made a single etymology and (usually) a single general definition serve for the whole group.[202] His marking of pronunciation is limited to the use of a single accent on words of more than one syllable; his definitions are relatively brief; and the bulk of his work is given over to very numerous illustrative quotations, arranged in chronological order and provided, at least in the *Encyclopædia metropolitana*, with fairly precise references, though not with dates. It is these quotations, gathered by wide reading in authors from the Middle English period to the nineteenth century, but only these quotations, that partially justify the traditional description of Richardson's work. His etymologies too often insult the simplest principles of historical linguistics.

Fortunately for Richardson's reputation, few readers seem to have bothered much with his etymologies or with his advocacy of Tooke's notions, so that he is remembered honorably, if he is remembered at all, as a precursor of the *OED*. A closer look at his *New Dictionary* breeds disappointment. Not only does Richardson follow Tooke in particular factual errors, as when he says that "Addle . . . becomes ail; as idle becomes ill, by sliding over the D, in pronunciation";[203] "he appears to take it for granted that the author of the Diversions of Purley proves everything that he asserts, and that all rational and philosophical English etymology must be founded on his system."[204] In short, his borrowed method is so perverse that the possibility of calling it historical becomes dubious.

Two illustrations will make the difficulty clear. The first is chosen from the "Advertisement" which was printed in the 1826 edition of Richardson's *Illustrations of English Philology* and which was intended to show, by parallel extracts, the superiority of Richardson's *Dictionary* to Johnson's. According to Tooke and Richardson, Johnson had failed because he had not given true etymological definitions like Richardson's of *clergy:* "A fragment of any thing; *sc.* cast into the urn or vessel; and hence, a lot." This "meaning," Richardson is compelled to recognize, is hopelessly remote from use; he therefore includes among his examples two explanations by Hooker and Gibbon, saying, "For the application of the word, see particularly the examples from Hooker and Gibbon." Our second passage, also from the *Illustrations*, is one small part of "A Critical Examination of the Dictionary of Dr. Johnson," which fills two hundred pages. In this passage, Richardson attacks Johnson's analysis of the meanings of *by* on the grounds that the "twenty-five supposed meanings" which Johnson listed are not in the word itself, which has only one meaning, but "in the context of the sentence, or in some *subaudition* to be inferred from it." *By* is treated, after Tooke, as the imperative of *be;* and "We mean to gain by you" is transmogrified, by "subaudition," to "We mean to gain, be you the means of our gain."[205] It must obviously be an odd distinction between *meaning* and *application* that requires such necromancy for its defense.

Richardson himself was perfectly aware of his difficulty and discussed it more than once. Like Tooke, he was trying to maintain that words have only one meaning, which is immutable; and at the same time he felt obliged to do justice to the obvious facts of semantic change. On the latter point, his critics said, Tooke had gone wrong, believing "that the meaning and force of a word, now and for ever, must be that which it or its root originally bore."[206] Richardson replied with the distinction between meaning and application. Tooke had meant only that a word has just one etymology, and therefore just one etymological meaning; but the word may be used in many different *applications* "founded upon this meaning, and inferred from it."[207] This was only to say that every word, at some stage of its history, had just one meaning, from which all its later meanings can be traced—a statement which could be most easily defended by treating every word whose meanings could *not* plausibly be traced to a single source as not one word but two. Yet Richardson did not ultimately succeed in making Tooke's doctrine seem a truism, a commonplace. "The meaning or intention of the speaker in using the word," he continued, "may be very different from the meaning of the word itself; but there must be some inference or deduction in the mind of the speaker, known to the hearer, which will warrant the usage."[208] That is, only etymologists can converse.

Richardson's arguments are no more impressive when he employs them in the closely related dispute with critics who sought meanings inductively, not etymologically. His univocal meaning destroys semantic history; his varied applications re-create it; and meaning and applications are reconciled by "subaudition." Repeating the distinction "between the intrinsick meaning of a word, and the application of it to things, differing, perhaps, in all respects, except one, which will authorize such application," Richardson insists again that for every legitimate application the etymological meaning must furnish a cause. "The meaning is uniform, unvarying, and invariable; the application and subaudition as unlimited as the numberless necessities of speech." Mere observation of usage would never reveal such secrets as that *mirth* and *murther* both mean "that which dissipates," but that with *mirth* the subaudition is "care," while with *murther* it is "life." The ultimate consequence is the same: only the etymologist can rightly understand speech and judge of its propriety.[209]

To say, then, that Richardson's method was historical demands a certain subaudition. It was, and it was not.

Primarily, it was derived from the theories of Horne Tooke, which were also the premises of Richardson's bitter attacks on Johnson; and though etymology was central to Tooke's work, semantic change, in his system, occupies a very equivocal position. If the stern critic were to be treated sternly, Richardson's contribution to English lexicography might be limited to the collection of more and earlier quotations than Johnson had collected.

Noah Webster was just the man to be stern with everyone but Noah Webster. While Richardson was publishing in the *Encyclopædia metropolitana*, Webster was at work on his *American Dictionary*. Webster published in 1828, Richardson's separate edition came out by 1837, and the two found themselves in competition with one another, with Todd's Johnson, and with Joseph Worcester. Inevitably, Webster and Richardson, to say nothing of Webster and Worcester, disliked one another. Though the conflict of dissimilar ideals of lexicography would alone have been enough to strain relations, Richardson asked for trouble, in 1834, by smugly criticizing the less courteous of his American rivals: "The Author is conscious that he should be chargeable with great want of courtesy if he passed unnoticed the American Dictionary of Dr. Webster. His *censure*, however, must be short. Dr. Webster disarmed and stripped himself for the field, and advanced unaided and unshielded to the combat. He abjured the assistance of Skinner and Vossius, and the learned elders of lexicography; and of Tooke, he quaintly says, 'I have made no use of his writings.' There is a display of oriental reading in his Preliminary Essays, which, as introductory to a Dictionary of the English Language, seems as appropriate and useful as a reference to the code of Gentoo laws to decide a question of English inheritance. Dr. Webster was entirely unacquainted with our old authors."[210] Webster did not take this criticism tamely. In an essay on the "State of English Philology," he complains, for example, that he has been the innocent victim of unprovoked assault. "Richardson, or his publisher, in a prospectus of his dictionary, has attacked me without provocation, and in violation of all the rules of courtesy."[211] Such conduct was unforgivable—in others, and Webster replied with a blast against Richardson and all his countrymen. "In proof of the low state of etymological knowledge in Great Britain," he says, "I will advert to Richardson's Dictionary";[212] and he proceeds to advert with true Columbian vigor. Little emerges from the controversy except that each man had a fondness for his own eccentricities. Webster and his supporters berated Richardson because Richardson, in following Tooke, had adopted a faulty etymological arrangement, had given meager definitions, and had included vast numbers of useless quotations, especially from old authors. Richardson scorned Webster because Webster, in his pursuit of oriental lore, had *not* followed Tooke, or had not followed him closely enough, had not included numerous quotations from old authors, etc. An unprejudiced modern reader, admitting the value of Richardson's quotations and Webster's definitions and conceding the strength of their challenge to the supremacy of Johnson, still must conclude that neither Webster nor Richardson was Johnson's equal as a man or even, all things considered, as a lexicographer. They had his shoulders to stand on.

With Webster, however, as with Richardson, use did not prevent abuse. Patriotic, enterprising, pugnacious, and happily blind to the limits of the possible and the probable, Webster was born for controversy and unlikely exploits. "Virginians," he wrote with the New Englander's unique capacity for pious self-esteem, "have little money and great pride, contempt of northern men, and great fondness for dissipated life. They do not understand Grammar."[213] There was no least chance that America's "critick and coxcomb general"[214] could so much as modify those lovable qualities; but he made the effort, just as he tried to reform American spelling and to correct the grammar of the King James Bible. Such a wizard would not be put off by the reputation of Samuel Johnson; and since Webster, though perhaps not a great man (as Sir James Murray called him), was certainly not Jefferson's "mere pedagogue of very limited understanding and very strong prejudices,"[215] his criticisms are much more significant than Tooke's.

The favorable criticisms may be disposed of quickly enough; they are neither very numerous nor very long. For example, in the Preface to his *Compendious Dictionary* of 1806, Webster compared Johnson and Bailey. "On Bailey's orthography, etymologies and definition of mathematical terms, Johnson has made little improvement. The excellence of Johnson's work consists chiefly in presenting to the reader the various different significations of words distinctly arranged and exemplified. On this part of the work, the author has bestowed uncommon pains, and has usually displayed critical discernment aided by extensive and various reading."[216] A year later, Webster's circumstances had changed, and with them his opinions. Under criticism by Charlestonian omniscients for his Yankee impudence in trying to improve on Johnson, he discovers so many errors in the *Dictionary* that the confidence reposed in it "is the *greatest injury to philology* that now exists." From his vantage point on the advancing front of philologic knowledge, Webster in 1807 can concede small merit to his predecessor. "What are the excellencies in the work to which it owes its reputation? To this inquiry the answer is obvious: Dr. Johnson has given many definitions of words which his predecessors had omitted, and added illustrations which in many instances are very valuable."[217] It will be noted that the nature of Johnson's merits remained the same, whereas their degree varied inversely with the pressure of his competition on Webster. That competition apart, Webster no doubt thought very well of Johnson, of whom he sometimes spoke in superlatives. "Dr. Johnson was one of the greatest men that the English nation has ever produced; and when the exhibition of truth depended on his own gigantic powers of intellect, he seldom erred. But. . . ."[218]

A catalogue of Webster's militant adversatives leaves no part of Johnson's work untouched. The Preface comes off best. "In the preface to Johnson's Dictionary we have a splendid specimen of elevated composition, not indeed perfectly free from faults, but generally correct in diction as well as in principle."[219] "Generally correct" would be much too favorable for Johnson's history of the language. "In the history of the English language the author has proved himself very imperfectly acquainted with the subject. He commences with a most egregious error in supposing the Saxon language to have been introduced into Britain in the fifth century."[220] This was Webster's opinion in 1807, when he felt that Johnson's work had suffered because Johnson had neglected both "the primitive English or Saxon" and the Celtic, under the false impression "that the Saxons and Welsh were nations totally distinct";[221] and though Webster's own stores of etymological misinformation were not so great in 1807 as they later grew to be, he persisted unshaken in the conviction that Johnson's "whole scheme of deducing words from their original is extremely imperfect."[222] The same wretched imperfection deformed Johnson's grammar, and for the same reason. It abounds with errors and contains "very few of the material and important facts which would serve to illustrate the history of the language and of the several nations from which it is derived."[223] Future grammarians had much to do, for "this field of inquiry has never been fully explored; it is a fruitful field, and hereafter the cultivation of it is to produce a valuable harvest."[224]

In the body of Johnson's *Dictionary*, Webster found fault not only with the etymologies but with every department of the work, from the word-list on. His objections to the word-list, in which he noted the familiar sins of defect and excess, showed small originality; but his complaint against Johnson's "vulgar and cant words" was more distinctive. Whatever their historical value, some such words always seemed to Webster "too low to deserve notice" by a pure-minded lexicographer;[225] and in 1807 his indignation against the favorite of aristocratic Charleston was unbounded. "Alas, had a native of the United States introduced such vulgar words and offensive ribaldry into a similar work, what columns of abuse would have issued from the Johnsonian presses against the wretch who could thus sully his book and corrupt the language."[226] Webster, of course, would have known precisely how to reply to those "columns of abuse."

Like moral purity, pure orthography was dear to Webster's heart, although he reserved the right to redefine it from time to time. Vacillation in others was not tolerable. "It is considered as a material fault, that in some classes of words, Johnson's orthography is either not correct upon principle or not uniform in the class."[227] Nor had Johnson done better in orthoëpy than in orthography, for he had not even shifted the position of his accent from the vowel, when it was long, to the following consonant, when the vowel was short; and despite great progress in pronouncing dictionaries, his editors had done nothing to improve this outworn technique. "Another great fault, that remains uncorrected, is the manner of noting the accented syllable; the accent being laid uniformly on the vowel, whether it closes the syllable or not. Thus the accent is laid on *e* in *te'nant* as well as in *te'acher*, and the inquirer cannot know from the accent whether the vowel is long or short."[228]

As to the all-important definitions, Johnson's are faulty in several ways, although the general opinion is otherwise and "uncommon praises have been bestowed upon the author's power of discrimination."[229] Johnson fails to distinguish rightly among words that are nearly synonymous; and even within his treatment of single words, he often inverts or disregards the true order of the definitions, because he has not discovered the one primary sense.[230] Like his method, his knowledge often fails him. "In numerous instances, Johnson has mistaken the precise sense of legal terms," which Lawyer Webster has dealt with more successfully; or, again, if Johnson's definition of a term in the arts or sciences was correct in his own day, it has grown "erroneous or defective" with the Advance of Mind.[231] "The great number of passages" which he cites "from authors, to exemplify his definitions," only makes matters worse. Often the quotations throw no light, or a false light, on the meanings supposedly exemplified;[232] for almost no one except Webster knows how to write English. "Let me only add that in the course of thirty years' reading I have not found a single author who appears to have been accurately acquainted with the true import and force of terms in his own language. And a multitude of errors committed by writers, evidently from their misapprehending the import of words, are cited as authorities by Johnson instead of being noticed with censure."[233] The "rags and tatters of barbarism" were no fit heritage for posterity.

If all Webster's thinking about language and lexicography had been on this level, he would never deserve the precedence over Tooke which we have given him; and the worst of Webster is yet to come. In 1828 the basis of his etymologizing was simple fantasy. Accepting the scriptural account of the dispersion, he believed that "the primitive language of man," spoken by "the descendants of Noah . . . on the plain of Shinar, . . . must have been the original Chaldee," and that "all the words of the several great races of men, both in Asia and Europe, which are vernacular in their several languages, and unequivocally the same, are of equal antiquity, as they must have been derived from the common Chaldee stock."[234] Thus the native element in modern English consists of "words which our ancestors brought with them from Asia," and the Danish and Welsh loans are also "primitive words," derived from the language of Japheth and his descendants.[235] Webster could believe all this "forty years after Sir William Jones, twenty after Schlegel, a dozen after Bopp, and half a dozen or more after the first volumes of Jacob Grimm";[236] he could believe it after actually reading Jones. "It is obvious," he wrote, "that Sir W. Jones had given very little attention to the subject [of etymology], and that some of its most common and obvious principles had escaped his observation."[237]

For such invincible ignorance, it is best to attempt no excuse; and if one looks for redeeming features in Webster's practice as a dictionary-maker or in other aspects of his theory, some of the praise which usually is given him begins to appear a little strained. Thus his contributions to the technique of English lexicography were few. The determining influence of his American spellings is more easily asserted than proved; his marking of pronunciation was crude, indefinite, and old-fashioned; his etymologies are sometimes frenetic; and he is greatly inferior to Johnson and Richardson in the provision of authorities. Without Todd's Johnson as a sort of working base, moreover, Webster's accomplishment would have been distinctly lessened: in the first ten pages of his letter *C*, Webster cites Johnson by name more than twenty times and sometimes uses him without citation, taking over entry-words, definitions, authorities, and etymologies.

In his theory, Webster was no more original than Johnson had been. The essence of his linguistic patriotism is the simple statement that lexical change will follow cultural change, that in the vocabulary of a language permanence is not always good and change not always bad; and Webster did not always act in the liberal spirit of that generalization, which really has no more to do with America than with China or Peru. Too often he entangled himself in chauvinistic absurdities, as when he suggested that the golden age of English was past in Britain but future in America. One is tempted to say that he might gladly have been less nearly right, if only the facts had permitted him.

But it is much too easy to make fun of Webster. He read and wrote incessantly, he collected an enormous amount of varied information, and he never lost sight of the one great idea which governed all his work. It was an idea, like Tooke's notions of the structure and history of English, that made conflict with Johnsonian doctrines inescapable. Johnson had believed that linguistic change is cyclic, that "every language has a time of rudeness antecedent to perfection, as well as of false refinement and declension"; and, believing also that the golden age of English was in the past, he had once hoped that he might fix the language.[238] When this hope was shattered, he made the minimal retreat and sought, for the honor of his country, to "give longevity to that which its own nature forbids to be immortal."[239] Since "all change is of itself an evil,"[240] linguistic change should be retarded when it could, and a return to the language of the past, if it were possible, would involve little or no loss. "From the authors which rose in the time of Elizabeth, a speech might be formed adequate to all the purposes of use and elegance. If the language of theology were extracted from Hooker and the translation of the Bible; the terms of natural knowledge from Bacon; the phrases of policy, war, and navigation from Raleigh; the dialect of poetry and fiction from Spenser and Sidney; and the diction of common life from Shakespeare, few ideas would be lost to mankind, for want of English words, in which they might be expressed."[241]

In that statement, despite his general approval of Johnson's Preface, Webster rightly found less sense than sentiment. Johnson was hardly in his grave, he answered, "when new discoveries in natural history originated a language almost entirely new." And it was not only the changing sciences which required new words. No language could or should be fixed, and most certainly not English as it spread itself across the continents. New ways of life would also demand new words and make old words obsolete, until at length each English-speaking country would form its "distinct dialect," the American being chief.[242] Over the years, Webster reiterated his simple statement that American English in his day was and must be different from the British English of Johnson's time; for whatever inconsistencies there may have been in his thinking, he held steadily to the belief that American English was and of right ought to be. He was quite clear on this point in 1789: "numerous local causes, such as a new country, new associations of people, new combinations of ideas in arts and science, and some intercourse with tribes wholly unknown in Europe, will introduce new words into the American tongue. These causes will produce, in a course of time, a language in North America, as different from the future language of England, as the modern Dutch, Danish and Swedish are from the German, or from one another."[243] He was quite clear in 1800: "New circumstances, new modes of life, new laws, new ideas of various kinds give rise to new words, and have already made many material differences between the language of England and America. . . . The differences in the language of the two countries will continue to multiply, and render it necessary that we should have *Dictionaries* of the *American language*."[244] And he was equally clear in 1828: "It is not only important, but, in a degree necessary, that the people of this country, should have an *American Dictionary* of the English language; for, although the body of the language is the same as in England, and it is desirable to perpetuate that sameness, yet some differences must exist. Language is the expression of ideas; and if the people of one country cannot preserve an identity of ideas, they cannot retain an identity of language. Now an identity of ideas depends materially upon a sameness of things or objects with which the people of the two countries are conversant. But in no two portions of the earth, remote from each other, can such identity be found. Even physical objects must be different. But the principal differences between the people of this country and of all others, arise from different forms of government, different laws, institutions and customs. . . . A great number of words . . .

[therefore] require to be defined in a phraseology accommodated to the condition and institutions of the people in these states."[245]

Reading such bills of linguistic rights, Americans, at least, can forgive Webster a great deal of nonsense about Chaldee and the sons of Noah; and, happily, this most sensible of his theories carried over into his practice. Realizing and accepting the inevitability of lexical change, he included a good many scientific and technological terms even in his *Compendious Dictionary*, a mere "convenient manual" which Webster hoped might serve until his great work could be completed. In 1828 he went further, for the *American Dictionary* added (he said) some 12,000 words to the list in Todd's Johnson and an even greater number of definitions. If Webster's extension of the word-list was an important step in the evolution of the modern "utility dictionary," in his definitions he met Johnson on his own ground and stood the comparison without dishonor. Though it is sometimes hard to see any clear plan in his ordering of the meanings of a word, and though he may have included *too much* encyclopedic information, he fairly won the title which Murray gave him, "a born definer"; and in that capacity, as Krapp said, "Webster reveals a clearness of mind, soundness of judgment and catholicity of interest that puts him intellectually in the same class with Franklin."[246]

The reception accorded the *American Dictionary*, at home and abroad, is a little hard to judge. Since it did not serve precisely the same purposes as either the Johnson or the Richardson, it was not calculated to drive either immediately from the market; but it was not so violently American that it could not be generally useful in England as well as in the United States. Apparently, the first editions did enjoy considerable success on both sides of the Atlantic. An English edition, well subscribed, very quickly appeared in periodical instalments and won some favorable reviews. The *Westminster* was generally favorable in 1831;[247] James Martineau and "*Professor Jameson*, of Edinburgh," early declared Webster superior to Johnson;[248] in 1840 Richard Taylor, the editor of Tooke, called Webster's much the best of all English dictionaries;[249] in 1850 John Ogilvie, though not totally disinterested, passed the same judgment;[250] and after the Webster-Mahn of 1864, Websterian leadership was rather generally conceded.[251] It had not always been so, particularly in the 1830's, when the *Quarterly Review* said bluntly that "Dr. Webster's quartos were hardly worthy of being reprinted in England,"[252] when Richardson said that Johnson had no rival,[253] and when the popular *Penny Cyclopædia* reported the continued acceptance of the Johnson as a standard.[254] As late as 1857, Trench could still dismiss the *American Dictionary* as having no value in his eyes.[255]

That dismissal left Trench by no means unprovided with other dictionaries to praise, condemn, or ignore. In the decades of Johnson's declining influence, immediately before and after Trench's paper, a fourth competing lexicographer shared the field with Johnson, Richardson, and Webster. Joseph E. Worcester began his dictionary-making by editing *Johnson's English Dictionary, as Improved by Todd, and Abridged by Chalmers; with Walker's Pronouncing Dictionary, Combined* (Boston, 1827). Two years later, he abridged the *American Dictionary*,[256] so that when he published the first of his own dictionaries, in 1830, he had the most thorough knowledge of two at least of his rivals. His career had begun successfully enough. His edition of the abridged Johnson had been called "the most complete manual of the kind that has yet appeared,"[257] and his *Comprehensive Pronouncing and Explanatory Dictionary* (1830) still seemed to Krapp in 1925 a better work than Webster's *American*.[258] Worcester's next important effort, *A Universal and Critical Dictionary of the English Language*, appeared at Boston in 1846 and was notable for its great extension of the word-list. "The Dictionary of Johnson," Worcester wrote, "as corrected and enlarged by Todd, and Walker's Critical Pronouncing Dictionary, have been made, in some degree, the basis of the present work";[259] for Johnson was supreme for definitions and authorities, Walker for pronunciation.[260] Webster and Richardson, however, were not ignored. With his usual modesty and sober good sense, Worcester pointed out that although Johnson's *Dictionary* had won most general acceptance as a standard, the "most considerable" of his British successors, Richardson, had done much for anyone who wanted to study the history of the language, while Webster had produced "the greatest and most important work on English lexicography" since 1755.[261] "It is a work of great learning and research, comprising a much more full vocabulary of the language than Johnson's Dictionary, and containing many and great improvements with respect both to the etymology and definitions of words; but the taste and judgment of the author are not generally esteemed equal to his industry and erudition."[262] Perhaps the last remark might have been spared.

Of Worcester's other compilations, only the last, *A Dictionary of the English Language*, needs comment here. Published in 1860 at Boston, a Worcester stronghold in the developing War of American Dictionaries, it was Worcester's masterpiece. The *London Athenæum* pronounced it "the best existing English lexicon," H. B. Wheatley found it "most admirable," and the *Quarterly Review* for 1873 confirms the impression that for some few years Worcester's was accepted in England as the best practical dictionary available.[263] Its fortunes in America, though complicated by the Dictionary War, were probably parallel to its English career: after the 1864 revision of Webster's *Dictionary*, the Worcester gradually lost ground until it disappeared with the edition of 1886. It was a solid, useful book, based on Worcester's *Universal and Critical* and therefore ultimately on Johnson and Walker, but made yet more "universal" by the inclusion of some thousands of additional words which had hardly been subjected to very severe criticism. The relative merits of Webster and Worcester are not measured by their relative familiarity to the modern student.

IV

Centennials provoke silly answers to sensible questions. What has Johnson's *Dictionary* meant to the English-speaking world? The answer, we believe, is implicit in what we have said about the influences that went into the *Dictionary* and those that emanated from it; and if we are wrong, if we have not already given the answer, we will come no closer to it by reducing the complexities of the tradition which we have followed to an arbitrary formula. We prefer the honest dulness of summary.

Our studies in the tradition of English lexicography seem to us to have been mutually confirmatory. Johnson's *Dictionary*, as we said in the beginning, was indeed a booksellers' project, whose favorable reception at home and abroad was carefully prepared; but it so nearly realized the contemporary lexicographic ideal that it was ultimately pushed aside more by changes in that ideal and changes in the English language itself than by the competition of other single-handed lexicographers. The early comparison between Johnson and the academies could be repeated, somewhat altered, a century later; for his *Dictionary* was superseded only by the Philological Society's historical dictionary and by the "utility dictionary" of the Merriam Company, with its succession of post-Websterian editors and their corps of assistants.

To these obvious conclusions, we have followed three obvious lines of inquiry. The critical reception of the *Dictionary*, we hardly need repeat, *was* generally favorable. There were objections, and extreme objections, notably to Johnson's word-list and his etymologies; but at least until the third decade of the nineteenth century, his work was widely accepted as a standard in both method and content. Until the very notion of the standard and standardizing dictionary was called in question, Johnson remained a powerful force to be reckoned with.

In the beginning, skilful advertising helped the *Dictionary* establish its dominance over numerous and persistent competitors. Throughout the eighteenth century and well into the nineteenth, this dominance was maintained, and even when the *Dictionary* no longer came so close to giving complete satisfaction as it once had done, the attempt was made merely to supplement it or to keep its essential virtues unchanged in revised and extended editions. Advertising, supplements, and editions revised by Johnson and by others must be considered in the attempt to state the avenues and extent of Johnson's influence in lexicography.

That influence was powerful and lasting, on the Continent and in America as well as in England itself. Only the grammar and the history of the language were of little but negative importance. For the glossarists, Johnson illustrated a method; to the synonymists, he provided materials; with his work, the work of the orthoëpists was often combined as its natural extension. General lexicographers were commonly content to use the *Dictionary* as a mine, without attempting greatly to extend its limits, at least until Richardson and Webster. Richardson, for all his criticisms, made his chief constructive effort in the collection of more and earlier quotations than Johnson had collected. Webster, equally critical, recognized the inevitability of lexical change and tried to do justice to developments since Johnson by extending the word-list and adding or improving definitions. Neither Richardson, however, nor Webster, nor Worcester, Johnson's three great nineteenth-century rivals before the *OED*, directly challenged Johnson with just the kind of dictionary he had made; all three of them were in his debt; and ultimately no one of the three can be adjudged his equal.

The magnitude of his achievement remains.

Notes

Chapter I

1. See Philip B. Gove, "Notes on Serialization and Competitive Publishing," *Oxford Bibliographical Society Proceedings & Papers*, V (1936–39), 309; and cf. pp. 111–14 above.

2. Quoted from Stanley Rypins, "Johnson's Dictionary Reviewed by His Contemporaries," *PQ*, IV (1925), 283; cf. also Harry R. Warfel (ed.), *Letters of Noah Webster* (New York, 1953), p. 284.

3. See DeWitt T. Starnes and Gertrude E. Noyes, *The English Dictionary from Cawdrey to Johnson, 1604–1755* (Chapel Hill, 1946), *passim;* Vera E. Smalley, *The Sources of "A Dictionarie of the French and English Tongues" by Randle Cotgrave (London, 1611): A Study in Renaissance Lexicography* (Baltimore, 1948), *passim;* Albert H. Marckwardt (ed.), *Laurence Nowell's Vocabularium Saxonicum* (Ann Arbor, 1952), pp. 1–19; DeWitt T. Starnes, *Renaissance Dictionaries* (Austin, 1954), *passim;* James Sledd, "Nowell's *Vocabularium Saxonicum* and the Elyot-Cooper Tradition," *SP*, LI (1954), 143–48.

4. Sir John Hawkins, *Life of Samuel Johnson* (London, 1787), p. 175; H. B. Wheatley, "The Story of Johnson's Dictionary," *Antiquary*, XI (1885), 13; G. B. Hill (ed.), *Johnsonian Miscellanies* (New York, 1897), II, 95, n. 1; Percy W. Long, "English Dictionaries before Webster," *Papers of the Bibliographical Society of America*, IV (1909), 31; Starnes and Noyes, *op. cit.*, pp. 184–89, 280; W. K. Wimsatt, Jr., *Philosophic Words* (New Haven, 1948), p. 21.

5. Cf. Arthur Golding's prefatory verses to the *Alvearie* of John Baret (1573); Baret's own statement in his "preamble" to the letter *E;* Gabriel Harvey's remarks in a letter of 1580 (G. G. Smith, *Elizabethan Critical Essays* [Oxford, 1904], I, 102); and esp. Mulcaster's *Elementarie* (1582), pp. 187, 264, in E. T. Campagnac's ed. (Oxford, 1925).

6. Quoted from Hermann M. Flasdieck, *Der Gedanke einer englischen Sprachakademie in Vergangenheit und Gegenwart* (Jena, 1928), pp. 23 f.

7. Skinner, *Etymologicon*, sig. a2^{v}.

8. Quoted from Eleanor N. Adams, *Old English Scholarship in England from 1566–1800* (New Haven, 1917), p. 185.

9. Flasdieck, *op. cit.*, pp. 30 f.

10. Dryden, *Works*, ed. Sir Walter Scott (London, 1808), VI, 235; *Essays of John Dryden*, ed. W. P. Ker (Oxford, 1926), II, 110.

11. Quoted from George H. McKnight, *Modern English in the Making* (New York, 1928), p. 363.

12. *The Works of Shakespear* (Dublin, 1747), I, xx.

13. Bonamy Dobrée (ed.), *The Letters of Philip Dormer Stanhope, 4th Earl of Chesterfield* (London, 1932), V, 1877.

14. *Works* (Oxford and London, 1825), VII, 442; V, 20.

15. Mary Segar, "Dictionary Making in the Early Eighteenth Century," *RES*, VII (1931), 211.

16. *Works*, V, 53; G. B. Hill and L. F. Powell (eds.), *Life of Johnson* (Oxford, 1934–50), I, 298; see above, pp. 146–47.

17. Hill and Powell, *op. cit.*, I, 182; cf. III, 405.

18. P. 170.

19. *Works of Johnson* (Oxford, 1825), I, xxii.

20. *Diversions of Purley* (London, 1840), p. 119, n. 1. The work was originally published in two parts in 1786–98. For further discussion of Horne Tooke, see pp. 183–85 above.

21. Hill and Powell, *op. cit.*, I, 176, n. 2, 255, 535; *The R. B. Adam Library Relating to Dr. Samuel Johnson and His Era*, II (London and New York, 1929) [19]; Gove, *op. cit.*, pp. 307–9; see pp. 105–11 above.

22. Hill and Powell, *op. cit.*, I, 183; Joseph Wood Krutch, *Samuel Johnson* (New York, 1944), p. 124; Gove, *op. cit.*, pp. 308 f.; see pp. 111–14 above.

23. Gove, *op. cit.*, *passim;* see pp. 147–49 above.

24. *Works*, V, 247; Hill and Powell, *op. cit.*, III, 405.

25. Cf., for example, John Wilkins, *An Essay towards a Real Character, and a Philosophical Language* (London, 1668), sig. a2^r; Philip Miller, *The Gardener's Dictionary* (2d ed.; London, 1733), Preface; Ephraim Chambers, *Considerations Preparatory to a Second Edition of "Cyclopædia"* (London, n.d.), p. 3.

26. I (1755), 61–62.

27. Hill and Powell, *op. cit.*, I, 359.

28. Starnes and Noyes, *op. cit.*, pp. 56–57, 79, 100, 120–21.

29. *Ibid.*, pp. 56 f.

30. See Otto Funke, *Englische Sprachkunde* (Bern, 1950), p. 36.

31. *Fac-simile of the Sale Catalogue of Dr. Johnson's Library* (London, 1892), p. 28.

32. Starnes and Noyes, *op. cit.*, pp. 128–30, 164–68.

33. Tooke, *op. cit.*, p. 119, n. 1.

34. Starnes and Noyes, *op. cit.*, pp. 279–80.

35. L. F. Powell, "Johnson and the *Encyclopédie*," *RES*, II (1926), 335–37.

36. See Lowth's *A Short Introduction to English Grammar* (London, 1762), sigs. a2^v, a3^r. For further notes on the influence of Johnson's grammar and history, see pp. 177–81 above.

37. "Dissertatio epistolaris," pp. 148 ff.

38. *Dictionary* (London, 1755), "History," sig. F1^v.

39. *Ibid.*, sig. F2^r.

40. *Thesaurus*, I, i, 196, 222–25, 231; *Dictionary*, "History," sigs. E1^r, E2^r.

41. Marckwardt, *op. cit.*, p. 21; Adams, *op. cit.*, pp. 63–64.

42. Charles Carpenter Fries, *American English Grammar* (New York, cop. 1940), pp. 61–63.

43. Sig. a2^v.

44. See H. G. Baker, "The Contribution of John Wallis to the Methods and Materials of English Grammarians" (University of Michigan diss., 1937), *passim*.

45. *Thesaurus*, I, i, 10; "Grammar," sig. b1^r; James Greenwood, *An Essay towards a Practical English Grammar* (2d ed.; London, 1722), pp. 68 f.

46. Sig. a1^r.

47. *A Grammar of the English Tongue* (3d ed.; London, 1714), pp. 62, n. 1, 82.

48. So far as we know, this debt was first noted by Gustaf L. Lannert in his *An Investigation into the Language of "Robinson Crusoe" as Compared with That of Other 18th Century Works* (Uppsala, 1910), p. 67.

49. See the chapter on Johnson in Baker's dissertation cited in n. 44.

50. "Grammatica linguae Anglicanae," *Opera mathematica*, III (Oxford, 1699), 43–44; *Dictionary*, Preface, sig. A2^r; "Grammar," sig. c1^r.

51. Tooke, *op. cit.*, p. 119, n. 1.

52. Hill and Powell, *op. cit.*, I, 218 f.; Hill, *op. cit.*, II, 347 f.; *DNB*, *s.v.* "Chambers"; *Boswell's Note Book, 1776–1777* (London, 1925), p. 19.

53. Flasdieck, *op. cit.*, pp. 119 f.

54. Chambers, *op. cit.*, p. 4.

55. *Ibid.*, p. 3.

56. *Cyclopædia* (London, 1741–43), I, ii.

57. *Considerations*, p. 4.

58. *Cyclopædia*, I, xxiii, ii.

59. *Ibid.*, pp. xx–xxi.

60. *Ibid.*, pp. xv, xix.

61. *Ibid.*, p. xvii.

62. See the eds. of the *Vocabolario* published at Venice in 1623 and at Florence in 1691 and 1729—all of which we have examined—and the collected prefaces included in the *Dictionnaire* (7th ed.; Paris, 1884).

63. S. Haverkamp (ed.), *Sylloge altera scriptorum de linguæ Græcæ pronunciatione* (Leiden, 1740), p. 232.

64. Wilkins, *op. cit.*, p. 10.

65. *Cyclopædia*, I, xvii.

66. P. 41.

67. P. 376.

68. P. 273.

69. *Op. cit.*, p. ix.

70. *Esquisse d'une histoire de la langue anglaise* (Lyon, 1947), p. 165.

71. See Harold B. Allen, "Samuel Johnson and the Authoritarian Principle in Linguistic Criticism" (University of Michigan diss., 1940), pp. 169–71; and cf. p. 37 above.

72. Tooke, *op. cit.*, p. 119, n. 1.

73. Rypins, *op. cit.*, pp. 283–84; Warfel, *op. cit.*, p. 285.

74. The definition of *cough* is by no means a unique instance. Cf. the entries under *butter*, *drunkenness*, and *eclipse* in Johnson and in Chambers. The phrasing of these entries will be found somewhat similar, and Chambers' diction is at least as Latinate as Johnson's. Johnson's "idiosyncratic" definitions are amusingly misrepresented in the familiar anthology of Woods, Watt, and Anderson, *The Literature of England* (rev. ed.), I, 1029, which (mis)quotes the "typically Johnsonian" definition of *thunder*—a definition borrowed by Johnson from Muschenbroek and attributed to Muschenbroek by name in the *Dictionary*.

75. *Cyclopædia*, I, xx.

76. *Ibid.*, I, xxi.

77. See James Sledd, "A Footnote on the Inkhorn Controversy," *Studies in English*, XXVIII (Austin, 1949), 49–56; Starnes and Noyes, *op. cit.*, p. 43.

78. These and other words on which Johnson commented are listed in Allen's dissertation, cited in n. 71.

79. *Lexicography* (London, 1948), p. 14.

80. *Physico-grammatical Essay*, p. 11.

81. "Grammar," sig. c2r; Preface, sig. B1r.

82. Wheatley, *op. cit.*, pp. 11–12.

83. *Catalogue of Johnson's Library*, p. 13; the *Annotazioni sopra il Vocabolario degli accademici della Crusca* (Venice, 1698) was published as by Alessandro Tassoni, but the real author was Giulio Ottonelli. See the *Biographie universelle*, XVII, 331, and XXXI, 486.

84. See the Preface to the *Vocabolario* (Florence, 1729).

85. Starnes and Noyes, *op. cit.*, pp. 151–59; *Catalogue of Johnson's Library*, p. 22.

86. Evidence on this point may be found in the ledgers and accounts of the printers William and Andrew Strahan (cf. R. A. Austen-Leigh, *The Story of a Printing House* [2d ed.; London, 1912], *passim;* Austen-Leigh, "William Strahan and His Ledgers," *Library*, 4th ser., III [1923], 261–87). William Strahan's "Folio Book" marked "B 1739" is the Ledger A of the microfilm deposited in the Bodleian Library by William Todd. On fol. 60v of that ledger, under date of October, 1747, Strahan charges the partners in "Martin's English Dictionary" for printing 2,000 copies of 34½ sheets of that work, for transposing the articles and correcting copy, and for cuts. The charges were paid by James Hodges on July 28, 1749 (fol. 61r). The early date of the charges might seem to raise some doubt concerning Martin's possible use of the *Plan*.

87. According to Starnes and Noyes, Lloyd's dictionary "belongs in a discussion of a universal language rather than in that of lexicography" (*op. cit.*, p. 231). In a study on which we are now engaged, we hope to show that this conclusion is not altogether just.

88. See Gertrude E. Noyes, "The Beginnings of the Study of Synonyms in England," *PMLA*, LXVI (1951), 951–70.

Chapter II

1. We have made no attempt to trace editions of the *Plan* beyond 1755.

2. In 1779, Johnson remarked to Boswell: "Dodsley first mentioned to me the scheme of an English Dictionary; but I had long thought of it" (G. B. Hill and L. F. Powell [eds.], *Life of Johnson* [Oxford, 1934–50], III, 405). See *ibid.*, I, 71, n. 3, for a collection of statements about his rapidity of composition.

3. *Ibid.*, I, 166.

4. See pp. 60–61 above.

5. To facilitate the location of all passages cited in this essay which also appear, in one form or another, in the printed *Plan,* we include references, whenever they are appropriate, to the text in the Oxford edition (1825) (cited as "Oxford") of Johnson's *Works.*

6. These are pp. 1, 2, 3, 4, 5, and 10.

7. In his discussion of "The Text of Johnson's Letters" (*TLS*, September 26, 1942, p. 480), R. W. Chapman remarks that Johnson, whose hand is "almost always rapid," not infrequently "omits a word" (n. 6). Also, in the Introduction to his edition of the *Letters* (Oxford, 1952), he says that he has "preserved Johnson's occasional inadvertences, such as the omission or repetition of small words, partly because they furnish some indication of his state of health or his state of mind, partly because they show the sort of error to which he was prone" (I, viii).

8. For *as*, see p. 4, l. 4; for *be*, p. 6, l. 12 and p. 17, l. 1; for *to*, p. 7, l. 22 and p. 14, l. 2; for *can*, p. 17, l. 22.

9. The *to* was probably added by a reader (see the preceding note).

10. Oxford, V, 9–10.

11. *Ibid.*, p. 16.

12. The use of the comma after *simple* is clearly a mistake; it may indicate that the stroke connecting the *e* of *simple* and the *s* of *swain* is to be broken.

13. The appearance of the comma after *swain* suggests that it may have been added by Johnson while he was revising the fair copy.

14. Oxford, V, 12–13.

15. *Ibid.*, p. 18, l. 6.

16. *Ibid.*, p. 18, l. 8.

17. *Ibid.*, p. 20, l. 6.

18. *Ibid.*, p. 15, l. 18.

19. *Ibid.*, p. 8, l. 28.

20. *Ibid.*, p. 13, l. 24. In making this change, Johnson may have suddenly decided to alter his manner of expression.

21. *Ibid.*, p. 8, ll. 27–28; p. 14, l. 9.

22. For a recent study of the friendship between Johnson and Taylor see James Gray, "Dr. Johnson and the King of Ashbourne," *University of Toronto Quarterly*, XXIII (1954), 242–52.

23. See p. 53 above.

24. Chapman, *Letters*, I, 23.

25. See the account of Taylor's life in the *DNB.*

26. Oxford, V, 13, ll. 22–23.

27. *Ibid.*, p. 9, ll. 10–12.

28. *Ibid.*, p. 3, par. 3; p. 6, par. 3.

29. *Ibid.*, p. 8, ll. 34–35. Johnson later substituted *Brow* for *Plow* (see pp. 91–92 above).

30. On p. 6, the reader also writes "Queer. Sense" opposite Gay's "The Drunkard's flight [*sic*] require sono'rous Lays" (*The Shepherd's Week*, "Saturday," l. 4), cited, along with a line from *Paradise Lost* (Book II, l. 619), to show the difficulty of giving "rules" concerning the pronunciation of "polysyllables" (Oxford, V, 8, par. 3). Johnson later substituted another line from *Paradise Lost* for the one from Gay (see p. 71 above).

31. Oxford, V, 13, par. 3.

32. *Essay on Man*, ii, 17.

33. Oxford, V, 19, par. 1.

34. *Macbeth*, Act III, scene 1, line 102; *A Letter from Italy, to the Right Honourable Charles Lord Halifax* . . . , l. 118.

35. Oxford, V, 15, par. 9. Johnson later substituted another passage from *Macbeth* for that containing *file* (see p. 56 above).

36. Oxford, V, 13, par. 2.

37. See p. 55 above.

38. Oxford, V, 9, ll. 20–25.

39. The paragraph in the "Scheme" containing this remark was later deleted (see p. 66 above).

40. The definitions in Faber's *Thesaurus* are commonly written in Greek, German, and French, as well as in Latin.

41. See p. 55 above.

42. See, especially, pp. 11–44.

43. Oxford, V, 20, ll. 3–8.

44. See n. 8.

45. Oxford, V, 7, l. 36.

46. For a discussion of the numerous connections between various dictionaries produced by members of the Stephanus family and early English-Latin–Latin-English dictionaries see DeWitt T. Starnes, *Renaissance Dictionaries* (Austin, 1954), *passim.*

47. Although derivatives are listed alphabetically, they are defined only under root words, to which cross-references direct the reader.

48. Fair copy, p. 6; Oxford, V, 3, l. 25.

49. See p. 49.

50. Fair copy, p. 27; Oxford, V, 12–13.

51. Oxford, V, 15, par. 9.

52. *Ibid.*, p. 9, par. 4.

53. *Dictionary* (1st ed.), "Grammar," sig. a1r.

54. Oxford, V, 6, ll. 3 ff.

55. See "The Editor's Preface" to Harrison's edition of the *Dictionary* (London, 1786), and cf. pp. 127–29 above.

56. Oxford, V, 3, ll. 15–17.

57. *Ibid.*, p. 4, ll. 25–31.

58. *Ibid.*, pp. 7–8. In addition to the changes cited in the text, another piece of evidence suggests that Johnson had begun rewriting the "Scheme": the title of the piece has been crossed out by three short lines, apparently made by Johnson's own hand.

59. See p. 90.

60. Oxford, V, 1–3, 21–22; 4; 6–7; 16; 16–17; 19; 20.

61. *Ibid.*, p. 5. Johnson later substituted *peculiar Words* for *Dialect* (see p. 91 above).

62. Oxford, V, 5–6.

63. *Ibid.*, p. 5, par. 3. The difference between the number of words in pars. 12, 13, and the first part of 14 (a total of 159 words) and *one* estimate (117 words) of the number on the missing half of p. 3 of the "Scheme" suggests that the paragraph was added in the lost manuscript. But since another estimate might put the total number of words on p. 3 as high as 244 (which is the actual number on p. 4 of the unrevised "Scheme") and, consequently, the number on the missing part of the page at 157, it is clear that the paragraph may have appeared in the "Scheme."

64. Paragraph 13 of the "Scheme" (fair copy, par. 27) was presumably completed on the missing p. 8; the longer part, on p. 7, is almost identical to the corresponding part of par. 27 of the fair copy. Paragraph 14 of the "Scheme" (fair copy, par. 37) presumably began on the missing p. 9; the last part, on p. 10, is similar to the corresponding part of par. 37 of the fair copy.

65. See pp. 72–76 above.

66. See the first (quarto) edition (1747) of the *Plan* (Oxford, V, 14–15). W. R. Keast's recent argument ("Johnson's *Plan of a Dictionary:* A Textual Crux," *PQ*, XXXIII [1954], 341–47) that pars. 47–49 are not "a proper part of the final text" (p. 342) of the *Plan* seems, in the absence of further evidence, to be unconvincing. Professor Keast be-

lieves that Johnson intended to substitute the paragraphs dealing with *arrive* for those which treat *ground* but that, despite Johnson's intention, the "survivals" remained in the text. He rests his case largely on the "striking" "breakdown in the coherence" of the text at this point; at par. 47, he asserts, the "expository pattern" followed in this section of the work "breaks down" (p. 342). For our part, we continue to be impressed by the fact that, as Mr. Keast notes, these paragraphs are primarily illustrative and that Johnson is not consistent in the number of examples he presents either at various stages in the composition of the piece or, indeed, in other parts of the printed *Plan;* in the "Scheme," for instance, he gives one illustration of the "burlesque" sense of words, but in the fair copy the number is increased to two. We also attach more significance than does Mr. Keast to the fact that the first ("Scheme") version of these paragraphs differs markedly from the printed version; this indicates that, at least at one stage beyond the "Scheme," Johnson intended these paragraphs to be a part of the *Plan.* We are doubtful, too, that the breakdown of "coherence" is as striking as Mr. Keast believes it is; granted the illustrative nature of the paragraphs, the expository movement seems clear enough, although admittedly not so smooth as it might be. Almost any reader, we think, when he comes to the beginning of par. 47 ("*Ground*, the earth," etc.) would assume that Johnson is about to present an example parallel to that presented in par. 43 ("To *arrive*, to reach the shore," etc.), and he would know this to be true when he begins reading par. 48. Finally, and most important, we are disturbed (as is Mr. Keast) by Johnson's failure, on several different occasions, to delete three paragraphs which, according to Mr. Keast's theory, he had decided to omit at a fairly early stage in the composition of the *Plan;* as we point out (see pp. 67 f., 71 ff.), Johnson almost certainly revised at least parts of the fair copy before sending it to Taylor; he certainly revised at least parts of it after its return from the readers; and he certainly revised the proofs at least once.

67. Oxford, V, 3–4.

68. *Ibid.*, pp. 8–9.

69. It should be pointed out that the amanuensis, while making the fair copy, may have erred in combining the two paragraphs into one; in the first edition (p. 23) of the printed *Plan*, however, the paragraphing is the same as that in the fair copy. The text in the Oxford edition (V, 15) consists of two paragraphs.

70. The first part of par. 50, it will be recalled, presumably appeared on the missing page (32) of the fair copy.

71. Oxford, V, 6.

72. See pp. 71–76.

73. Oxford, V, 1, l. 14; 6, ll. 15–16; 19, l. 34.

74. *Ibid.*, p. 11, l. 8.

75. *Ibid.*, p. 19, ll. 30 ff.

76. *Ibid.*, p. 5, l. 4; p. 9, l. 15.

77. *Ibid.*, p. 4, l. 24; p. 14, l. 20.

78. Hill and Powell, *op. cit.*, I, 184 f. (see p. 51 above).

79. *Ibid.*, VI, 425 (see p. 98 above).

80. Johnson later changed *tralatitious* to *metaphorical* (see p. 91 above).

81. Oxford, V, 4, ll. 25 ff.; 8, par. 4; 11, l. 29.

82. See p. 91 above.

83. Oxford, V, 13, par. 2. The lines from Davies appear in *Nosce Teipsum*, ll. 119–20; for the source of the quotation from Addison, see n. 34.

84. The line from Milton appears in *Paradise Lost* (Book I, l. 540); for the source of the line from Gay, see n. 30.

85. Oxford, V, 3, ll. 30 ff. Johnson later rewrote the sentence (see p. 71 above).

86. For Chesterfield's note see pp. 91–93.

87. Oxford, V, 11, l. 24.

88. *Ibid.*, p. 14, ll. 13–16.

89. *Ibid.*, p. 12, par. 2.

90. Johnson makes no reference, in the first edition of the *Dictionary*, to this specific use of *make*.

91. *divide* should obviously be *decide*. Presumably Johnson did not notice this error until he was correcting the proofs of the *Plan* (of course, the printer may have caught it): *decide* appears in the first edition (p. 30, l. 6).

92. Oxford, V, 19, par. 3.

93. *Ibid.*, p. 1, l. 6. At some point in the revision of the fair copy, Johnson changed *employment* to *Drudgery*.

94. Oxford, V, 7, l. 28.

95. *Ibid.*, p. 12, l. 28.

96. *Ibid.*, p. 21, ll. 12–13.

97. *Ibid.*, p. 4, ll. 8–10; pp. 4–5, ll. 37, 1–3.

98. *Ibid.*, p. 1, l. 9.

99. Hill and Powell, *op. cit.*, I, 185; for the complete passage see p. 98 above.

100. "L'Allegro" (l. 80).

101. Oxford, V, 10, l. 23.

102. *Ibid.*, p. 21, l. 13.

103. *Ibid.*, p. 2, ll. 12–13. In this passage, also, Johnson substituted *Tongues* for *Languages*, perhaps in order to avoid the repetition of the latter, which is used in the following sentence.

104. Oxford, V, 3, l. 37; 7, ll. 11–12.

105. *Ibid.*, p. 5, ll. 22–23; p. 6, ll. 21–22. The latter passage is one of many which Johnson revised again while he was reading the proofs of the *Plan* (see pp. 76–78 above).

106. Oxford, V, 2, ll. 5–8; 12, ll. 22–24; 2, l. 17.

107. *Ibid.*, p. 1, ll. 12–14.

108. *Ibid.*, p. 6, ll. 13–16.

109. *Ibid.*, pp. 6–7.

110. The passage is from Joseph of Exeter's *De bello Troiano*, ll. 506–12. Johnson probably used the edition by J. Morus (London, 1675); the passage is on p. 23 of that edition.

111. Oxford, V, 6, ll. 7–8.

112. We have not been able to locate the quotation from the elegant author.

113. Oxford, V, 16, par. 3.

114. *Ibid.*, p. 20, ll. 33–36.

115. See p. 65.

116. We suggest that Strahan *may* have printed the first edition of the *Plan* because, as entries in his ledgers prove, he printed both the second (octavo) edition of the work and the first edition of the *Dictionary* itself (see pp. 83, 107 ff. above). Some of his ledgers for 1747 are apparently lost.

The evidence that the fair copy served as printer's copy consists of marks on pp. 12, 23, 34, and 44 which coincide exactly with the beginnings and endings of the signatures in the first edition. "The marking of the signatures," it has been said, is "the one infallible test" identifying printer's copy in the eighteenth century (Frederick A. Pottle, "Printer's Copy in the Eighteenth Century," *Papers of the Bibliographical Society of America*, XXVII [1933], 73). So far as we can tell, there are no other printer's marks on the fair copy. The verso of

p. 18 contains a series of arithmetical calculations, almost certainly in Johnson's hand, but we do not know what these refer to.

117. See p. 227 below.

118. Fair copy, pp. 4, 5; Oxford, V, 2, ll. 32–33; 3, l. 14.

119. Fair copy, pp. 15, 2; Oxford, V, 7, l. 24; 2, l. 5.

120. Oxford, V, 22.

121. This collation is based on an examination of a copy belonging to Herman W. Liebert. Although some earlier commentators (e.g., Robert F. Metzdorf, "Notes on Johnson's *Plan of a Dictionary*," *Library*, 4th ser., XIX [1938–39], 200) have doubted that the title-page is E2 folded back, examination of this copy, which is uncut and in a blue paper wrapper, shows that the title-page and E1 are conjugate.

122. "Johnson's *Plan of a Dictionary*," *RES*, II (1926), 216–18.

123. *Ibid.*; Metzdorf, *op. cit.*, pp. 198–201, 363; and Herman W. Liebert's unpublished paper, "The Bibliography of Johnson's *Plan of a Dictionary*," to which we are indebted.

124. The line division is different in a total of 8 lines (on pp. 2, 4, and 7).

125. The type in l. 1 on p. 34 has been "awkwardly leaded to fill the space" left by the removal of "the redundant *the*" (Liebert); cf. Metzdorf, *op. cit.*, p. 199.

126. We have also discovered two other variants: (1) the Cambridge University copy of the *Plan* has a large 1 instead of the right-hand bracket at the top of p. 18; thus: [181; (2) the Rosenbach copy has *likewlse*, instead of *likewise*, on p. 26, l. 1.

127. See Chapman, *op. cit.*, p. 217; Metzdorf, *op. cit.*, pp. 198, 200; R. W. Chapman and Allen T. Hazen, "Johnsonian Bibliography: A Supplement to Courtney," *Oxford Bibliographical Society Proceedings & Papers*, V (1936–39), 130.

128. The penetrating criticism and generous assistance of Professor Fredson Bowers and Professor Arthur Friedman have been invaluable to us in our discussion of the printing of the first edition of the *Plan*.

129. The 28 copies—5 "Chesterfield" and 23 "Non-Chesterfield" (of which 7 contain the error on p. 34)—on which our discussion is based include: 3 copies (including 1 "Chesterfield") belonging to Herman W. Liebert; 1 copy in the University of Chicago Library; and microfilms of these copies: 4 (including 1 "Chesterfield") in the British Museum, 4 (including 1 "Chesterfield") in the Yale University Library,

2 in the Harvard University Library, 1 in the Bodleian Library, 1 in the Cambridge University Library, 1 in the Library of Congress, 1 in the Hertford College Library (Oxford University), 1 belonging to the Historical Society of Pennsylvania, 1 in the Huntington Library, 1 ("Chesterfield") in the (London) University College Library, 1 in the University of Rochester Library, 1 belonging to the Rosenbach Company, and 1 in the Rylands Library. In addition, Mr. and Mrs. Donald F. Hyde have answered all our inquiries about the 4 copies (including 1 "Chesterfield") in the Hyde collection.

130. *General Advertiser* for March 20, 1747. The same announcement appears in later numbers of the *General Advertiser* and also in other newspapers (see p. 142 above).

131. Letter of Wray dated August 8, 1747, in British Museum Add. MS 35,401.

132. XXXIX, 233–34. The complete text of this brief review—which consists of a paragraph in the section entitled "NOUVELLES LITERAIRES. *DE LONDRES*." and which no one, apparently, has noted before—is as follows: "Il n'est pas surprenant que peu de Nations aient de bons Dictionnaires de leur langue. La tâche est aussi pénible que peu brillante, & convient mieux à une Société qu'à un particulier. C'est à leur Académie que les François doivent tous leurs Dictionaires [*sic*]. Quoiqu'un pareil établissement soit jusqu'ici simplement souhaité dans cette ville, un particulier travaille depuis quelque tems à un Dictionnaire complet, & il vient d'en publier le plan dans une Lettre à Mil. *Chesterfield*. Ce Seigneur accoutumé à favoriser les projets utiles, & connoissant mieux que personne les beautés & les difficultés de sa langue, a encouragé l'Auteur qui se nomme *Johnson*, à poursuivre un travail aussi ingrat. Celui-ci expose dans sa Lettre la méthode & les regles qu'il a dessein de suivre. On ne peut rien ajouter à la finesse de ses vues, & à la délicatesse des détails dans les quels il entre. Son Ecrit confirme que pour être bon Critique il faut être bon Philosophe. L'histoire des mots est liée avec celle de la succession des idées, & il ne faut pas moins de bon sens que de lecture pour suivre une langue dans ses progrès & dans ses bisareries, qui souvent cessent de l'être, lorsqu'on en démèle les raisons. Mr. *Johnson* aporte tout ce qu'il faut pour le succès, & ceux mème qui ne font pas de l'Anglois une étude particuliere ne liront pas sans fruit une Lettre écrite avec une pureté & une élégance peu communes. Si l'Ouvrage est dans le mème goût, les Anglois n'auront pas à se plaindre de l'avoir longtems attendu."

133. Benjamin Martin, *Miscellaneous Correspondence*, I (London, 1755), 86. Martin says: "As the Plan of this Work cannot but be sufficiently known from the great Numbers of it distributed *gratis* for several Years past, we shall only say, that in the Opinion of good Judges, the Work has great Merit, perhaps more than any other single Hand could have given it."

134. So far as we know, only D. Nichol Smith's bibliography of Johnson in the *CBEL* (II, 615) suggests that the date of the octavo was "probably" 1755.

135. XVI, 601–12.

136. The announcement about the *Dictionary* in the *Public Advertiser* for February 27, 1755, contains no mention of the *Plan*, but that for March 1 adds the note: "Where may be had, gratis, The Plan of this Dictionary, Address'd to the Right Hon. The Earl of Chesterfield." The same note also appears in the announcement printed in the *London Evening-Post* for March 1–4, 1755. Announcements in the *Public Advertiser* throughout most of March contain the same note, but the announcement for April 1, 1755, drops the offer of free copies of the *Plan.*

137. R. A. Austen-Leigh, *The Story of a Printing House* (2d ed.; London, 1912), facsimile opposite p. 24.

138. This collation is based on an examination of the copy belonging to Herman W. Liebert.

139. These include: 1 copy belonging to Herman W. Liebert, 1 copy in the Newberry Library; and microfilms of the following: 2 copies in the British Museum, 2 copies in the University of Texas Library, 1 copy in the Bibliothèque Nationale, 1 copy in the Bodleian Library, 1 copy in the Cambridge University Library, 1 copy in the Harvard University Library, 1 copy in the Rylands Library, and 1 copy in the Yale University Library. In addition, Mr. and Mrs. Donald F. Hyde have answered our inquiries about the 2 copies in the Hyde collection.

Chapter III

1. Bonamy Dobrée (ed.), *The Letters of Philip Dormer Stanhope, 4th Earl of Chesterfield* (London, 1932), I, 182–85.

2. See pp. 46–47.

3. Dobrée, *op. cit.*, I, 183.

4. C. E. Vulliamy, *Ursa Major* (London, 1946), p. 35; Joseph Wood

Krutch, *Samuel Johnson* (London, 1948), p. 117; Sidney L. Gulick, Jr., "Johnson, Chesterfield, and Boswell," in *The Age of Johnson: Essays Presented to Chauncey Brewster Tinker* (New Haven, 1949), pp. 329–40; Benjamin Boyce, "Johnson and Chesterfield Once More," *PQ*, XXXII (1953), 93–96.

5. For a discussion of the possible identity of this person see p. 51 above.

6. *Bibliotheca Boswelliana* (London, 1825), p. 99. Another comment about the fair copy is obviously incorrect: it is *not* the "Original Manuscript of the Plan of Johnson's Dictionary, addressed to Lord Chesterfield." As we have already pointed out (see pp. 66–68), the fair copy was prepared by an amanuensis from a manuscript of Johnson's which is now lost and which the amanuensis, to judge from the character of his mistakes, was not always able to decipher.

7. In the Introduction to the *Private Papers of James Boswell from Malahide Castle* (privately printed, 1928), Geoffrey Scott says that "the great majority" of the Johnsonian manuscripts listed in the *Bibliotheca*—the number is some twenty—"must have belonged to Boswell, though some few may have been purchased after his death" (I, 9). Mrs. Donald F. Hyde in her "History of the Johnson Papers" (*Publications of the Bibliographical Society of America*, XLV [1951], 106, 109 ff.) traces the "Scheme" and the fair copy of the *Plan* from the 1825 sale to the present but says nothing of their earlier movements (she tells us that, so far, she has been able to discover nothing about the previous history of the two documents).

8. John Wilson Croker (ed.), *Boswell's Life of Johnson: Including Their Tour to the Hebrides* (London, 1866), p. 57, n. 1. Earlier in the same note Croker expresses the opinion that only Robert Dodsley, not "a noble Lord," as Boswell has it, "communicated with" Chesterfield about the *Dictionary*.

9. (Oxford, 1887), I, 185, n. 2. Similarly, in his *Bibliography of Samuel Johnson* (Oxford, 1915), W. P. Courtney notes that "Mr. Croker had seen the draft which contained the remarks of his lordship and of another person: 'Johnson adopted all these suggestions' " (p. 20). The Chapman-Hazen supplement to Courtney (R. W. Chapman and Allen T. Hazen, "Johnsonian Bibliography: A Supplement to Courtney," *Oxford Bibliographical Society Proceedings & Papers*, V [1936–39], 130) directs the reader to the *Adam Catalogue* "for fac-

similes of Johnson's autograph draft and of the final manuscript with his autograph corrections."

10. G. B. Hill and L. F. Powell (eds.), *Life of Johnson* (Oxford, 1934–50), I, 185, n. 2.

11. *Op. cit.*, p. 331, n. 3.

12. Willard Connely, in *The True Chesterfield* (London, 1939), pp. 261, 489, comes nearest to being the honorable exception. He cites as his authority "photostats of the MS. in the R. B. Adam Library," quotes or paraphrases five of Chesterfield's comments on about the first "two-thirds of the Dedication," and adds that "he let the rest go, with only one or two minor marks"; yet with the evidence apparently before him, Connely can say that it was "a proof of the Dedication" which Johnson submitted to Chesterfield.

13. In his Introduction to the *Catalogue of the Johnsonian Collection of R. B. Adam* (privately printed, 1921), Professor Charles G. Osgood, while discussing the manuscripts of the *Plan*, comments as follows: "The phrases of address" to Chesterfield "are all wanting in the first draft except a casual one near the beginning. This is enough, however, to show that the purpose of dedicating to him lay in Johnson's mind at least the greater part of a year if not longer, and that it was not altogether so unpremeditated as Boswell's account leaves one to infer" (p. 14). Professor Osgood, whose remarks are reprinted in *The R. B. Adam Library Relating to Dr. Samuel Johnson and His Era* (I [London and New York, 1929], vii), seems to imply that Johnson had decided to dedicate the *Plan* to Chesterfield before April 30, 1746; but this, as we point out (pp. 58, 89, 96), is very unlikely.

14. See chap. ii above.

15. "Scheme," p. 4.

16. Italics ours.

17. The comments of Professor James L. Clifford have been useful to us here and elsewhere, but he is not responsible for our interpretation.

18. The evidence on which this conclusion is based may be stated briefly. The first version of the sentence quoted in the text includes the phrase *settled, and settled*, which was presumably written before April 30, 1746. Part of this phrase was queried, supposedly after April 30, by one of the readers (perhaps John Taylor; see p. 51) of the "Scheme," who drew a line above the second *settled*. Later Johnson crossed out the line, and still later he struck out the whole passage containing the

phrase and substituted for it the passage referring to Chesterfield's views on spelling.

19. In the fair copy as revised by Johnson (pp. 12 f.), the sentence reads: "When all the Words are selected and arranged, the first part of the work to be considered is the ORTHOGRAPHY, which was long vague and uncertain, and at last when its fluctuation ceased, was in many Cases settled but by accident, and in which, according to your Lordship's observation [changed from *as your Lordship observes* by Johnson's own hand] there is still great Uncertainty among the best critics, nor is it easy to State a Rule by which we may decide between custom and Reason, or between the Equiponderant Authorities of Writers alike eminent for Judgment and Accuracy." In the quarto edition (p. 9), the sentence is much the same: "When all the words are selected and arranged, the first part of the work to be considered is the ORTHOGRAPHY, which was long vague and uncertain, which at last, when its fluctuation ceased, was in many cases settled but by accident, and in which, according to your Lordship's observation, there is still great uncertainty among the best critics; nor is it easy to state a rule by which we may decide between custom and reason, or between the equiponderant authorities of writers alike eminent for judgment and accuracy."

20. We have been guided in our search by Sidney L. Gulick, Jr., *A Chesterfield Bibliography to 1800* (Chicago, 1935), pp. 90–95.

21. See J. H. Neumann, "Chesterfield and the Standard of Usage in English," *MLQ*, VII (1946), 468–69.

22. See Dobrée, *op. cit.*, I, 143. In a letter to Lord Hardwicke dated October 28, 1746, the Duke of Newcastle says: "Chesterfield accepts" (Sir Richard Lodge [ed.], *Private Correspondence of Chesterfield and Newcastle, 1744–46* [London, 1930], p. 147).

23. We owe this observation to Professor W. R. Keast.

24. "In the revised manuscript copy of Johnson's *Plan of a Dictionary*," Mr. Adam pointed out a good many years ago, "Chesterfield's notes are easily distinguished by his handwriting" (*The R. B. Adam Library*, Vol. III, "Corrections and Additions"). For another specimen of Chesterfield's writing see also *ibid.*, III, 61 ff. We have taken the precaution of comparing the comments on the fair copy with other specimens of Chesterfield's hand in the Bodleian Library. To facilitate location of passages from the *Plan*, we give references both to the fair copy (cited as "FC") and, as in the preceding chapter, to the Oxford edition (1825) of Johnson's *Works.*

25. The second reader also commented on this word (see pp. 69–70 above).

26. FC, reverse of p. 7; Oxford, V, 4.

27. FC, reverse of p. 8; Oxford, V, 5.

28. See p. 69 above for the second reader's comment on *flexions*.

29. FC, reverse of p. 22; Oxford, V, 11.

30. FC, reverse of p. 16; Oxford, V, 8. Earlier, the first reader of the "Scheme" had written *plough* in the margin opposite this passage (see p. 52 above).

31. FC, reverse of p. 15; Oxford, V, 8.

32. FC, reverse of p. 20; Oxford, V, 10.

33. *A Letter from Italy, to the Right Honourable Charles Lord Halifax* . . . , l. 118.

34. "Davis" is Sir John Davies, and the quotation is from *Nosce Teipsum*, ll. 119–20. The bracketed parts of Johnson's sentence were on a corner of a page which has now been torn off; we have supplied them from the quarto edition.

35. The second reader thought the usage improper in both Addison and Davies (see p. 69 above). Readers of the "Scheme" also commented on the phrase (see pp. 52–53).

36. FC, reverse of p. 27; Oxford, V, 13.

37. FC, reverse of p. 17; Oxford, V, 9. Pope's couplet is from "Epistle V: To Robert, Earl of Oxford, and Earl Mortimer," ll. 9–10; Rowe's is from the Prologue (ll. 3–4) to *The Fair Penitent.*

38. "Sir William Yonge sent me word that" *great* "should be pronounced so as to rhyme to *seat*, and that none but an Irishman would pronounce it *grait*" (Hill and Powell, *op. cit.*, II, 161).

39. See pp. 68–71.

40. Cf. n. 28.

41. *divide* should clearly be *decide* (see p. 216, n. 91).

42. FC, reverse of p. 40; Oxford, V, 19.

43. Dobrée, *op. cit.*, I, 120, 143, 161; III, 656, 760–64, 771, 773, 786, 1068, 1078 f., 1096, n. 1, 1113, 1120, 1167, 1182 f.

44. See Hill and Powell, *op. cit.*, I, 182; III, 405; *The Letters of Samuel Johnson*, ed. R. W. Chapman (Oxford, 1952), I, 69 (". . . it was by his [Dodsley's] recommendation that I was employed in the work").

45. Hill and Powell, *op. cit.*, I, 535.

46. FC, pp. 3 f.; Oxford, V, 2.

47. Dobrée, *op. cit.*, I, 183, 207; Ralph Straus, *Robert Dodsley* (London and New York, 1910), pp. 43, 51, 67, 200, and *passim.*

48. We have no way of estimating the frequency of the correspondence between Chesterfield and Dodsley. So far as we know, only three letters have survived—two by Dodsley, dated "*Dec.* 19th [1757]" and "Jan. 5th," 1758 (Straus, *op. cit.*, p. 224); one by Chesterfield, dated "*Bath*, 22 *December*, 1757" (Dobrée, *op. cit.*, V, 2273). In quoting (pp. 200–201) from Chesterfield's letter of December 22, Straus says that it was written late in 1758. He seems to be unaware that the letter is almost certainly an answer to Dodsley's of December 19, 1757, from which he quotes at length (p. 224). All three letters deal with the production of Dodsley's tragedy *Cleone.*

49. Hill and Powell, *op. cit.*, I, 183.

50. In the *General Advertiser* for March 20, 1747, the *Dictionary* is advertised as "*now Preparing for the* PRESS, *and in good Forwardness.*"

51. See pp. 57–58 for additional evidence of Johnson's first steps in transforming the "Scheme" into the *Plan.*

52. Hill and Powell, *op. cit.*, I, 184 f.

53. Dr. L. F. Powell suggests that the "noble Lord" was "perhaps William, 3rd Earl of Jersey" (*ibid.*, VI, 425), who was Whitehead's patron, and in whose London house the poet was apparently living (as a tutor to Jersey's son) in 1747 (see the account of Whitehead's life in the *DNB;* Hill and Powell, *op. cit.*, I, 31).

54. Hill and Powell, *op. cit.*, I, 259–61; IV, 332.

55. Letter of Birch dated August 8, 1747, in British Museum Add. MS 35,397; letter of Wray (cited also on pp. 82, 143) dated August 8 (Add. MS 35,401).

56. For the full text of the review in the *Bibliothèque raisonnée* see p. 219, n. 132. For further discussion of Maxwell's proposals see pp. 144–46.

57. Hill and Powell, *op. cit.*, I, 264 f.

58. See p. 82 above.

59. See pp. 82–83.

60. *The World*, No. 100 (November 28, 1754).

61. Cf. the "celebrated letter."

62. Hill and Powell, *op. cit.*, I, 264 f. At about the same time, of course, Johnson also substituted *patron* for *garret* in l. 160 of *The Vanity of Human Wishes* (*The Poems of Samuel Johnson*, ed. David Nichol Smith and Edward L. McAdam [Oxford, 1941], p. 28). According to

Straus (*op. cit.*, p. 356), Vol. IV of Dodsley's *Collection of Poems*, in which the text of the poem containing the substitution first appeared, was published on March 18, 1755.

63. Hill and Powell, *op. cit.*, I, 261–63.

64. *Ibid.*, I, 264 f.

65. British Museum Add. MS 35,350.

66. XVI, 601–12. Cf. p. 82 above.

67. *Gentleman's Magazine*, Vol. XXIV (December, 1754); *London Magazine*, Vol. XXIII (December, 1754); and *Scots Magazine*, Vol. XVI (December, 1754). Cf. p. 82 above.

68. XVI, 565. Chesterfield's name is also given at the beginning of the reprint in the *Gentleman's Magazine* (XXIV, 551).

69. XVII (1755), 91; cf. pp. 135–36 above.

70. A. De Morgan, "Dr. Johnson and Dr. Maty," *Notes and Queries*, 2d ser., IV (July–December, 1857), 341.

Chapter IV

1. Strahan's "Folio Book" marked "B 1739," fol. 67^{v}. This book, as we have said, is the Ledger A of the microfilm deposited in the Bodleian Library by William Todd.

2. "Folio Book" (Todd's Ledger A), fols. 71^{v}, 85^{v}.

3. "Folio Book," fol. 86^{r}.

4. British Museum Add. MS 35,397, fols. 140, 222, 307^{r}. The facts which we have here presented are obviously relevant to the dating of the letter, No. 38 in Dr. Chapman's edition, in which Johnson asks Strahan "to go to Mr Millar and represent to him our manner of going on, and inform him that I know not how to manage, I pay three and twenty shillings a week to my assistants, in truth without having much assistance from them, but they tell me they shall be able to fall better in method, as indeed I intend they shall. The point is to get two Guineas" (R. W. Chapman [ed.], *The Letters of Samuel Johnson* [Oxford, 1952]). In his note (I, 41), Chapman dates this letter "not later than Apr. '50."

5. "Folio Book," fols. 67^{v}, 81^{v}, 85^{v}, 86^{r}.

6. G. B. Hill and L. F. Powell (eds.), *Life of Johnson* (Oxford, 1934–50), I, 183, 186, 189, 304.

7. *Ibid.*, p. 255.

8. In the *Bibliotheca Boswelliana*, Lot 3157 was "Five Letters ad-

dressed to Dr. Johnson; one containing . . . Evidence of the deplorable Circumstances of Dr. Johnson in 1751." Several times during that year, Johnson was compelled to ask John Newbery for small sums (Chapman, *op. cit.*, Nos. 32–34).

9. Chapman, *op. cit.*, No. 35.

10. The statements of the early biographers, several of whom seem to touch on this same matter, are conflicting. Boswell's story of the final exchange with Millar is familiar: "Mr. Andrew Millar, bookseller in the Strand, took the principal charge of conducting the publication of Johnson's Dictionary; and as the patience of the proprietors was repeatedly tried and almost exhausted, by their expecting that the work would be completed within the time which Johnson had sanguinely supposed, the learned authour was often goaded to dispatch, more especially as he had received all the copy-money, by different drafts, a considerable time before he had finished his task. When the messenger who carried the last sheet to Millar [*sic;* not Strahan] returned, Johnson asked him, 'Well, what did he say?'—'Sir, (answered the messenger) he said, thank God I have done with him.' 'I am glad (replied Johnson, with a smile,) that he thanks God for any thing' " (Hill and Powell, *op. cit.*, I, 287).

Boswell's story does not fit badly with Johnson's letter, and one might be tempted to find in it a motive for Johnson's alleged request that his pay be increased: the job had outlasted the wages, and Johnson had to live. His contract had commenced by midsummer of 1746 (Chapman, *op. cit.*, I, 29), so that his optimistic three years had already become more than five; yet Chapman doubts that he had, "so early as '51, 'received all the copy-money' " (*ibid.*, p. 38). Two of the earliest biographers, Thomas Tyers and William Cooke, seem to have had no such doubts. In *A Biographical Sketch of Dr. Samuel Johnson* (1785; publication No. 34 of the Augustan Reprint Society), Tyers reports: "The money was all gone before the task was completed. . . . A refreshing fee was perpetually necessary . . . to the amount of three hundred additional pounds. . . . When Johnson came to settle with his employers, said Andrew Millar, they produced their receipts for the money they had advanced, most of which were for small sums. He was confounded to find the balance against himself . . . and that he had been working nine years for nothing. . . . The booksellers generously made him a present of the difference" (pp. 7–8). According to Cooke, whose *Life of Johnson* (1785) was printed anonymously for the bookseller Kearsley,

Johnson, while making the *Dictionary*, "found the money all expended before the work was finished. In this dilemma, he called upon the Booksellers for an additional *five hundred pounds;* which was objected to on their part, and, by some, called an *imposition*, as departing from the original agreement. He was then obliged to tell them 'the Work must be suspended:' but this had no effect; and a law-suit was talked of for some time: at last, after much grumbling, they made a virtue of necessity, and paid him the money" (*The Life of Samuel Johnson, LL.D.* [London, 1785], pp. 40* f.). Cooke repeats this anecdote as one which had been often told and much discussed.

A very similar version appeared a little later in the life of Johnson in Harrison's edition of the *Dictionary*, p. 9: "In the course of his arduous task, Johnson finding himself, with all his exertions, most miserably poor, applied to the booksellers for an augmentation of the agreed price; this was not only refused, but he was menaced with a suit in equity, to compel him to proceed under the original contract: but, at length, finding he despised their threats, and convinced that nothing less than a compleat acquiescence could induce him to go on, they prudently put the best face on the business, and acceded to his proposition. It was probably at a meeting to settle this new arrangement, and not at the conclusion of the work, that Johnson had received a trifle more than he would have been entitled to from the first agreement, which was then allowed him, with the addition of a tavern supper; after which he was to proceed at so much a sheet, as the best possible way of avoiding any future misunderstanding."

Harrison's "Life" is a poor performance, distorted by his bitter rivalry with Longman and the other proprietors of the *Dictionary;* his remarks on the tavern supper are intended to refute Sir John Hawkins' account of the booksellers' liberality and of the dinner at which they produced receipts to show that they had paid Johnson more than his contract demanded. Of this sum, Hawkins had written, "Johnson, who was no very accurate accountant, thought a great part would be coming to him on the conclusion of the work; but upon producing, at a tavern-meeting for the purpose of settling, receipts for sums advanced to him, which were indeed the chief means of his subsistence, it was found, not only that he had eaten his cake, but that the balance of the account was greatly against him" (Sir John Hawkins, *Life of Samuel Johnson* [London, 1787], p. 344). The booksellers, Hawkins concluded, generously forgave the debt and paid for the "entertainment" at the tavern.

Hawkins' version, with its emphasis on the booksellers' generosity, may be considered in some sense "official"; it was repeated by Arthur Murphy, who wrote his *Essay* at the request of the "proprietors of Johnson's Works," including Longman, Harrison's rival. Murphy on Johnson's overpayment for the *Dictionary* is brief and to the point: "For his subsistence, during the progress of the work, he had received at different times the amount of his contract; and when his receipts were produced to him at a tavern-dinner, given by the booksellers, it appeared, that he had been paid a hundred pounds and upwards more than his due" (*An Essay on the Life and Genius of Samuel Johnson, LL.D.* [London, 1792], p. 78).

One more account, again by a rather untrustworthy witness, is perhaps worth quoting. In the *Gentleman's Magazine*, LXIX (1799), 1171, a correspondent who signs himself "W. N." writes that at the time when Francis Stewart was helping Johnson with the explanation of "low cant phrases," "the Doctor was, in the printing-house phrase, *out of town*, that is, had received more money than he had produced MS. for." In order to exert some pressure, "the proprietors restricted him in his payments, and would answer no more demands from him than at the rate of a guinea for every sheet of MS copy he delivered; which was paid him by Mr. Strahan [*sic;* not Millar] on delivery; and the Doctor readily agreed to this." Though W. N.'s remarks do not maintain a consistently high level of accuracy, his claim should be noted that he was somehow employed in the business of Strahan's payments to Johnson; and at least his reference to Stewart rings true, for it was Stewart who took Johnson the proprietors' message which provoked the threat of a strike.

Perhaps, then, something can be made of the conflicting statements of the biographers; perhaps they are not hopelessly conflicting. It is clear that the proprietors had no reason to goad Johnson to dispatch after April, 1753, at the latest. By that time he had finished the first volume of the *Dictionary;* and the printing of the second volume, which overlapped that of the first, was done in haste (Chapman, *op. cit.*, I, 41 n.). Late 1751, and 1752, are likely dates for the most energetic goading. When the goading, however, occurred as effect, its cause, the running-out of the copy money, must also have operated; so that if Chapman is right in thinking that the copy money had not run out by November, 1751, it may have run out not too long afterward. Johnson's threat to strike would then force the proprietors to do one of three things: pay him a regular weekly stipend, pay him for every sheet of copy that he turned in, or do both. Payment by the sheet would be to their interest; until his progress became more rapid, payment by the week would be to Johnson's. Any likely compromise would probably involve an ultimate shift to payment by the sheet—a shift which several of the biographers report.

Conjecturally, it might be said that when Johnson's work took longer than he had expected and than the proprietors thought proper, they threatened to cut off his weekly payments. He had already made up his mind that something must be done to alleviate his situation, and replied with a threat to strike. After some skirmishing, in which tempers were a little ruffled, a new understanding was reached. Johnson was paid for copy on delivery, and in the end received considerably more than his original contract had specified.

11. "Folio Book," fol. 85^{v}.

12. *Ibid.*, fol. 86^{r}.

13. *Ibid.*, fol. 81^{v}.

14. W. N. in the *Gentleman's Magazine*, LXIX (1799), 1172.

15. Cf. Chapman, *op. cit.*, Nos. 52, 53, and 56, and Chapman's notes on them.

16. R. A. Austen-Leigh, *The Story of a Printing House* (2d ed.; London, 1912), facsimile opposite p. 24. The facsimile reproduces fol. 10^{r} of what Strahan calls his "Little 8vo." (Ledger B in Todd's microfilm). The entry clearly summarizes earlier records of which some seem now to be lost.

17. Giuseppe Baretti, *Epistolario* (Bari, 1936), I, 98; Lacy Collison-Morley, *Giuseppe Baretti* (London, 1909), pp. 88–90.

18. Chapman, *op. cit.*, Nos. 52 and 53, with Chapman's notes.

19. *Ibid.*, Nos. 56, 62, 63, and 64, again with Chapman's notes.

20. *Public Advertiser*, February 27, 28; March 1 ff.; April 1; *London Evening-Post*, March 1–4 ff.; March 29–April 1 ff.; *London Gazette*, March 18–22, 22–25.

21. Cf. nn. 16 and 20.

22. *Public Advertiser*, October 10, 1755.

23. W. R. Keast, "The Preface to *A Dictionary of the English Language:* Johnson's Revision and the Establishment of the Text," *Studies in Bibliography: Papers of the Bibliographical Society of Virginia*, V (1952–53), 129–46.

24. Cf. Philip B. Gove, "Notes on Serialization and Competitive

Publishing," *Oxford Bibliographical Society Proceedings & Papers*, V (1936–39), 305–22; and see pp. 147–49 above.

25. Cf. pp. 147–49 above.

26. Chapman, *op. cit.*, No. 72: "The Dictionary sells well."

27. For other views, cf. R. W. Chapman and Allen T. Hazen, "Johnsonian Bibliography: A Supplement to Courtney," *Oxford Bibliographical Society Proceedings & Papers*, V (1936–39), 138; Gove, *op. cit.*, p. 309; Hill and Powell, *op. cit.*, I, 290, n. 1.

28. Hill and Powell, *op. cit.*, I, 305.

29. *Jackson's Oxford Journal*, June 7, 1755; *London Evening-Post*, June 5–7; *Public Advertiser*, June 6; etc.

30. See, for example, the *London Evening-Post* from June 14–17 to December 11–13, 1755.

31. Cf. the advertisements, devoted chiefly to the newly published octavo abridgment, in the *London Evening-Post* throughout January, 1756.

32. "Little 8vo." (Todd's Ledger B), fol. 59^{r}.

33. Todd's Ledger D, fol. 28^{r}.

34. Todd's Ledger E, fol. 44^{v}.

35. If the printing of the second edition or the printing of complete copies of the second edition was *finished* by this time, the edition had not only been planned but partially printed before April 15. The Scott-Bailey began printing *after* that date, unless unpublished sheets of the Johnson had got into the wrong hands.

36. Todd's Ledgers A, fol. 91^{v}; B, fol. 9^{r}; and D, fols. 20^{v}–21^{r}.

37. "Folio Book" (Todd's Ledger A), fol. 97^{v}.

38. Todd's Ledgers B (fols. 16^{r}, 37^{r}, 60^{r}), D (fols. 23^{v}, 41^{r}), E (fols. 25^{r}, 46^{r}), and F (fol. 46^{r}).

39. Hill and Powell, *op. cit.*, II, 155.

40. Chapman, *op. cit.*, No. 295.

41. *Ibid.*, Nos. 268, 275.1, 277, 278, 278.1; cf. also Hill and Powell, *op. cit.*, II, 143, n. 3.

42. Book K in Todd's microfilm, fols. 9 ff.

43. Todd's Ledger D, fol. 28^{r}.

44. Hill and Powell, *op. cit.*, II, 498 (Appendix B).

45. Keast, *op. cit.*

46. Typical examples of Johnson's revisions may be found under *abiding* n.s., *ableness*, *abolishment*, *abominable*, *abominably*, *abominate*, *abomination*, *abortion*, *abortive*, *abortment*, *above* prep., *bezoar*, *but* conj.,

cardinal's flower, *chill* adj., *declaratory*, *draw* v.n., *drill* v.a., *fated*, *follow* v.a., *have*, *hold* v.a., etc. For the text of the Preface see Keast, *op. cit.*; and for additions to the grammar cf. the last paragraph on nouns and the last paragraph before "Etymology." Errors (mostly negligible) are introduced or left uncorrected under *act* n.s., sense 5; *after* adv., sense 1; *air* v.a., sense 1; *assert* v.a., sense 2; *defluxion; dubious;* etc. The confusion in the alphabetical order beginning with *fire* n.s. was in the first edition and remained through the sixth; the fourth edition repeats or introduces a surprising number of small errors between *unassailable* and *unpardoned*, some of which the fifth or sixth corrected. For further comment and illustration see Arthur Sherbo, "Dr. Johnson's Revision of His Dictionary," *PQ*, XXXI (1952), 372–82, to which we are indebted.

47. Unfortunately, the catalogue is hard to come by; Sotheby and Company, who answered our questions with their usual courtesy, have no copy on their own premises. Substantial quotations from the catalogue are given, however, in the *Bulletin of the John Rylands Library*, XII (1928), 9, and in *Book-Prices Current*, XLII (October, 1927–August, 1928), 519.

48. Alfred J. Horwood, "The Manuscripts of the Rev. Walter Sneyd, of Keele Hall, Co. Stafford," *Third Report of the Royal Commission on Historical Manuscripts* (London, 1872), Appendix, p. 290.

49. Aleyn Lyell Reade, *Johnsonian Gleanings* (London, 1909–52), I, 14; II, 98; III, 67–69, 129; IV, 137, 145–46; and *passim;* Reade, *The Reades of Blackwood Hill* (London, 1906), pp. 238–39, 245; Hopkins, *Dr. Johnson's Lichfield* (New York, 1952), *passim.*

50. Our remarks on Johnson's sale catalogue have profited from the generous criticism of Dr. L. F. Powell, though he is in no way responsible for them.

51. On the Sotheby facsimile page, the fourth sense of *abomination* is printed, "The cause of pollution"; at the end of the definition, Johnson has written, "a Scriptural sense." In the fourth edition, "The cause of pollution" has become sense 5, but without the addition. Similarly, the fourth edition adds another sense of *abortive*, of which no hint appears in the facsimile. The rearrangement of the quotations under this word, in the fourth edition, is quite different from the rearrangement which the facsimile indicates.

52. We are at work on a detailed study of the Museum copy. W. P. Courtney notes its existence (*Bibliography of Samuel Johnson* [Oxford,

1915], p. 55) but describes it wrongly as "an imperfect copy" of the third edition "from 'A' to 'Jailer.'"

53. Our whole discussion makes it plain that sheets 2N through 3U1 do not belong to the fourth or any later edition. They cannot belong to the second edition, since in them the weekly numbers of that edition are nowhere indicated. They are not of the third edition, since they do not have the shortened references; that is, where the third edition has simply "*Bacon*," "*Milton*," "*Shakespeare*," or the like, the Museum sheets have "*Bacon's Essays*," "*Milton's Comus*," "*Shakesp. Henry* VI," etc. On the other hand, press figures, catchwords, and signatures are identical with those in the first edition, from which the collation of scattered pages reveals no differences. The effectiveness of such tests appears from the fact that they immediately and obviously distinguish an undoubted third edition from an undoubted first edition.

54. Though the family affinities of this gentleman were somewhat involved, he seems to have been a relation of the Pigotts of Chetwynd, an old Shropshire family, who, in turn, were somehow related to the Sneyds of Keele and whose extensive connections lead again to the fringes of Johnson's acquaintance. Cf. MSS Top. Salop. c. 5, fol. 39^{v}, and Pigott e. 2, fol. 9, in the Bodleian.

55. Austen-Leigh, *op. cit.*, facsimile opposite p. 24.

56. We owe this information to Professor Edward Robertson, Librarian of the John Rylands Library, and Dr. Frank Taylor, Keeper of Manuscripts there. In a search of the eighteenth-century correspondence among the Sneyd MSS, which the Rylands Library now holds, and an examination of the library papers of Ralph Sneyd (d. 1870) and his brother the Rev. Walter Sneyd (d. 1888), Dr. Taylor found nothing else of any relevance.

57. *General Evening Post*, October 1–4, 1785; *Morning Chronicle, and London Advertiser*, October 5.

58. Book J in Todd's microfilm, *passim;* British Museum Add. MS 38,730 (indexed); William H. Peet, "Booksellers' Sales in the Eighteenth Century," *Notes and Queries*, 7th ser., IX (January–June, 1890), 301; Cyprian Blagden, "Booksellers' Trade Sales, 1718–1768," *Library*, 5th ser., V (1951), 243–57.

59. Our account is based on the *General Evening Post* (hereafter cited as "*GEP*") and the *Morning Chronicle, and London Advertiser* ("*C & A*"), for October–January, 1785–86.

60. *C & A*, October 12, 13, 18, 22, 1785; *GEP*, November 29–December 1, 1785; etc.

61. *C & A*, October 11, 12, 15, 18–20, November 1, 14, 16, 17, 30, December 3, 5, 12, 31; *GEP*, October 11–13, 25–27, November 1–3, 12–15, 24–26, November 29–December 1, December 1–3, 8–10, 17–20, 24–27; etc.

62. *C & A*, October 14, 17, 24, 26, 28, November 26, December 3, January 10; *GEP*, October 13–15, 15–17, 20–22, 22–25, 25–27, November 3–5, 24–26, December 3–6.

63. Frederick Whiley Hilles (ed.), *Letters of Sir Joshua Reynolds* (Cambridge, 1929), pp. 140–41; Austen-Leigh, *op. cit.*, pp. 32 f.

64. Todd's Ledger F, fols. 96^{v}–97^{r}.

65. *C & A*, October 18, 22.

66. Cf. the life of Johnson in Harrison's edition of the *Dictionary;* also *C & A*, October 15 and November 1.

67. *C & A*, October 24.

68. Todd's *Johnson's Dictionary* (London, 1818), I, iii–vi.

69. In the Rylands *Bulletin* for 1955 we more fully discuss the Reynolds copy and its use by the proprietors.

70. Inscription in the first volume.

71. In the left-hand margin, by the quotation from Tillotson under sense 2 of *eat* v.a., Johnson wrote:

"eating cares
Lydian airs   Milton";

the sixth edition copies mechanically:

"*Eating* cares,
Lydian airs.   *Milton.*"

72. In the left-hand margin, by the quotation under *declaratory*, Johnson wrote "in law"; his note was too obscure to be used in the sixth edition. He changed the accents on *predicable* n.s. and *predicament*, but the sixth edition accents the words as the fourth had done. Presumably, such minute changes might more easily be overlooked by a page-scanning copyist than by a compositor. It must be admitted, however, that other failures to introduce Johnson's corrections into the sixth edition cannot be explained in this way.

73. E.g., in par. 24 of the Preface, the fourth edition has the reading "a perpetual repetition by one general acknowledgment"; the fifth,

sixth, and seventh have "a *general* repetition . . ." (italics ours). The statement of our hypothesis, of course, is deliberately simplified.

74. He corrected the spelling of *unassailable*, combined the two entries for *ungentleness* into one, rightly inserted *not* before *cancelled* in the second definition of *unpardoned*, several times restored the alphabetical order, etc. The seventh edition corrects some errors that remain in the sixth, and perhaps some corrections were made while the sixth edition was passing through the press. We have considered the possibility that in the entries after *Umbo*, differences between the fourth and sixth editions might derive, in various ways, from lost Johnsonian corrections; but collation throughout the letter *U* (*V*) reveals no unmistakably Johnsonian change.

75. This chapter was written in January, 1954, repeatedly revised, and finally submitted to the publisher in the autumn. Meanwhile, in the spring, we had learned the present location of the Sneyd copy, had addressed to Col. Richard Gimbel the first of several requests for possible information, and had discussed the problem of Johnson's revisions with friends and colleagues. Since Col. Gimbel found himself unable to answer our questions about the Sneyd copy or to permit us to examine it, we learned only that it might possibly be exhibited at Yale University in April, 1955; and our arrangements for publication were already complete when Mr. Herman W. Liebert informed us that Col. Gimbel had confirmed his earlier tentative consent to the exhibition. In January, 1955, we still do not know the conditions under which the exhibition will be held. It seems best, therefore, to let our speculations stand as they were written, when Col. Gimbel himself could give no assurance that further information concerning the Sneyd copy would be available in the foreseeable future. To suppress them would only extend the duplication of effort which already seems inevitable.

Chapter V

1. Vedder M. Gilbert, "The Altercations of Thomas Edwards with Samuel Johnson," *JEGP*, LI (1952), 326–35. Our account, however, is based directly on Edwards' manuscript copies of his letters.
2. MS Bodl. 1012, p. 187.
3. *Ibid.*, pp. 208 ff.
4. *Ibid.*, p. 211.
5. XVII, 91.

6. G. B. Hill and L. F. Powell (eds.), *Life of Johnson* (Oxford, 1934–50), I, 285.

7. Gertrude E. Noyes, "The Critical Reception of Johnson's *Dictionary* in the Latter Eighteenth Century," *MP*, LII (1955), 191: "Johnson is his own best critic."

8. *London Quarterly Review*, XI (1858), 74.

9. A. F. M. Willich, *Three Philological Essays, Chiefly Translated from the German of John Christopher Adelung* (London, 1798), p. clxxi.

10. *European Magazine*, LI (1807), 45.

11. Allen Walker Read, "Projected English Dictionaries, 1755–1828," *JEGP*, XXXVI (1937), 359.

12. *Remarks on the Last Edition of Shakespeare* (London, 1783), p. 44.

13. ". . . the Galic is the language of Japhet, spoken before the Deluge, and probably the speech of Paradise" (William Shaw, *A Galic and English Dictionary* [London, 1780], Preface).

14. "Observations on the Derivation of the English Language," *Archaeologia*, IX (1789), 335.

15. *Ibid.*

16. *Blackwood's Edinburgh Magazine*, XLV (1839), 457.

17. "A. B. D." in *Gentleman's Magazine*, LVIII (1788), 7.

18. Quoted from Whitaker's *History of Manchester* by Herbert Croft, *Gentleman's Magazine*, LVIII (1788), 91.

19. Joseph E. Worcester, *A Dictionary of the English Language* (Boston, 1860), p. lvi.

20. Cf. pp. 29–32 above.

21. *Deformities of Dr. Samuel Johnson* (2d ed.; London, 1782), p. 13.

22. Richard Chenevix Trench, *On Some Deficiencies in Our English Dictionaries* (London, 1857), p. 4.

23. III, 385.

24. Pp. 233 f. Cf. p. 219 above.

25. See pp. 82, 107.

26. British Museum Add. MS 35,397, fols. 63, 67; Add. MS 35,401, Wray's letter of August 8.

27. The Countess of Cork and Orrery (ed.), *The Orrery Papers* (London, 1903), II, 6, 8, 43; Add. MS 4,303, fols. 126, 130; Hill and Powell, *op. cit.*, I, 185.

28. *Orrery Papers*, II, 43.

29. Add. MS 35,397, fols. 140, 222.

30. Professor James L. Clifford, quoting Sotheby's catalogue, to which he had been referred by Mrs. Donald F. Hyde.

31. Add. MS 35,397, fol. 307; and cf. p. 107 above.

32. Arthur Sherbo, "Dr. Johnson's *Dictionary:* A Preliminary Puff," *PQ*, XXXI (1952), 91.

33. Cf. p. 211, n. 86, above.

34. According to Strahan's ledgers, Martin's first edition was of 2,000 copies, his second of twice that size (Strahan's "Folio Book" marked "B 1739" [Todd's Ledger A], fols. 60^{v} and 89^{v}).

35. Of Maxwell's numerous promises, the thirteenth is perhaps amusing enough to quote at length. Like Johnson, Maxwell intended to include quotations which would be delightful or instructive in themselves. "This he is the better enabled to perfect, by the Help of References digested in such a Manner, that entire Discourses of the most ingenious and approved Authors on the most important and curious Subjects will be inserted: Each Sentence standing as an Authority for the Signification of some one principal Word in that Sentence, which by the Help of the References aforesaid may be put together by the Reader at Pleasure. The Design, which the Compiler has principally in View in this Branch of his Work, is a Defence of Natural and Revealed Religion in general, of the Christian Religion in particular, and of the Rights of the Subject." For all the elaboration of his proposals, Maxwell expected "(God willing) in about a Year and a half's Time to put the Work to the Press" ("Literary News," *Literary Journal*, V, No. 1 [March, 1747–March, 1748], 221 f.). He never did.

36. See the December numbers of the three magazines, and the appendixes in the last two; cf. also pp. 82, 103 above.

37. Cf. pp. 82–83 above.

38. Hill and Powell, *op. cit.*, I, 323.

39. Cf. Stanley Rypins, "Johnson's Dictionary Reviewed by His Contemporaries," *PQ*, IV (1925), 281.

40. Cf. A. De Morgan, "Dr. Johnson and Dr. Maty," *Notes and Queries*, 2d ser., IV (1857), 341.

41. In his thirty-eighth paragraph, Johnson speaks of "inserting great numbers of compounded words, as may be found under *after*, *fore*, *new*, *night*, *fair*, and many more." W. R. Keast, noting that *fair* is wrong, has recently suggested *semi* as a possible correction ("The Preface to *A Dictionary of the English Language:* Johnson's Revision and the Estab-

lishment of the Text," *Studies in Bibliography: Papers of the Bibliographical Society of the University of Virginia*, V [1952–53], 132 f.). Since there is no reason to assume that Johnson's list is alphabetical and since *semi* does not fit well in a group of native English forms, the *Monthly* reviewer's guess is probably better: "*Fair* seems to be an error of the press, and intended to have been *far*, from whence we have *far-fétch*, *far-fétched*, *far-piercing*, *far-shooting*, &c." (XII, 300, n. 14). In the body of the *Dictionary*, *far*, which could easily be read as *fair* in Johnson's hand, is listed as frequent in compounds.

42. *A Letter from a Friend in England to Mr. Maxwell, Complaining of His Dilatoriness in the Publication of His So-long-promised Work: with a Character of Mr. Johnson's English Dictionary, Lately Published, and Mr. Maxwell's Justification of Himself* (Dublin, 1755).

43. On May 6, 1755, Garrick's friend Claude-Pierre Patu wrote from Paris to ask Garrick's opinion of the *Dictionary* (*Private Correspondence of David Garrick* [London, 1831–32], II, 389). For Garrick's verses see W. P. Courtney's *Bibliography of Johnson* (Oxford, 1915), p. 42. They appear in the *Scots Magazine*, XVII (1755), 197, and in the *Gentleman's* and *London* magazines, as cited by Courtney.

44. *Les Registres de l'Académie françoise, 1672–1793* (Paris, 1895), III, 67.

45. *Ibid.*, p. 153.

46. Cf. Philip B. Gove, "Notes on Serialization and Competitive Publishing," *Oxford Bibliographical Society Proceedings and Papers*, V (1936–39), 305–22; DeWitt T. Starnes and Gertrude E. Noyes, *The English Dictionary from Cawdrey to Johnson, 1604–1755* (Chapel Hill, 1946), chap. xxii. We have made a fresh examination of the evidence.

47. Todd's Ledger A, fol. 97^{v}.

48. P. 314.

49. In *Jackson's Oxford Journal* for December 20 and 27, Johnson's octavo is announced for January 5; the same date is given in the *Public Advertiser* for December 20, the *Daily Advertiser* for December 22, etc. The eighty-first number of the Scott-Bailey is announced in the *London Evening-Post* for November 16–18, 1756.

50. Henry B. Wheatley, "Chronological Notices of the Dictionaries of the English Language," *Transactions of the Philological Society* (1865), p. 254.

51. In *Lloyd's Evening Post*, for example, and the *London Chronicle*; cf. also p. 113 above.

52. *London Chronicle*, October 18–20, 1759.

53. Gove, *op. cit.*, p. 322.

54. April 12–14, 1757.

55. See p. 114 above.

56. In this account, we follow mainly Allen Walker Read, "British Recognition of American Speech in the Eighteenth Century," *Dialect Notes*, VI, Part VI (1933), 313–34.

57. *Eclectic Review*, III (1807), 303–10.

58. *Ibid.*, p. 304.

59. George Mason, *A Supplement to Johnson's English Dictionary* (New York, 1803), p. i.

60. John Seager, *A Supplement to Dr. Johnson's Dictionary* (London, 1819), p. v.

61. *Ibid.*

62. Preface, sig. b1.

63. *Monthly Review*, 3d ser., VII (1828), 541, in the notice of a stereotyped edition of the *Dictionary*.

64. Cf. p. 130 above.

65. Todd's "Advertisement," reprinted in Joseph E. Worcester (ed.), *Johnson's English Dictionary, as Improved by Todd, and Abridged by Chalmers; with Walker's Pronouncing Dictionary, Combined* (Philadelphia, 1839), p. xxvi. Worcester's book first appeared in 1827.

66. *Quarterly Review*, CXXXV (1873), 452 f.

67. *London Quarterly Review*, XI (1858), 77 f.

68. *Edinburgh Review*, CIX (1859), 380.

69. Charles Richardson, *Illustrations of English Philology* (London, 1826), p. 5. The *Illustrations* was first published in 1815.

70. Chalmers' abridgment appeared in 1820. For its combination with Walker, see pp. 176–77 above.

71. For the date, see Wheatley, *op. cit.*, pp. 287 f.

72. *Edinburgh Review*, CXXVIII (1868), 56.

73. *Quarterly Review*, CXXXV (1873), 452 f.

74. Noah Webster, *A Compendious Dictionary of the English Language* (Hartford and New Haven, 1806), p. v.

75. Anthony Vieyra, *A Dictionary of the Portuguese and English Languages* (new ed.; London, 1813), Part II.

76. British Museum Add. MS 32,325, fol. 143.

77. Jacob Serenius, *An English and Swedish Dictionary* (2d ed.; Harg and Stenbro, 1757), pp. 1 f.

78. (2d ed.; Uppsala, 1801), "Foeretal." Presumably Brisman used the octavo.

79. I (1756), 37.

80. (3d ed.), IX, 574.

81. Arthur G. Kennedy, *A Bibliography of Writings on the English Language* (Cambridge and New Haven, 1927), p. 100, No. 2728.

82. From *Die deutsche Gelehrtenrepublik* (1774) in *Klopstocks Werke*, XII (Leipzig, 1817), 280.

83. Leonard L. Mackall, "Goethe's Lines in Johnson's Dictionary," *Archiv*, CXIX (1907), 169–70.

84. Courtney, *op. cit.*, p. 58.

85. Wheatley, *op. cit.*, p. 281. Our list could be extended indefinitely. For example, since writing the first draft of this chapter, we have seen the *Wörterbuch* (Leipzig, 1793–94) of Johannes Ebers, who in his "Vorrede" gives Johnson pride of place in an account of the recent cultivation of the English language. Ebers used the sixth edition of the *Dictionary* (1785).

86. Courtney, *op. cit.*, p. 67.

87. *Dictionnaire de la conversation et de la lecture par une société de savants sous la direction de M. W. Duckett*, VII (2d ed.; Paris, 1854), 559.

88. Willich, *op. cit.*, p. clxxix.

89. F. A. F., "Die englische Lexikographie in Deutschland seit Adelung (1783)," *Archiv*, VIII (1851), 252 f.

90. *London Evening-Post*, August 7–10, 10–12, 1756; *Jackson's Oxford Journal*, August 7, 1756. Among the proprietors of Thomas' dictionary, which was published in two volumes in 1758 as *An Abridgement of Ainsworth's Dictionary*, were Hitch and Hawes, Millar, and the Longmans.

91. *Abridgement*, p. vii.

92. Francesco Alberti di Villanova (1737–1800), *Dizionario francese-italiano e italiano-francese* (1772); we have used the first Italian edition (Venice, 1777). We have not seen Alberti's *Dizionario universale critico enciclopedico della lingua italiana* (6 vols.; 1797–1805), though obviously it might also show traces of Johnson's influence.

93. A. Boyer, *Dictionnaire royal françois-anglois et anglois-françois* (new ed.; Lyons, 1768), I, iii: "nous sommes redevables de celles dont on a enrichi la partie Angloise, au savant Dictionnaire de *Samuel Johnson*, qui fait autant d'honneur à l'érudition qu'à la sagacité de son Auteur."

94. *Ibid.*, pp. iv f.

95. Courtney, *op. cit.*, p. 67.

96. *Historical and Literary Memoirs and Anecdotes, Selected from the Correspondence of Baron de Grimm and Diderot with the Duke of Saxe-Gotha, between the Years 1770 and 1790* (London, 1814), I, 436 f. Cf. Maurice Tourneux, *Correspondance par Grimm, Diderot, etc.*, XII (Paris, 1880), 94; also *Les Registres de l'Académie françoise, 1672–1793* (Paris, 1895), III, 432.

97. Monti, *Proposta* (Milan, 1819), II, Par. I, 1–52.

98. *Ibid.*, p. 22.

99. Lacy Collison-Morley, *Giuseppe Baretti* (London, 1909), pp. 89 f.; cf. also Giuseppe Baretti, *Epistolario* (Bari, 1936), I, 98.

100. Allen T. Hazen, *Samuel Johnson's Prefaces and Dedications* (New Haven, 1937), pp. 4 ff. For further discussion of Baretti's debt, see C. J. M. Lubbers-van der Brugge, *Johnson and Baretti* (Groningen, 1951).

101. II, iii.

102. Joseph Baretti, *A Dictionary, Spanish and English, and English and Spanish* (new ed.; London, 1794), "Advertisement."

103. Collison-Morley, *op. cit.*, pp. 293, 321.

104. *Works* (Oxford, 1825), V, 97.

105. Robert Nares, *A Glossary; or, Collection of Words . . . Which Have Been Thought To Require Illustration, in . . . Shakespeare, and His Contemporaries* (London, 1822), p. vii.

106. *Ibid.*

107. In 1756, in the *Literary Magazine*, Johnson used this phrase when he criticized the Americanisms in Lewis Evans' *Geographical, Historical, Political, Philosophical, and Mechanical Essays.* We take the quotation from H. L. Mencken, *The American Language, Supplement I* (New York, 1945), p. 3; and Mencken took it from Read, "British Recognition of American Speech in the Eighteenth Century," p. 317, which we have also consulted.

108. Johnson's words of encouragement to Boswell when Boswell showed him part of "a dictionary of words peculiar to Scotland." In the quotation, we follow John Jamieson in the Preface to the original edition of his *Etymological Dictionary of the Scottish Language*. The passage in question is reprinted in the new edition of Jamieson (Paisley, 1879), I, viii f.

109. *Ibid.* (new ed.), I, ix, xvii.

110. *A Vocabulary, or Collection of Words and Phrases Which Have Been Supposed To Be Peculiar to the United States of America* (Boston, 1816), pp. 11, 18.

111. *Ibid.*, pp. v–vi.

112. Quoted from the *Westminster Review*, XIV (1831), 57.

113. (3d ed.; London, 1844), p. 3.

114. *A Letter to the Honorable John Pickering* (Boston, 1817), pp. 7, 11, 26 f., 53 f. For further discussion of Webster's opinions, cf. pp. 191 ff.

115. Lloyd, *An Alphabetical Dictionary* (London, 1668), sig. aaa2, etc.

116. We here follow Gertrude E. Noyes, "The Beginnings of the Study of Synonyms in England," *PMLA*, LXVI (1951), 951–70.

117. John Trusler, *The Distinction between Words Esteemed Synonymous* (3d ed.; London, 1794–95), pp. vi f. The changed title had appeared in the second edition (1783).

118. P. xiii in the 1799 ed.

119. Cf. the title-page of the 1792 ed.

120. Wheatley, *op. cit.*, p. 260.

121. (1792 ed.), Preface, sig. A2v.

122. Noyes, "Study of Synonyms," p. 965.

123. *Ibid.*, p. 967.

124. *Ibid.*, pp. 966–68.

125. *Ibid.*, p. 968.

126. When Taylor argues that "a synonymist is prone to error who 'leans too much on usage, which is transient, too little on etymology which is immutable' " (Noyes, "Study of Synonyms," p. 960), it seems probable that he is thinking of Johnson's dependence on illustrative quotations; but since we have not been able to see his book, we can make no positive statement. Crabb is careful to say that his "selection of authorities has been made by an actual perusal of the authors, without the assistance of Johnson's dictionary" (*English Synonymes* [new ed.; New York, 1830], p. v). The disclaimer establishes the opposite practice as the rule.

127. Noyes, "Study of Synonyms," p. 964.

128. *Ibid.*, p. 970.

129. Worcester, *Dictionary of the English Language*, p. lvii.

130. Esther K. Sheldon, "Pronouncing Systems in Eighteenth-Century Dictionaries," *Language*, XXII (1946), 39. In our account of the pronouncing dictionaries, we draw heavily on this article and on Shel-

don, "Walker's Influence on the Pronunciation of English," *PMLA*, LXII (1947), 130–46.

131. Cited by Hans Stichel, *Die englische Aussprache nach den Grammatiken Peytons* (*1756*, *1765*) (Darmstadt, 1915), p. 6.

132. Courtney, *op. cit.*, p. 63.

133. Cf. the notice in the *European Magazine*, XVIII (1790), 45.

134. G. B. Hill (ed.), *Johnsonian Miscellanies* (New York, 1897), II, 50.

135. *A Defence of Mr. Kenrick's Review* (London, 1766), p. 7 n.

136. Cf. the title-page of his *Dictionary*.

137. Cf. his "Grammar," sig. a1^{r}, and his Preface, sig. A2^{v}.

138. Quoted from Wheatley, *op. cit.*, pp. 259 f.

139. Information from Worcester, *Dictionary of the English Language*, p. lvii.

140. *Ibid.*

141. Robert Nares, *Elements of Orthoepy*, pp. 271 f.

142. *Ibid.*, pp. 269 f.

143. *Ibid.*, p. 272.

144. Wheatley, *op. cit.*, p. 262.

145. Worcester, *Dictionary of the English Language*, p. lvii.

146. Wheatley, *op. cit.*, p. 268.

147. Worcester, *Dictionary of the English Language*, p. lvii, quoting the *Penny Cyclopædia*.

148. *Ibid.*

149. Wheatley, *op. cit.*, p. 262.

150. Thomas Sheridan, *A Complete Dictionary of the English Language* (London, 1790), sigs. C1^{v}–C2^{r}. This is the 3d edition of Sheridan's work.

151. *Ibid.*, sig. B3^{r}.

152. Courtney, *op. cit.*, p. 64.

153. Worcester, *Dictionary of the English Language*, p. lviii, quoting B. H. Smart's Preface to Smart's *New Critical Pronouncing Dictionary* of 1836 (*Walker Remodelled*, as the proprietors, Cadell among them, chose to call it).

154. John Walker, *Critical Pronouncing Dictionary* (stereotype ed.; New York, 1823), pp. 3–6.

155. George Philip Krapp, *The English Language in America* (New York, 1925), II, 352.

156. Wheatley, *op. cit.*, pp. 282–88.

157. Cf. W. Bohnhardt, "Zur Lautlehre der englischen Grammatiken des 17. und 18. Jahrhunderts," *Phonetische Studien*, II (1889), 71.

158. *European Magazine*, XVIII (1790), 45.

159. Sterling Andrus Leonard, *The Doctrine of Correctness in English Usage, 1700–1800* (Madison, Wis., 1929), pp. 200 ff. But Leonard seems to be wrong in saying that "before Dr. Johnson issued his dictionary, the idea that English has a subjunctive mode seems not to have been suspected"; cf. Ivan Poldauf, *On the History of Some Problems of English Grammar* (Prague, 1948), pp. 67, 272, 308 f. In general, Leonard is so busy fighting eighteenth-century notions that he lacks the time and detachment to study them thoroughly and present them fairly.

160. Harold B. Allen, "Samuel Johnson and the Authoritarian Principle in Linguistic Criticism" (University of Michigan diss., 1940), pp. 346 f.

161. Priestley, *The Rudiments of English Grammar* (3d ed.; London, 1772), p. xxiii.

162. *Monthly Review*, XXVI (1762), 27.

163. *Ibid.*, XXXIX (1768), 184.

164. *Ibid.*, LIII (1775), 446.

165. *Ibid.*, LXXVI (1787), 360.

166. See p. 17.

167. *Short Introduction*, pp. iv–v.

168. *A Regular English Syntax* (5th American ed.; Philadelphia, 1792), p. vi. The first edition appeared in 1767.

169. *A Grammatical System of the English Language* (Boston, 1792), p. iii. We quote from the 5th edition (Boston, 1799).

170. *Works* (Oxford, 1825), V, 12 f.

171. *Ibid.*, V, 25.

172. Cf. *Edinburgh Review*, XCII (1850), 312; *Westminster Review*, XIV (1831), 69.

173. See pp. 12, 148 above; L. F. Powell, "Johnson and the *Encyclopédie*," *RES*, II (1926), 335–37; Kennedy, *op. cit.*, p. 15, No. 361.

174. George Ellis, *Specimens of the Early English Poets* (London, 1801), I, 205–8; G. M. C. Denina, "Comment la langue angloise s'est formée de la celtique & anglo-saxonne ...," *Mémoires de l'Académie Royale* (Berlin), *Classe de belles-lettres* (1796), p. 64.

175. Ellis, *op. cit.*

176. *Deformities of Dr. Samuel Johnson* (2d ed.; London, 1782), p. 54.

177. Noah Webster, *Compendious Dictionary*, p. v.

178. Joseph Worcester, *A Universal and Critical Dictionary of the English Language* (Boston, 1846), p. lxiv.

179. Cf. R. O. Williams, *Our Dictionaries* (New York, 1890), pp. 26, 31 f.

180. For a discussion of Tooke's theories see Otto Funke, *Englische Sprachphilosophie im späteren 18. Jahrhundert* (Bern, 1934).

181. *Diversions of Purley* (London, 1840), p. 25.

182. *Ibid.*, pp. 25 f., 631 f., 683 f.

183. *Ibid.*, p. 14.

184. *Ibid.*, pp. 23 f., 77.

185. *Ibid.*, p. 48.

186. *Ibid.*, pp. 193 f.

187. *Ibid.*, pp. 65 f.

188. *Ibid.*, p. 329.

189. *Ibid.*, pp. 52, 345.

190. *Ibid.*, pp. 184–87.

191. *A New Dictionary of the English Language* (London and New York, 1837–39), Preface, p. 56. The Preface and "Preliminary Essay" are sometimes bound in the first volume, sometimes in the second.

192. *Works*, V, 14.

193. *Ibid.*, pp. 36, 38; cf. p. 24 above.

194. We quote from p. 1 of an undated "Address to the Public, from the American Publisher of Richardson's English Dictionary," in the University of Chicago library. According to the "Address," the quotation in our text is from Richardson's "original prospectus."

195. *Illustrations of English Philology* (London, 1826), p. 17. The first edition is dated 1815.

196. Richardson, *Dictionary*, Preface, p. 39.

197. *Illustrations*, pp. 8–16; "Address to the Public, from the American Publisher," p. 1.

198. *Illustrations*, p. 248; review of the *Illustrations* in the *Monthly Review*, LXXXII (1817), 81 f.

199. In 1818, Richardson's dictionary began to appear as part of the *Encyclopædia metropolitana*, which was published serially from 1817 to 1845. The prospectus for the *Dictionary* as a separate publication appeared in 1834; the first number was reviewed in the *Spectator* for January 3, 1835; and by the spring of 1837 publication was complete, although a supplement appeared as late as 1856. Of the copies which we have seen, both bear on their title-pages the name of William Jackson of

New York as well as that of Pickering of London; one copy dates the first volume 1837, the second volume 1839; and in the other copy both volumes are dated 1838. By 1837, Noah Webster was in print with "Errors in Richardson's Dictionary"; cf. the description of his *Mistakes and Corrections* (New Haven, 1837) in the British Museum Catalogue. Attacks by Webster or his supporters on the American edition of Richardson apparently prompted the "Address to the Public" which we have quoted.

200. *Spectator*, No. 474 (July 29, 1837), p. 714, quoted in an advertisement of the *New Dictionary* which is bound in at the back of Richardson's *Study of Language* (London, 1854).

201. Quoted from Worcester, *Dictionary of the English Language*, p. lvii.

202. On p. iii of the "Advertisement to the English Lexicon" in Vol. XIV of the *Metropolitana*, the organization of Richardson's entries is outlined as follows:

"These are the main divisions which it will be incumbent upon the lexicographer to observe in the explanation of different words; and they may be thus methodically disposed:

"1. The etymology, with the literal meaning, applied literally or to material objects: with the words similarly applied.

"2. The metaphorical application of this meaning to the human mind; and the words similarly applied.

"3. The application consequent or inferred from the literal meaning.

"4. The application consequent, or inferred from that which is metaphorical.

"But the greater portion of language will admit of this comprehensive yet simple distribution:—

"The etymology, and literal meaning, literally and metaphorically employed; with the words of similar application."

203. *S.v.* "Addle."

204. *Quarterly Review*, LIV (1835), 311.

205. *Illustrations*, pp. 70–72.

206. Archbishop Whately, quoted by Richardson, *On the Study of Language* (London, 1854), p. 191.

207. *Ibid.*, p. 193.

208. *Ibid.*

209. *Illustrations*, pp. 256–63.

210. Richardson's "original prospectus," quoted from the "Address to the Public, from the American Publisher," p. 2.

211. *A Collection of Papers on Political, Literary and Moral Subjects* (New York, 1843), p. 360.

212. *Ibid.*

213. Harry R. Warfel, *Noah Webster: Schoolmaster to America* (New York, 1936), p. 133.

214. Quoted *ibid.*, p. 203.

215. Jefferson's characterization from Warfel, *op. cit.*, p. 272; Murray's opinion from *The Evolution of English Lexicography* (Oxford, 1900), p. 43.

216. P. v.

217. "Letter to David Ramsay," in Harry R. Warfel (ed.), *Letters of Noah Webster* (New York, 1953), p. 289.

218. *An American Dictionary of the English Language* (New York, 1828), Vol. I, sig. G2^{r}.

219. *Letters*, p. 284.

220. *Ibid.*

221. *Ibid.*, pp. 265, 284.

222. *American Dictionary*, Vol. I, sig. G2^{r}.

223. *Letters*, p. 285.

224. *Ibid.*

225. *American Dictionary*, Vol. I, sig. G2^{r}.

226. *Letters*, p. 287.

227. *American Dictionary*, Vol. I, sig. G2^{r}.

228. *Ibid.* Cf. our account of Kenrick's system of accentuation, pp. 173–74.

229. *Letters*, p. 287.

230. *American Dictionary*, Vol. I, sig. G2^{r}.

231. *Ibid.*, Vol. II, "Advertisement."

232. *Ibid.*, Vol. I, sig. G2^{r}.

233. *Letters*, p. 288.

234. *American Dictionary*, Vol. I, sig. A4.

235. *Ibid.*, Vol. I, sigs. A4^{r}, B1^{v}.

236. Franklin Edgerton, "Notes on Early American Work in Linguistics," *Proceedings of the American Philosophical Society*, LXXXVII (1944), 26.

237. *American Dictionary*, Vol. I, sig. B4^{v}.

238. *Works*, V, 40, 18, 45 f. Cf. pp. 29–30 above.

239. *Ibid.*, p. 49.

240. *Ibid.*, p. 7.

241. *Ibid.*, p. 40.

242. *Compendious Dictionary*, p. xxii.

243. *Dissertations on the English Language* (Boston, 1789), pp. 22 f. We quote Warfel's edition for the "Scholars' Facsimiles."

244. Quoted from Warfel, *Noah Webster: Schoolmaster to America*, p. 289.

245. *American Dictionary*, Vol. I, sig. A2.

246. Murray, *op. cit.*, p. 43; Krapp, *op. cit.*, I, 368.

247. XIV, 56–93.

248. "British Notices of Webster's Dictionary," bound in at the beginning of Webster's *Collection of Papers on Political, Literary and Moral Subjects.*

249. *Diversions of Purley*, p. lii.

250. *The Imperial Dictionary* (Glasgow, 1850), I, ii.

251. "English Dictionaries," *Quarterly Review*, CXXXV (1873), 458.

252. LIV (1835), 309.

253. *New Dictionary*, Preface, p. 39.

254. *Penny Cyclopædia* (London, 1833–46), Vol. VIII, article "Dictionary."

255. Trench, *op. cit.*, p. 7 n.

256. Krapp, *op. cit.*, I, 371; Worcester, *Dictionary of the English Language*, p. lxi.

257. *North American Review*, new ser., XVIII (1828), 523.

258. Krapp, *op. cit.*, I, 372.

259. *Universal and Critical Dictionary*, p. iv.

260. *Ibid.*, p. lxvi.

261. *Ibid.*, p. lxiv.

262. *Ibid.*, p. lxv.

263. Stewart Archer Steger, *American Dictionaries* (Baltimore, 1913), p. 80; Wheatley, *op. cit.*, p. 280; *Quarterly Review*, CXXXV (1873), 458. It is amusing to compare the notice of the English edition of Webster in the *Gentleman's Magazine* for 1830: "A DICTIONARY of the English language, by an American, is an annunciation prone to excite alarm or ridicule; but nevertheless the fact is such, and we rejoice, because it may tend to prevent American-English from lapsing into that slang to which the late Mr. Mactaggart and others have pronounced it to be in speedy progress of approximation" (C, 439). Is Mactaggart really dead?

Index

Index

Index

Index

PRINTED IN U·S·A